Sunset Lives

Sunset Lives

British Retirement Migration to the Mediterranean

Russell King, Tony Warnes
and Allan Williams

Oxford · New York

First published in 2000 by
Berg
Editorial offices:
150 Cowley Road, Oxford, OX4 1JJ, UK
70 Washington Square South, New York, NY 10012, USA

looó8o4o25

© Russell King, Tony Warnes and Allan Williams 2000

Berg is the imprint of Oxford International Publishers Ltd.

Library of Congress Cataloguing-in-Publication Data

A catalogue record for this book is available from the Library of Congress.

British Library Cataloguing-in-Publication Data

A catalogue record for this book is available from the British Library.

ISBN   1 85973 357 3 (Cloth)
          1 85973 362 X (Paper)

Printed in the United Kingdom by Biddles Ltd, King's Lynn

Contents

List of Tables

List of Figures

Preface

This book investigates one of the most distinctive yet little-documented forms of transnational mobility – international retirement migration. It presents original research on the retirement of UK citizens to four contrasting regions in southern Europe – the Costa del Sol, the Algarve, Tuscany and Malta. The research was funded by the Economic and Social Research Council (ESRC Grant R000235688) over the three years 1995-7.

International retirement migration (IRM) lies at the intersection of three major research areas and literatures: migration studies, tourism and social gerontology. Understanding the nature and evolution of IRM involves combining perspectives from each of these fields, and it is no accident that each of the three authors can claim some expertise in at least one of them – King in migration, Williams in tourism and Warnes in gerontology. Pooling and integrating our respective strengths, we have tried to respond to the major epistemological challenge of this research, namely to create new knowledge, from various perspectives on a little-studied contemporary phenomenon. On theoretical issues, we saw a need to give less attention to the factors of income and employment differentials that traditionally have been invoked to explain international labour migration, and more regard to life-stage, cultural, attitudinal, recreational and environmental factors. One obvious link is to tourism: indeed the term 'residential tourists' is sometimes used to describe retired (and other) people who have settled permanently or semi-permanently in the same areas as those visited by large numbers of tourists, and whose retirement to these resort areas often follows a personal history of holiday-making in the same destination region. We also wanted to explore the complexity of IRM as a residential strategy for later life, given the likelihood that this involves a range of mobility patterns and multiple links to two (occasionally more) places, often expressed via seasonal or regular migrations.

Another key context framing the research is the changing regulatory roles of the national state and the European Union. IRM is embedded in important EU institutional and social policy considerations, including Articles 48 and 49 of the Treaty of Rome on free movement, the Single

European Act which removes barriers to property rights across member states, Article 8 of the Treaty of European Union (Maastricht) which bestows limited electoral rights, and the Social Charter which envisions the potential to harmonise pension and welfare systems across the Community. There is a need, therefore, to assess the extent to which supranational institutional and legal changes have contributed (and may contribute in the future) to increasing international retirement moves and to the types of problems – and solutions – encountered.

The social reconstruction of older people's lives provides another powerful organising principle that pervades the research presented in this book. It is increasingly realised within social gerontology that to combat the simplistic projections of the consequences of an increasing number of older people, which focus on the burden of the sick and the frail, more attention needs to be given to cohort differences and to the positive attributes of retirement and later life. The innovative residential settings and lifestyles associated with IRM are one manifestation of new, positive and developmental ambitions among older people drawn from a broad income spectrum and a range of occupational backgrounds.

We were fortunate in being able to integrate some of our research with that of other scholars working on related topics. Assisted by a grant from the 'Acciones Integradas' scheme operated by the British Council and the Spanish Ministry of Education and Science, we co-ordinated our field research in Spain with that of a Spanish research team led by Vicente Rodríguez at the Consejo Superior de Investigaciones Científicas in Madrid. Rodríguez's research on the retirement experiences of several north European nationalities in the Costa del Sol used similar research instruments to our own, and some instructive comparative analyses were published in a special issue of the *International Journal of Population Geography*, 4(2), 1998. Versions of our questionnaire were also used in smaller 'offshoot' surveys administered by Seán Damer in Cyprus and by Gabriella Lazaridis in Corfu. Damer's Cypriot research was also funded by ESRC and his full results, based on six months of participant observation in the Paphos district, and set out in his end-of-grant report, are referred to from time to time in this book. Another important ESRC research project was carried out by Keith Hoggart and Henry Buller on British homeowners in rural France. This project's research output was published as we were planning and launching our own survey, and once again comparative reference is made to the results of this French study, which incorporated a component of retirees.

Our choice of title needs a few words of explanation. *Sunset Lives* began as one of several working titles. Although we recognise its connotations of decline, we also appreciate its apposite, enigmatic and positive allusions, and it was the strong preference of the publisher. The metaphor for human life of the rise and fall of the sun is timeless and culturally universal. As for its appropriateness, the appeal and tonic effect of the sun infuses the migrants' own commentaries on their motivations and experiences.

On countless occasions the benefits of living in the south were explained to us by reference to the drier and warmer climate. The sun encourages an active life, reinvigorates and cheers, and longer winter days and sunny evenings enable more to be done and more to be seen.

Finally, it is our pleasure to acknowledge the invaluable help of several people in the carrying out of this research. The empirical research which lies at the heart of this book owes a great deal to the energy and talent of Guy Patterson, our Research Assistant on the project. Guy spent much of his time establishing fruitful and well-disposed contacts and managing the fieldwork. He worked almost uninterruptedly and with exceptional tenacity in Tuscany, Malta, the Costa del Sol and the Algarve between autumn 1995 and the end of 1996. It was largely due to his efforts that the project was able to build such a rich base of data and information – more than one thousand self-completion questionnaires, transcripts of 200 in-depth interviews, and extensive field notes from all four locations.

In Tuscany we owe a particular debt of gratitude to the staff of the British Consulate in Florence and to Raymond Flower, pioneer British settler in Chianti and an exemplary key informant. In Malta we are indebted to Stanley Davis of the British Residents' Association and to Julian Mamo of the UN International Institute of Ageing in Valletta, both of whom showed a close interest in our work and rendered valuable assistance. In the Costa del Sol we benefited from the help and advice of Vicente Granados of the University of Málaga, Joan Hunt of CUDECA, Yvonne Ward and Charles Betty; and in the Algarve our thanks go to Frank Gerhard of AFPOP, Michael and Jyll Pease, João Guerreiro of the University of the Algarve, and Carminda Cavaco and Jorge Gaspar of the University of Lisbon. At Sussex the maps were drawn by Hazel Lintott and Sue Rowland of the University's Cartography Unit, Mary Clarke undertook the herculean task of transcribing more than 200 recorded interviews, whilst the whole manuscript was prepared with great efficiency by Jenny Money of the School of European Studies. At Sheffield, Alex Burton, Merryn Gott and Charlotte Rees skilfully coded the questionnaires and built the survey data base, and Kate Smith carried out a thousand secretarial tasks with immense tact and care. To all these people, and to all our 'research subjects' who allowed us to trespass into their lives, our sincere thanks, not least for making the project, and the writing of this book, one of the most enjoyable research experiences imaginable.

Russell King, Tony Warnes and Allan Williams

Retirement Abroad

Introduction

Where a person lives in later life and how they spend their time are expressions of a multitude of influences, ranging from their personal health and functional capacity to the social, material and legal conditions of society. The activities and circumstances of each generation of older people have changed with their economic, social and family roles and their means of material support. Just as individual biographies differ, so the generational or cohort biographies are distinguished by the social, economic and political events through which the group has lived. This book is concerned with one rapidly growing trait of the current cohorts of British older people – the increasing propensity to retire to southern Europe. We call this general process 'international retirement migration' – IRM for short.

Retirement and settlement abroad have interlocking demographic, geographical, sociological and applied gerontological dimensions and implications. Our intention is not only to document the highly visible impacts of new concentrations of northern European retirees at various locations around the Mediterranean; we also wish to place these fascinating expressions of affluence, internationalism and a positive approach to old age in the wider contexts of migration, settlement abroad and social change. In this opening chapter, the focus is 'why do people migrate for retirement?' The question is tackled firstly by examining the underlying causes of the twentieth-century growth of retirement migration and the factors particularly associated with international moves. The second half of the chapter examines the diversity and evolution of residential mobility in old age, enabling our prime concern, 'environmental preference retirement migration', to be assessed in a wider context. Throughout, the emphasis is on British social, demographic and retirement trends; the wider European context is opened up in Chapter 2.

An uncontroversial first proposition is that the 'take-off' of international retirement migration and residence in Europe during the past three decades has come about both through radical improvements in older people's incomes and assets, and through major transformations in the age group's preferences and opportunities. If this is almost self-evident, the problem is to specify the pertinent changes and to assess their relative importance. 'Increased resources' and 'changed preferences' are tackled first, by describing important changes in 'old age' during the lifetimes of the oldest people alive today. It is a selective account, featuring those changes which have had greatest impact on people's residential preferences and decisions, and particularly the increasing 'taste' for and achievement of overseas retirement residence. As the means with which to acquire a home abroad is clearly a control, sections of the chapter examine the rising standard of living, the growth of owner-occupation and the elaboration of pensions entitlements. Attention is also given to the characteristic social networks and ties at the end of working lives and in early retirement – strong indicators of 'locational constraints'. We examine whether there are discernable trends both in the retiree age group's responsibilities for others and in their own need for care and support. Are these ties reducing, so enabling more of the latest generation of retirees to make radical, long-distance moves abroad?

The Growing Preference for Retirement Abroad

Most of those who retire abroad have made several choices: to stay or move, where and when to go, who goes with them, to rent or buy, what kind of dwelling to move to, and whether to keep other properties. The research questions are about which options have increasing favour and why. It could be that the desire to live in a warm climate has recently increased, in which case the growth is not entirely explained by raised incomes and wealth: many moves abroad could be substitutions for moves within the British Isles. Similarly, the almost startling growth of a few expatriate retired concentrations in southern Spain may not indicate a great change in the propensity of the British and other northern Europeans to live abroad, but only a displacement from more scattered destinations in several Mediterranean countries or, more likely, from the Antipodes and North America. If, however, both rising incomes and housing assets have been influential, it is likely that internal and external retirement moves have grown in parallel.

An important question for both the origin and the destination countries is whether the 'taste' for overseas residence in later life will remain a minority enthusiasm or become a mass habit. By raising our understanding of the underlying reasons for the growth of international retirement migration, we will increase our ability to distinguish long-term trends from the 'noise' of local developments. Among the factors that influence economic behaviour, including people's decisions about what kind of dwelling to buy or rent, preferences (or tastes or wants) logically precede expressed demands and actual transactions. The first task is therefore to understand the aspirations and motivations that underlie the wish to live abroad.

Box 1.1 Mr and Mrs Morgan: from working lives in Britain to a new start in retirement

Mr Morgan had worked as a fireman and lived in south-east London for most of his adult life. He retired in 1992 at the age of 51 years.

I could have gone on for another few years but there was no increase in the pension. Most people at that stage are thinking of a second career after they retire. The nearer you get to the finishing line, things start to happen. I made my mind up ten years before I retired that ... I would not have a second career.

For ten years before retirement the couple had been taking holidays in Spain. In 1987, they bought a small flat near Málaga as a holiday home, for they loved the climate and the outdoor life of southern Spain, but it was too small and noisy to be a permanent home. On Mr Morgan's retirement, the couple sold their London home and the holiday flat. The proceeds were used to buy a new home in Spain, a smallholding 'well into the country. This is a small village with about 1,500 inhabitants. We are on the edge of the mountain range.' They had just enough money to do this, and had reasoned that if they lived spartanly and maintained the house themselves, they would get by.

They had never previously lived abroad and when asked if they had ever visited another country, replied that 'they had been to Jersey'. Both Mr and Mrs Morgan enjoy travelling throughout Spain, and value the company of a few close friends.

We both have many hobbies – those pictures on the wall ... those are my worst examples, I sold 30 of them the other week... That is one hobby and another is hens and aviaries. I also play golf. My wife has similar hobbies so between us, we don't have enough hours in the day. This is the secret of living here at our age.

Mr Morgan is frequently called upon by the local English-language newspapers and radio stations to comment upon local affairs, and to relate some of his fire-service experiences. This has encouraged him to write short stories, fulfilling one of his long-held ambitions. They both give thoroughly positive reports of their life in Spain.

One way to explore these questions is to examine the biographies of those who have achieved their goal of retirement abroad. We begin by considering the pathways to southern Spain of two couples, the Morgans and the Taylors, whose accounts are paraphrased in Boxes 1.1 and 1.2 (with changes to the names and distinguishing facts). The biographies have been selected for their contrasts, but both couples represent the pathways taken by many others. The two accounts vividly demonstrate both the substantial differences in people's attractions and pathways to an overseas retirement destination, and paradoxically that there are several shared aspirations. The contrast between the lifetime Londoner from a steady public-service occupation, and the privately-educated and cosmopolitan

Box 1.2 Mr and Mrs Taylor: a cosmopolitan pathway to retirement in Spain

The second profile is of an 'expatriate' couple. Mr Taylor was born in 1928 of British parents in Latin America, where his father worked for an international oil company. He attended boarding school in the UK, but was evacuated to Venezuela during the war when 11 years of age. He learnt Spanish, and after the war returned for national service in the Royal Navy, in which he served for thirty-two years as a pilot. He was stationed at various times in Cyprus, Gibraltar, Singapore and Aden, and during a period in Chatham met and married his first wife. They enjoyed the naval life and at the overseas postings the couple normally lived in married quarters. Mr Taylor now has no close relatives or strong links in the UK: his father remained in Venezuela, his uncles worked in Africa, and most of his other relatives including his brothers were expatriates.

Mr Taylor explained,

> When I was about 32, I came back to Gibraltar [and] began to think of retiring here. I liked the weather, and the people who were friendly. They seemed sincere. I met most of them in bars or on the golf course.... I suppose it was when I was about 49 that I first thought seriously about [the practicalities].

He realised that he had few savings, no permanent home, and needed to accumulate capital. It was taken for granted among his expatriate acquaintances that the quickest way to raise the money for a house was to work in a Middle Eastern country. Many of his friends planned to retire to Cyprus or Spain for, as Mr Taylor explained, 'they all love warm weather'. Mr Taylor retired from the Navy at 50 years of age and then spent eight years as an air-crew trainer for a Middle East state, saving enough money for a house in that time. The couple considered retiring to Australia and to Argentina (where a sister lived), but decided on Spain: the cost of housing and the climate were the main attractions. They looked for a quiet place with a good sports club nearby. Mr Taylor is now well settled in a dominantly British community, where he finds his command of Spanish much valued. Separated from his first wife, he and his new partner are both active in social and community organisations and give positive reports of their life in Spain.

expatriate reminds us that although international retirement migration is selective of the upper two-thirds (or so) of the income spectrum, most educational, occupational and residential history backgrounds are found among British retirees abroad. The correspondences in their preferences are all the more striking. They moved for intricate reasons, but critical to both cases was a strategy to conserve their personal finances and to maximise their level of retirement living. Also shared were strongly held environmental and social preferences. For the Morgans and the Taylors, as for many others, the most consistently shared preference, expressed by some in an unqualified panegyric, was to live in a Mediterranean climate and especially to have the benefit of warm winters.

For both couples, retirement to the Costa del Sol realised a carefully nurtured ambition. Few of their counterparts forty years ago developed similar ambitions and, among those who did, most were unable to make the move. Such a preference was rare, because few were aware of the Costa del Sol or its equivalents elsewhere around the Mediterranean, and hardly any visited foreign resorts on holiday. During the early postwar decades, a different world view prevailed, oriented to the British Empire, and there was much less attraction to the European continent than is found today. There are inevitably exceptions to this generalisation of cohort change (notably the long-established British connections with Florence and Tuscany), but before the 1970s most of those who wanted to move to the seaside in retirement had mainly English Channel resorts in mind, although some with far-flung family connections considered Australia, New Zealand, South Africa and the United States. The rising experience of holidaying abroad over the last generation and the growing preference for retirement in Europe will be examined more fully in Chapter 2. On the ability or means to move, the predecessors of the Morgans and Taylors were much more likely to have had to work until 65 years of age, if only because their lifetime real incomes were substantially lower. Their savings would also have been much less, many fewer were owner-occupiers in the housing market or received occupational pensions, and the opportunities and incentives to take early retirement were rare. These changes in old-age lives – or the changes in the cohort or group biographies of education, work, income, marriage, family relationships and much else besides – have been very important as both the context and the controlling factors in the generation of international retirement migrants. They are, as it were, the supply-side factors, to which our focus now turns.

How Later Life Has Changed

An individual on the threshold of retirement has experienced six decades of learning, socialisation, effort and experience. Much of a person's make-up is their biography. More directly pertinent to the individual's available choices at the transition to retirement is not just whether he or she has a spouse or partner (so they do not act independently), or have caring and support responsibilities towards others, but also the extent to which the person is inclined to pursue their own ambitions and pleasure, or alternatively to dedicate themselves to others' well-being.[1] Our main concern is with change through time in group profiles or 'cohort differences'. Five sets of changes in twentieth-century society can be identified for their strong influence on the 'social construction' of old age and on aspirations for later life: the spread of retirement, increased survival, rising affluence, greater education and improved housing.

The spread of retirement

Large reductions in the economic activity rates of older men have occurred during the twentieth century, while older women's participation

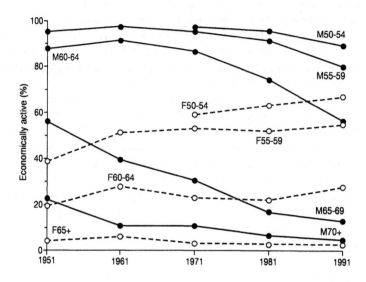

Figure 1.1 Economic activity rates of older men and women, Great Britain, 1951-91 (Various census tabulations; Walker and Maltby (1997: Table 5.2).)

has increased. In 1901, almost 60 per cent of the male population of England and Wales aged 65 and over was occupied and the corresponding figure for women was 13.4 per cent. The figures were virtually unchanged in 1911 and 1921, and declined in 1931, but 'the most rapid decline has come about since the Second World War, with the percentage of economically active men aged at least 65 years falling from 30 to 10 between 1951 and 1981. Because of a rise in married women's employment, the percentage of the female population aged at least 60 in employment was about the same (8 per cent) in 1981 as in 1951' (Johnson, Conrad and Thomson 1989: 64). From 1971 to 1996, the percentage of men in their early sixties who were economically active fell from 86.6 to 49.6 (Figure 1.1). In other words, changed employment policies and practices mean that in 1996 around 520,000 men could expect roughly five years more retirement than if they had reached the end of the working lives twenty-five years before. The simultaneous spread of early retirement (with lump sum payments offered as incentives), and of owner-occupation, have been key factors in encouraging migration and settlement abroad.

Survival

For every person approaching their own or their partner's retirement, a fundamental consideration is the anticipated duration of remaining life and good health. Retirement has recently lengthened through both

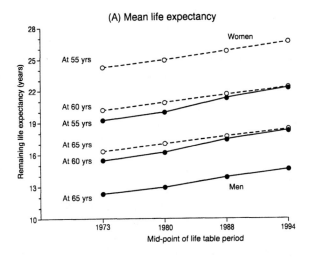

(A) Mean life expectancy

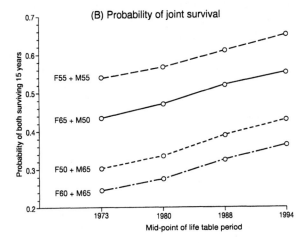

(B) Probability of joint survival

Figures 1.2a and 1.2b Improvements in survival around retirement ages, England and Wales, 1973-94 (Office of National Statistics (1997: Table 49); OPCS (1976: Table 22; 1983: Table 23; 1991: Table 15).)

earlier retirement and reduced mortality. Average life expectancy at birth in England and Wales increased from 44.1 years for men and 47.8 years for women born in the 1890s, to 58.7 and 62.9 years respectively for those born in 1930-2. By 1993-5, the male and female life expectancies at birth were 74.1 and 79.4 years (Office of National Statistics 1997: Table 49). These period life expectancies are calculated from the life table at the time of birth but, because mortality conditions have improved through the century, the attained durations have been greater. On the other hand, the rise in average life expectancy exaggerates the improvement in adult mortality, for most of the reduction has been in infant mortality. A better indication of the changing survival prospects of older people is the remaining life expectancy at later ages. At age 45 years, it increased by 15 per cent for men (from 22.2 years) from the 1890s to the early 1930s, and for women by 17 per cent (from 24.2 years). Since the 1930s, improvements have been faster, so that remaining life expectancy at 65 years of age increased by 25 per cent (to 14.6 years) from the early 1950s to 1993-5, and by 28 per cent for women (to 18.3 years). Figure 1.2a plots gender-specific life expectancies at 55, 60 and 65 years over the period 1973-94. There is of course great variation: at any age a few unlucky people do not reach their next birthday, while a few 65-year-olds will live for more than forty years.

Given that couples comprise the great majority of households who retire abroad, it is of interest to estimate their joint survival probabilities (Figure 1.2b). This is done simply by multiplying the probabilities for the man and the woman. Consider the changed prospects of a man aged 65 years and a woman of 60 years. From the 1950s to the 1970s, these ages were not only the eligibility ages for UK state pensions (as they still are) but also approximated the actual ages at which employed men and women entered retirement. The 1972-4 England and Wales mortality rates indicate that the probability of both the man and the woman surviving a further fifteen years was one quarter. Just twenty-one years later, that probability has increased by a half to 0.36. The survival probabilities of other hypothetical couples are plotted on Figure 1.2b. Many men and women retire today at 55 years, obviously raising the chances of a long remaining life. Even in 1972-4, more than a half of male-female couples of that age would have survived without loss for fifteen years, and that probability has subsequently improved by one-fifth to 0.65. The average period before the joint probability of a death reaches 0.5 is now a little over twenty years, compared to just under sixteen years in 1972-4. It follows that a couple that invests in a radical change in their lives when they are both 55 years of age can, on average, expect their shared lives to extend a quarter more years than if they had been making the same change in the early 1970s.

Average life expectancy is an abstract (and unreal) concept and few members of the general public could cite the figure for their age let alone joint probabilities, but there is a general awareness that survival has improved, and this is changing people's view of the balance of gains and losses of a radical move in their late fifties. The effect will continue into the next decades, but it should be noted that the cohorts born since 1947 are experiencing increased young adult mortality, so long-term projections are uncertain (for details see Office of National Statistics 1997; Warnes 1998).

Increased experience of secondary and further education

Changes in aspirations and preferences have been an important precondition of increased retirement abroad. Although more difficult to monitor and assess, one foundation of changed attitudes and behaviour has

Table 1.1 Educational participation, England and Wales 1901-61 and Great Britain 1980-1

	School education				Further and higher education		
Year	Years of full-time school	% 5-16 year-olds at school	Teacher years per pupil	Annual rate of increase	Year	%19-20 year-olds at university	% 19-20 year-olds in FE/HE	Annual rate of increase
1901	7.6	53.6	0.16		1900	0.8	1.2	
1931	9.1	63.2	0.28	2.0	1924	1.5	2.7	4.1
1951	10.3	71.8	0.39	1.7	1954	3.2	5.8	7.1
1961	11.1	77.0	0.44	1.1	1961	4.1	8.3	20.4
1980-1	12.8	82.5	0.65	2.0	1981	7.0	11.8	7.1

Sources: Department of Education and Science (1983: Tables 7, 29); Halsey *et al.* (1972: Table 6.11).
Notes: Data are school and FE/HE populations for the reference years. The average birth years of school pupils would be around 10 years earlier, and for FE/HE students about 20 years earlier. All pupil data are for 'listed' schools not differentiating state from private establishments. Annual rates of increase are from the previous year.

surely been the growth of education (Evandrou 1997). The simplest comparative indicator of educational experience in successive generations has been the school leaving age. Even when brought up to date as the 'terminal age of full-time education', the measure is crude and understates the increase of 'inputs' and attainments (Table 1.1).[2] Many now in their eighties and nineties left school at 14 years of age, having characteristically been taught to script elegantly, to be adept at mental arithmetic, and to respect books and learning. Those with ambition were given the tools to educate themselves further. Among those now in their seventies, the average age on leaving school was around 15 years, and more than two-thirds left before that birthday (Halsey, Sheehan and Vaizey 1972). In contrast, among today's early retirees in their fifties, the average age of leaving was around 16½ years, and only 5 per cent withdrew before 15. Such a pace of change will continue for many decades. By the mid-1950s a national system of grammar, secondary modern and technical schools was in place, so that the cohort presently (1999) in their sixties will be the last not universally to have received five years of secondary schooling. Plentiful research evidence demonstrates associations between educational experience and the entry into white-collar and professional occupations. While an analogous effect upon attitudes and expectations cannot be demonstrated, the likelihood is that rising education will continue to raise the share of young retirees who take a developmental approach to later life.

Improved housing standards and the rise of owner-occupation

The consequences of educational gains on people's lives have been modified by inter-related changes in occupations and earnings, tastes, the use of leisure time and, in a radical way, housing standards and tenure. The rising standard of living has enabled greatly increased 'housing consumption' – bringing improved space standards, basic amenities and ancillary facilities (utility rooms, garages, recreation rooms). These changes have been encouraged by government policies that have promoted owner-occupation. Since around 1960, savings have been invested in property at an exceptional pace, fuelling several phases of rapid house-price inflation, but also providing more and more retirees with an asset by which to finance a move abroad. According to successive General Household Surveys, in 1973 barely a half of householders (49 per cent) aged 60-64 years were owner-occupiers, while just fifteen years later the share had increased to 62 per cent.

More widespread property ownership, improved housing quality, increased leisure, and the rapid adoption of the car, telephone and television, have all fostered more home-centred lives. In-home entertainment and activities (hobbies, study and paperwork) have become a pervasive aspect of domestic routines. Another rapid diffusion has now begun, of cable and satellite communication technology and its applications to home-centred entertainment, shopping, banking and diverse domestic services, from delivered meals to counselling by phone. One likely implication of the 'networked home' is that some locational constraints are reduced. Home lives can be much the same in a city suburb or a village, and also potentially in Malta or the Algarve. Even the contacts maintained with friends and relatives can now be little different if they are 150 or 2,500 km away. If the specific location of a dwelling has less control on the quality of in-home lives, and modern services are ubiquitous, then other factors, including climate and landscape, may exert greater influence on a rising proportion of residential decisions.

Personal relationships, obligations and locational ties

Many people do not consider moving away from their accustomed residential area at retirement either because of other people's ties (their spouse or partner may still be employed), or because local contacts with individuals and organisations are important facets of their lives. A minority intensely engage with local social networks or community activities, while many more have strong family and friendship networks or caring responsibilities, most often for their own children, older relatives or grandchildren. Others depend upon the support or care of people who live nearby. To appreciate whether the *potential* number of long-distance retirement migrants is changing, it is therefore important to establish trends in the social arrangements that bind people to long-accustomed areas of residence.

Four categories of people are likely to be dependent on young retirees: spouses or partners; parents and other relatives of the preceding generation; dependent children (minors); and adolescents. The first two groups may be dependent financially, for care and emotionally; children require all those forms of support; and adolescents commonly expect accommodation and financial help. The majority of the dependent relationships involve co-residence and almost all imply a locational tie. Many factors influence the prevalence of the various dependencies – mortality or survival, past fertility, earlier migrations, and marriage, divorce and re-marriage. The picture is complicated by mutual dependencies between two households, as between an octogenarian parent and an early-retired child. Standard sources including censuses provide no information on these arrangements.

The influences on dependent relationships are several and the outcomes fluctuate. Social demographic research shows, for example, that low birth rates do not translate simply into a lowered prevalence among people in their fifties and sixties of caring responsibilities for children (Glaser and Grundy 1998). The pertinent variables include the rate of childlessness, the age at which the last child is born, the ages of partners and their children in second and later marriages, and the extension of adolescent dependency. Fertility and nuptiality fluctuated irregularly during the twentieth century and, when comparing adjacent generations, change may be the opposite of the long trend. For example, although during this century fertility fell, the birth rates of the 1940s' cohort were greater than the 1910s'. Other intricacies are readily uncovered:

> The cohorts born in the early decades of this century, as well as including relatively high proportions of never married women, also had higher rates of childless marriage than the later cohorts who married in the 1940s and early 1950s. Three surveys in 1962, 1977 and 1986 show a decrease in the proportion of childless elderly people ... [and] the proportion with large families also decreased between 1962 and 1986... The difference between having, for example, four as opposed to three or two children, is minimal [in its effects on living arrangements and caring responsibilities], compared with the difference between being childless and having one or two children (Grundy 1995: 7-8).

Despite the long-term decline of large families during the twentieth century, not even the trend in the share of 55-year-olds with dependent children and adolescents is clear. Early in the century, relatively high maternal and general mid-life mortality led to second marriages with much younger wives than husbands. By mid-century, that cause and effect had declined, but since the 1960s rising divorce and re-marriage have had similar effects. In England and Wales, around 9 per cent of women born in 1925 experienced re-marriage by their fiftieth birthday. The equivalent percentage for those born in 1940 was 15 per cent, and for those born in 1955 it is very likely to exceed 20 per cent (Clarke 1995: Figure 8). As regards adolescent children, the number who co-reside and are *de facto* financially dependent is influenced by their participation in further and higher education and by their independent household formation which, in turn, is associated with coupling and marriage behaviour. Beyond a certain level of affluence, the direct provision of housing accommodation for adolescent or young adult children becomes only a minor constraint on the acquisition of another home abroad.

Richard Wall (1995) has reviewed the changing living arrangements of older people in England during the twentieth century and before. The best comparative data combines successive censuses and special surveys and is for currently unmarried people. In 1921 approximately two-thirds of unmarried elderly men and women lived with at least one relative. 'By 1962, this proportion had fallen, but not dramatically so. The real change has occurred with a rise in the percentage ... who lived alone and a marked decline in the proportion living with non-relatives only.' His explanation stresses income influences:

> the rise between 1921 and 1962 in the proportion of elderly men living alone can be explained by the decline in the percentage who were in some senses already economically dependent, in that they budgeted separately from the non-relatives with whom they lived but lacked the wherewithal to establish their own households. About a third of the change in the residence patterns of elderly women can also be explained in this way.

After 1962, there is 'a spectacular fall in the percentage ... living with relatives'. There seems no doubt that improved affluence has had a large role in the reduced number of shared and complex households.

Dedicated surveys and much research have provided detailed data on caring responsibilities for parents or other elderly and sick people (although long-term trends are uncertain). The *General Household Survey* of 1990 had a special section on carers (OPCS 1992). It found that 19 per cent of men and 23 per cent of women aged 60-64 years were providing regular care to a sick, older or handicapped person (higher than for both working-age and older adults). Responsibilities for sick or frail parents do peak among people in their fifties and early sixties. Approximately one-third of those cared for by the 60-64 years age group were co-resident, and most of them were spouses. It can be inferred that among 1990 households headed by people in their fifties and early sixties, around 14 per cent had a regular caring responsibility in another household. Many others have strong emotional bonds or are restrained from moving by the possibility that sometime later the caring role will fall to them – by no means all are oppressed by the prospect. While three-generation households may have declined (certainly since the last postwar housing shortage), increasingly it is understood that multi-generational households neither contain nor reliably measure the prevalence of caring responsibilities or emotional bonds. These thrive and adapt between households as well as within four walls.

The support of older people

Older people through the ages have relied on diverse sources of material and practical (or instrumental) support, the range being from total dependence upon their own resources to extensive state-managed material, residential and medical services (as most comprehensively provided today in the Netherlands and Nordic countries). Whether a household is able to move on retirement is conditional not only upon whether they have sufficient income and assets, but also by the modes of their financial and instrumental support. Some forms imply strong ties to both localities and to the country where taxes have been paid. Reciprocal social relationships and care obligations, as within households and between close relatives, create restraints on moving. 'Welfare state' sources of support, including not only income benefits but also many subsidised and tax-financed social and health services, are commonly conditional upon residence in the home country. From the 1980s, the United Kingdom government increased the scope of its bilateral agreements with other countries by which pensions are paid to those resident abroad; and from the early 1990s, the ambitions of the European Union for a 'social Europe' began to have practical effect, by which citizens of any member country will have similar social entitlement in whichever member state they reside. The forms of income and welfare support are therefore relevant in several ways to international retirement migration. A decline of reciprocal or inter-generational family support and obligations releases local ties, while enhanced international portability of social and health service entitlements would encourage more to move. These themes will surface at many points in this book. As the most recent cohorts to reach retirement show many changes in the sources of their material and practical support, and further substantial alteration is likely, it will be helpful to outline the principal trends.

The elaboration of welfare states in Europe from the late 1940s to the 1960s coincided with a long-overdue period of high economic growth. As a share of all income, state benefits climbed for all UK pensioners from 42 per cent in 1951 to 59 per cent in 1981, since when the proportion has fallen back to just under one half (Table 1.2). During the 1990s, around 40 per cent of the recently-retired's income came from state benefits, while among older pensioners the share was 60 per cent. The most marked change in older people's sources of income in recent years has been the rise of occupational (and private) pensions, which by 1997 formed more than a quarter of the total – they were slightly more important as a share among the younger retirees.

The much-improved incomes of the older population of Britain and comparable countries over the last thirty years or so has therefore come about through the parallel elaboration of *state* and *employee-employer* old-age income schemes. This conjunction is now under stress from deep-seated changes in both the organisation of labour and the relationship between

13

Table 1.2 Components of income among people of pensionable age, 1930-1997 (%)

Year	Earnings	State benefits	Investment income	Occupational pensions
1929-31	35	44	14	5
1951	27	42	15	15
1961	22	48	15	16
1971	18	48	10	21
1981	17-5	51-66	14-13	17-16
1990-1	14-4	42-54	20-20	23-24
1996-7	18-2	39-59	14-14	28-25

Sources: For 1929-31, Gordon (1986); for 1951-71, Johnson *et al.* (1989: Table 3.1); for 1981 and later years, Office of National Statistics (1999: Table 5.3).
Notes: For 1981, 1990-1 and 1996-7, the left-hand figures are for the recently retired (single women aged 60-64 years, single men 65-69 years, couples with a man aged 65-69 years); right-hand figures are for the older people of pensionable age. The average of the two figures approximates the share for all pensioners.

governments and their electorates. With hindsight it seems likely that the UK Social Security Act of 1975 marked the zenith of state-organised, communal support of the older population. It introduced the State Earnings Related Pensions Scheme (SERPS), which would have much reduced poverty among widows and other dependants. When the long run of Conservative governments began in 1979, however, SERPS quickly attracted disaffection. The main objections were fiscal and macro-economic. The scheme implies a rising bill for the Social Security Fund and therefore locks future governments into high rates of 'payroll taxation'. Other dissonances with neo-liberal thinking were the high costs to employers and the elements of compulsion and state paternalism. A 1986 Act diluted many SERPS provisions and was the first retreat during the century of the state's role in organising the improvement of old-age incomes, heralding an increased emphasis on the individual's responsibility to make provision for an *enhanced* retirement income. In Britain and the rest of Europe, if we are still only at the beginning of such a shift, its continuation looks increasingly likely.

Incomes In Old Age

A key influence on the growth of retirement migration has been rising incomes and wealth. Having the means to move is a necessary precondition, but until recently old age has generally been associated with poverty. It should be stressed that very low incomes, if not 'absolute poverty', remain the norm in advanced old age, particularly among widowed women. Nevertheless, most northern European countries have seen more and more affluence among older people in recent decades. In broad terms, the average real income of a British pensioner household has doubled over the last twenty years or less (Johnson, Disney and Stears 1995).[3] This surge in real incomes has come mainly from occupational pensions and investments, but social security benefits have also increased (although since 1979 *not* the basic retirement pension). The trend in lifetime incomes is also impressive.[4] In units of the average income from employment in 1982, it was estimated that the lifetime income of the average married couple aged 60-64 years in 1986 was 46.1. For their equivalents in 2001 the prediction was 59.2, and for those fifteen years later 69.3, an increase of 50 per cent over thirty years.

The increases in old-age real incomes over recent decades have, however, been increasingly inequitable. Among those aged 50-74 years during 1979-89, 'the median income in the top decile rose 50 per cent in real terms, and in the bottom decile rose 10 per cent'. In the low income group, 'there were more unemployed 50-59 year olds in 1989 than in 1979, and greater dependence on state benefits' (Johnson 1993: 37). The trend has continued: by 1997 'the incomes of the top 20 per cent of pensioners had increased by 70 per cent since 1979' but for those in the lowest fifth of the income distribution, the increase was only 38 per cent (Hutton 1998: 613). Simultaneously there has been a marked change in the older age groups that are most associated with affluence and with poverty:

> The pre-retirement years [were previously] considered to be wealthy relative to other times in the life cycle, but ... the group now has the greatest disparity of living standards. Some are at the height of their earning power, have a partner who is also working, own their home, and have long contributed to an occupational pension scheme. Others, because of redundancy or poor health, dependency on means-tested benefits, and uncertain low-paid careers, are in very different circumstances (Hutton 1993: 427).

The welfare state has eased several of the financial insecurities that restrain both working- and middle-class older people's spending (Laslett 1989). The 1946 National Health Service principle that treatment is 'free at the point of delivery' has played an important part, while 'social security', social services and even state-financed universities have lessened the pressure on older people to conserve resources. There is, for example, less need to keep a reserve to help parents or adult children if, following redundancy, divorce or sickness, they meet financial difficulties (although admittedly other spending claims have increasingly entered people's calculations, such as private school and nursing home fees). Welfare spending has therefore made a substantial contribution to increasing the pool of retiring couples who have the resources to finance a move abroad.

General Features of Migration in Later Life

If the pioneer student of British migration, E. G. Ravenstein (1885), found over a century ago that most migrants moved 'to better themselves in material respects', the first half of this chapter has assembled ample grounds for an alternative hypothesis, namely that many retired people's residential moves are consumption decisions and a function of disposable income and accumulated wealth. How prevalent are international retirement moves and are they increasing? These questions are now addressed by reviewing the current knowledge of residential choices and migrations among older people. One aim is to place the comparatively infrequent overseas migrations in context, so as to judge whether they are a variant of the larger family of retirement moves or are different in kind. The account opens with a profile of older people's moves within Great Britain at the beginning of the 1990s, which compares the distances, destinations and motivations of the moves made by young and old elderly people. Then the evolution of long-distance 'retirement migrations' is described, from their earliest 'mass' manifestation in England during the interwar years. After reviewing some early forms of British overseas retirement, the chapter concludes by summarising the contemporary global dispersal of British pensioners.

Through later life, a succession of events of variable inevitability and prevalence change people's optimal residential locations and, as a direct consequence, the influences upon the migrations undertaken either to reduce 'locational stress' or to raise 'locational advantage'. The events include retirement, the last child leaving home, the redemption of mortgages, the maturity of life assurances and personal pensions plans, finding oneself unable to manage the home, income decline, bereavement, and sickness or disability. Broadly speaking, new opportunities occur more frequently in the earlier years of old age, and the constricting events more at greater ages. The contrast in opportunities is matched by the motivations. Moves made around the age of retirement tend to be for *positive* reasons: some to improve the residential environment, some for personal development, some hedonistic, and some to strengthen family or social interactions. They can therefore be influenced both by the locations of family and, more rarely, friends, and by environmental preferences or 'amenity' considerations. On the other hand, most moves made very late in life may be termed *defensive*: to conserve savings or to convert housing assets into income, to maintain independence, or to seek support, personal care or medical treatment.

Taxonomies of the causes, motivations and types of late-life migration have been suggested by several investigators (Meyer and Speare 1985). The earliest and most elaborate, by Robert Wiseman (1980; Wiseman and Roseman 1979), explored several implications of the changing life course on residential choices. More widely recognised, however, has been Eugene Litwak and Charles Longino's (1987) developmental model of later-life migrations. This associates three successive phases of later life with distinctive residential requirements and therefore migration objectives. The first, early retirement, is when positive environmental and amenity considerations prevail. The second marks the onset of frailty or ill-health, which increases the advantage of a location accessible to services and support (and begins our defensive stage). The third is when through chronic infirmity and dependency a person is unable to live independently and must move, either to live with or very close to informal carers, or into an institutional setting. All authors emphasise that chronological age does not control migration behaviour and that exceptional individuals abound – those who undertake ambitious changes in their eighties, and people in their early sixties who have to move into nursing homes. Nor does every older person experience every stage of the proposed sequence; and reversals do occur, so that most nursing homes have had residents who have moved back into the community.

More detailed generalisations about the origins, distances and destinations of migrations, and the ages, gender, marital status and household sizes of the migrants have emerged from some hundreds of European, North American and Anglophone studies of migration in old age. Several reviews and specialised studies are available (Longino 1996; Rogers, Frey, Rees, Speare and Warnes 1992; Warnes 1983, 1996). In the following discussion, we follow the usual British and European convention of defining migration as a permanent residential move over any distance.[5] Seven generalisations can be drawn from the corpus of research:

- The migration *rate* among people aged 60 years or more is generally low relative to the rates through the working ages.
- Most migrations by older people (as at all ages) are very short distance (<10 km). Generally moves made by older men are longer distance than those by older women.
- Long-distance migrations are mainly undertaken by the more affluent, owner-occupiers and married couples. The most characteristic long move is from a large metropolitan area to a region of lower population density and higher environmental amenity.
- Around the modal retirement ages, there is a modest and brief rise of the migration rates – this peak is more sharply defined among men than a similar rise at a slightly younger age for women. The average distance of retirement peak moves is comparatively long, and they are unusually dominated by couples without others.
- Among those aged 75 years or more, there is an exponentially rising rate of migration with increased age.
- At these advanced ages, women's age-specific rates of migration are higher than men's. Given that more women than men survive to these ages, the characteristic migrant in advanced old age is a widowed woman moving alone.
- In advanced old age, women tend to have a higher rate than men of migration into institutional accommodation.

Table 1.3 General and old-age rates of migration: Great Britain, 1960-1 to 1990-1 (% changing address within GB during year)

Migration rates by age in 1990-1   ratio

Age group	1+	1-49	50+	50-64	65-79	80+	50+/1-49
Rate	9.9	12.7	3.9	3.7	3.4	6.2	0.31

Migration rates by age, 1960-1 to 1990-1

	1960-1	1965-6	1970-1	1980-1	1990-1
1+ rate	9.8	9.9	11.1	9.0	8.7
60+ rate			5.5	4.4	3.6

Source: Various census tabulations.

The United Kingdom's decennial censuses collect the addresses on and one year before the census night of every enumerated person, enabling detailed profiles and analyses of migrants and migrations. Here we examine briefly the rates and relative frequency of different types of migration at successive stages of old age (Table 1.3). During 1990-1, 3.9 per cent of the over-fifty group moved, less than one-third of the rate for younger people. The annual rate increased from around 3.5 per cent among people in their sixties to 12 per cent among women and 10.5 per cent among men in their nineties and older. The strongest feature of the age functions for all marital status groups was a steep rise in the migration rate after 75 years of age. This exponential rise, dubbed the 'late age slope', is common to many Western countries and was first established by Rogers and Castro (1981). It has only recently been confirmed for the United Kingdom, largely because of poor age breakdowns in the pre-1991 census migration tabulations. While many people in advanced old age do move into residential and nursing homes and hospitals for their last weeks and months of life (Harrop and Grundy 1991), even in this age group the majority move into conventional housing, either to homes very close to children or other carers, or to join another household (Warnes and Ford 1995).

The other common departure from the generally low migration rates of old age is a short peak of mobility around the age of retirement. The 'retirement peak' is characteristic of long-distance migrations undertaken by the more affluent, married couples and owner-occupiers. Retirement-peak moves have been a marked feature of inter-state moves in the United States, with strong net flows from the populous north-eastern states to Florida, Arizona and California. In Great Britain, a large share originate in the London Metropolitan Area and other major cities. They were more pronounced in Great Britain in 1970-1 and 1980-1 than during 1990-1, possibly because of the lowering and spread of retirement ages described earlier.

The absence of census evidence of the growth of *long-distance* migration among older people is surprising, but two factors should be borne in mind. The substantial growth of owner-occupation will have tended to suppress the migration rate. Secondly, given the falling share of the over-sixty population that is in employment, a decrease in the average rate of mobility would be expected: the migration rate among the economically inactive may have increased. Other factors include the younger ages of 'retirement moves', which removes many from the statutory pension ages; and the rising number of dual-career and remarried (or partnered) couples, a growing proportion of which have the use of two or more homes. As such couples pass through their fifties and early sixties, some move the focus of their lives without a single legal change of address, as from London to the Cotswolds or to a Mediterranean coast. In such cases, neither a clear-cut migration nor any official enumeration of the change occurs.

Two-thirds of older households are now owner-occupiers, and it is easier for them to move during housing market booms than recessions. Such swings have a long history in the private housing market but recently have been severe. A time series on the annual totals and rates of GB internal migrations from the early 1970s, based on the National Health Service registers of patients (Owen and Green 1992; Stillwell, Rees and Duke-Williams 1996), shows one pronounced boom (during the late 1980s), two slumps (around 1981 and around 1991), and a variation of 30 per cent. The series suggests that the suppression of moves in the most recent housing slump around 1989-92 was stronger for older than for younger adults. This is a problem both for those keen to make a 'clean break' and those who cannot manage their present dwelling, and applies equally to international and internal moves when financed by the sale of a UK property. By mid-1998, the housing market had recovered strongly and the overseas property market was buoyant: in a radio interview a bullish spokesman for a property trade fair at the Brighton Conference Centre claimed that the British now own 2 million homes overseas and are buying once more at the late 1980s rate when the UK house-price boom enabled many to capitalise their assets and move abroad.

The Evolution of Retirement Migration

The extent to which international retirement migrations are generated by much the same processes as long-distance internal migrations or are different in kind is now considered. The histories of moving for retirement and of the development of recognisable retirement settlements are readily outlined: the earliest were connected with the growth of inland spas during the eighteenth century and of fashionable seaside resorts from the early nineteenth century. Accounts of the early resorts are abundant in social histories, for authors are drawn to the combination of social refinement, display, civilised pastimes and licentiousness, and to the zealous promotion of real and quack hydropathies by physicians and land promoters:

> Bath ... became the cynosure of elegance and one of Britain's top ten towns, its population of 2,000 in 1700 shooting up to 34,000 by 1800. 'Taking the waters' for medicinal reasons was the excuse, but in reality it was a holiday haven. Visitors flocked in to idle away time, ogle the exquisite, haggle matches for their daughters, and, above all, gamble... Bath was in turn imitated all over the country: Malvern Wells, Cheltenham, Buxton, Harrogate, Scarborough, all offered glimpses of glamour for ... widows wanting husbands, old men wanting health, and misses wanting partners (Porter 1990: 227).

Similar resort spas were established during the eighteenth century throughout Western Europe, but always with national and local idiosyncrasies. For example, 'the Germans are the world's most inveterate spa-cure addicts. It is an old tradition, dating back long before the days when Goethe took the waters at Marienbad in Bohemia; and, whereas in those times it was the privilege of an élite, today the practice has spread to all classes' (Ardagh 1988: 201). But in Germany, unlike France and Britain, the spa habit did not lay the foundations for a widespread aspiration to retire to the countryside or into pleasant small towns.

The conversion of the British nineteenth-century seaside resorts from playgrounds of the élite to day-trip and holiday destinations for the masses was a product of the railways and fostered the association of the seaside with leisure and retreat. This was echoed during the 1920s and 1930s by the first substantial exodus of retired people from large cities to coastal towns and adjacent rural areas, particularly in England and France, but also on the Belgian, Italian and northern Spanish coasts (Cribier 1982; Karn 1977; Warnes 1993). Despite widespread unemployment and stagnant real incomes, retirement migration from London and the Home Counties grew sufficiently to affect long stretches of the South Coast, and similar developments were seen on the North Wales, Lancashire and Yorkshire coasts, supported principally by moves from the West Midland, South Lancashire and West Yorkshire conurbations.

The same phenomenon occurred on the coasts of California and Florida in the United States. By the 1930s a large concentration of white-collar retirees had grown up in southern California. During the 1940s, retirement migration developed vigorously in the United States but was halted in Europe by the World War. In America, Social Security pensions and the booming war economy meant that older people could choose 'to leave the communities in which they had resided for 30 or 40 years and move a thousand miles or more into a strange but reputedly congenial environment' (Harlan 1954: 333). The scale of the redistribution prompted the first commercial handbook guides and substantial academic studies (Blanchard 1952; Burgess, Hoyt and Manley 1955). By 1950, St Petersburgh and Miami in Florida were thriving as fashionable resorts and provided permanent and winter residence for rich and retired people (Vesperi 1985).

In Europe retirement migrations revived during the 1950s and for two decades grew strongly. Different forms reflected technological and societal changes. Mains electricity, telecommunications and piped water were being supplied to rural areas which, with the rapid spread of car ownership, markedly raised their attractiveness for retirement. This encouraged the return of those city retirees with rural roots, a widespread component of retirement migration that was most apparent in France, following its accelerated urbanisation during the immediate postwar decades (Cribier 1970; Cribier and Kych 1993). Many European countries, from Ireland and Spain to Greece, saw similarly rapid urbanisation from the 1950s and strong rural-urban migration. Many first-generation urban workers never broke their ties with their native areas, and from the 1960s increasing numbers returned on retirement.

The enlargement and spread of the favoured British destinations has continued. By 1981 the popular retirement areas included the hills and vales of Dorset, Wiltshire and adjacent counties, the Welsh Borders and central Wales, north Norfolk, and a scatter of attractive rural areas further north. The trend was reinforced by the spread of both owner-occupation and early retirement. The continuing modernisation of rural areas also encouraged the conversion of vacant rural dwellings and declining villages to weekend-retreat, holiday and retirement functions. More intense 'circulation' between towns and the countryside had, however, blurred the processes, and even by the 1970s in counties to the west of London, such as Hampshire and Wiltshire, it was difficult to distinguish part-time or second-job commuters, early retirees and fully-fledged pensioners. The never sharp distinction between the peri-urban areas affected by long-range suburbanisation and those acquiring a retirement function is obscure, especially in the densely populated and prosperous rural areas of southern England. The same phenomenon characterised an extensive annulus around Paris, and probably could be identified around New York and a dozen European cities.

Despite the cyclical suppression of mobility among owner-occupiers in 1990-1, changes in the distribution of the British older population from 1981 to 1991 confirm the further elaboration of long-distance retirement-age moves. The fastest increases of the retirement-age population during the 1980s were in a broad band of English and Welsh counties, extending north-eastwards from Somerset and Dyfed (each side of the Severn Channel) to Lincolnshire and Norfolk, as though the vanguard of retirement settlers from the South-East had advanced 50 km to the north-west, beyond the Severn-Wash line to a Dovey-Humber frontier. They had also advanced south across the English Channel, both to adjacent Normandy and Brittany and to warmer destinations further south (Buller and Hoggart 1994). New forms of international retirement migration had emerged. By 1990, 29 per cent of the populations of the Lot and

Dordogne *départements* were aged 60+ years and 0.4 per cent of their residents were British citizens holding *cartes de séjour*, compared in all France respectively to 20 and 0.1 per cent (Hoggart and Buller 1993).

From the monitoring of retirement migration destinations in Britain, France, America and Australia, it became possible to formulate an evolutionary model. In its first phase, migrants tend to return to dispersed regions of birth and childhood (Law and Warnes 1982). While most evident in France during the third quarter of the twentieth century, the phase was muted in Britain, because rural-urban migration was largely completed before the First World War, and since mid-century the 'return component' of this country's retirement migrations has been less to scattered rural areas than 'down the urban hierarchy' to provincial towns and cities. One persistent form, however, has been returns to rural areas in the Republic of Ireland, while recently a comparable retirement stream has been established from London to the Caribbean islands (Byron and Condon 1996).

The second stage in the evolution occurs when childhood connections cease to be a factor in location choice, and instead accessibility, environmental attractiveness, housing availability and social support have rising influence. The relative importance and precise effect of these four factors depend upon specific time and place conditions. In England and France, retirement migration became sufficiently popular before mass car ownership to give accessibility by rail a strong influence, as exemplified most clearly in Britain during 1920-39 and the 1950s by movements to coastal resorts (Law and Warnes 1973). The third stage sees a return to more dispersed destinations. As more people wish to move, the favoured destinations necessarily multiply and disperse. And as those who move at retirement have higher real incomes and assets, they demand better housing and environments. Increasingly, the preference to live in attractive, 'unspoilt' landscapes is asserted, diverting migrants into rural areas, some of which were until recently poorly serviced and experiencing population decline. This dispersion has now attained an international dimension in the Americas, in Europe, and on the western Pacific rim from Japan to Australia.

Older People and Overseas Retirement in the Past

The recent growth of international retirement migration residence in Europe and North America is not unprecedented. For a century or more, various situations have brought about small concentrations of expatriate retirees. The extensive European worldwide empires of the nineteenth and early twentieth centuries took hundreds of thousands of Belgian, British, Dutch, French and German army personnel, civil servants and traders to the imperial lands. Many established their family homes, and raised and educated their children in the country. In some cases this has brought only a transitory presence and, in a few, the settlement has been reversed, as with the return from Algeria of around 800,000 *pieds noirs*,

French-origin settlers, to the home country during 1962-3, or the repatriation during the 1970s of the majority of Portuguese colonists from their country's possessions in southern Africa.

An interesting North American case is Cuba, which was occupied by the USA during the first three decades of the century and culturally colonised until the 1950s. Pioneer retirement migrants moved to the island during this period but, from 1956, 'the changes introduced by the Cuban Revolutionary Government determined that the great bourgeoisie and landlords and their followers ... abandoned the country' (Castellón 1991: 38). Since 1960 very few US citizens not of Cuban descent have considered retiring to the island, despite its environmental suitability, low cost of living and separation from Florida by just 150 km. Instead, other Caribbean destinations have been selected. 'Several identifiable expatriate retirement settlements have sprouted in the [Caribbean] island chains: from the more visible enclaves in the mature, high-impact tourist destinations – Bahamas, Bermuda, Cayman Islands and the US Virgin Islands – to the newer communities in ... the British Virgin Islands, Montserrat, Nevis, Saba, St Eustatius and St Vincent-Grenadines' (McElroy and de Albuquerque 1992: 128). The flows of affluent white Americans and Europeans for retirement and 'residential tourism' are supplemented by returns, from Britain and the United States, of Caribbean island natives and their spouses and partners at the end of their emigrant working lives (Byron and Condon 1996; McElroy and de Albuquerque 1988).

The legacy of colonial settlement and the diaspora of Europe's poor, disaffected and ambitious peoples that peaked a century ago have provided many opportunities for today's northern Europeans to retire abroad. We do not know when British, Scandinavian or German retirees began in number to sell up and join their brothers, sisters, cousins or children who had previously emigrated to North America and the southern hemisphere, but the displacement almost certainly pre-dates the jet plane. As will be seen later, these destinations still dominate the choices of British pensioners who live abroad. The flows are to widely dispersed destinations, have hardly any visible impacts and, consequently, like other mundane migrations, have attracted very little study.

Trends in the Number and Distribution of British Retirees Abroad

The last aspect of residential choices and mobility in later life which we examine to describe the context of retirement migration to southern Europe is the dispersion of British retirees across the world. Two sources give extended if not precise indicators of the trends: passenger destination data and social security statistics of the number of pensions paid abroad. The *International Passenger Survey* (IPS) samples between 0.1 and 5 per cent of passengers (depending on the route and time of year) entering or leaving the UK (Office of National Statistics 1998); it establishes the age, sex and citizenship of the traveller, and asks the purpose of the journey. If people are emigrants or immigrants, they are asked whether they are moving for work or study, but unfortunately migration for retirement is not distinguished. The weaknesses of the IPS data are the inconsistent and low sample fraction and the superficial inquiry into 'reasons'.

According to the IPS estimates, uprated for the population, since 1980 an average of 11,000 men and 6,500 women in late working-age (45-59 years for women, 45-64 years for men) have emigrated from the UK each year. The annual totals have fluctuated strongly: they are affected by the demand for labour and other economic conditions in the UK *and* in the rest of the world, and by changes in immigration law. The total rose during the mid-1980s to reach 23,000 in 1988, but then the housing market in southern England collapsed and the number of emigrants decreased. There was another emigration peak in 1993, and through the following three years the total oscillated around 17,000. On the other hand, the net change or balance of immigrations and emigrations has altered since 1980 from a net annual loss of around 4,500 to a net gain in 1996 of around 2,500. In other words, in-migration has increased while out-migration has fluctuated with no overall trend since 1980.

There have been fewer emigrants of pensionable age.[6] Since 1980, the annual average number of departures from the UK (after uprating the IPS counts) has been 2,400 men and 4,650 women, but the levels have fluctuated strongly. Throughout there have been net losses with a decreasing trend, from around 4,000 in 1980 to 1,000 by 1996. The outflows have a high female-to-male ratio, for which the principal explanation must be that a disproportionate number of pension-age emigrants are widowed, divorced or single women, leaving to live with or near relatives and friends settled abroad. This 'traditional' form of overseas retirement is motivated less by 'environmental preference' considerations than by the availability of concern, care and support.

The second source is the number of state pensions (or old-age income benefits) that are paid by the UK government to people resident in other countries. British pensioners receive their state benefits in more than 300 countries.[7] Beneficiaries fall into three categories: those receiving retirement pensions, widow's benefits, and unclassified. Widow's benefits are paid when the widow did not make sufficient National Insurance contributions to be entitled to her own pension, but her former husband did and so the couple were formerly in receipt of a married couple's pension. Not all beneficiaries are of pensionable age. In 1997, 763,000 British pensioners received their benefits overseas. Four countries accounted for two-thirds of the total: almost a quarter were in Australia, and at least 10 per cent in the United States, the Irish Republic and Canada. Mediterranean countries were also well represented, with 34,225 (4.5 per cent) in Spain and 24,536 (3.2 per cent) in Italy. There were 6,049 in Cyprus, 3,801 in Portugal, and 2,365 in Malta (Table 1.4).

During the 1980s the number of British pensioners who drew their benefits overseas was increasing by 9 per cent every year. The exceptional growth rate of 10 per cent during 1988-9 came at the end of the 'Lawson

Table 1.4 UK pensioners overseas, 1997 and changes 1994-7

Country	Beneficiaries in 1997		Change 1994-7	
	no.	% share	no.	%
Australia	180,252	23.8	8,790	5.1
Canada	125,788	16.6	2,227	1.8
USA	102,251	13.5	15,287	17.6
Irish Republic	82,156	10.8	7,794	10.5
Spain	34,225	4.5	6,128	21.8
South Africa	32,084	4.2	-1,404	- 4.2
New Zealand	28,889	3.8	- 3,332	- 10.3
Italy	24,536	3.2	5,132	26.4
Germany	23,005	3.0	2,940	15.1
Jamaica	22,405	3.0	2,940	15.1
France	14,089	1.9	2,359	20.1
Cyprus	6,049	0.8	857	16.5
Netherlands	5,357	0.7	783	17.1
Portugal	3,801	0.5	593	18.5
Barbados	3,120	0.4	860	38.1
Total	762,932	100.0	51,667	7.3

Source: Department of Social Security Benefits Agency, Pensions and Overseas Benefits Directorate, Newcastle upon Tyne, unpublished tabulations.
Note: The totals are slightly greater than the sum of the countries listed here because of minor countries omitted from the table.

boom' and the exceptional inflation of UK house prices. The rate moderated to around 4-5 per cent through the 1990s despite relatively low price inflation and subdued house sales. The overall total has increased threefold between 1981 and 1997, and among the more popular destinations, the United States had the highest rate of growth. It has UK immigrants scattered throughout its territory who attract 'joining' retirees (as in Australia, Canada, New Zealand and South Africa), and high amenity 'sunbelt' environments in Florida, California and Arizona that are attractive to 'environmental preference' retirement migrants. Some Caribbean destinations, such as Barbados and Jamaica, also had high rates of growth. European countries with sunbelt tourist and retirement locations were another group with rapidly rising numbers: indeed, by the late 1990s, the growth rate of UK pensioners in France, Italy, Spain and Portugal exceeded that of the United States (Table 1.4).

The relative attractiveness of other parts of the world has been decreasing. There have been absolute declines in South Africa and New Zealand

and below-average increases in Australia and Canada. Political changes, contrasting migration histories, and cohort differences will all have played a part. Each case requires specific study, but a general hypothesis appears plausible, namely that the importance of the family connections grounded in Britain's colonial history is declining, while the destinations of rising importance are associated with environmental preferences and the strengthening, since 1945, of the UK's economic relationships with western Europe. The dynamics of these changes raise many questions, but whatever uncertainties there are between the reported numbers of overseas UK pensions beneficiaries and the scale of retirement migration and settlement, the IPS and the pension data demonstrate unequivocally that international retirement is both heterogeneous and neither an exclusive nor a trivial component of population mobility.

Conclusion

The objective of this chapter has been to set our study of retirement migration from Britain to southern Europe in the context of older people's national and international residential choices and mobility. It has identified multiple reasons for the growth of migration at the retirement transition motivated by the wish for radical change in the residential environment and lifestyle. Among the prime influences, increasing longevity, earlier retirement, and raised incomes and assets appear most instrumental. These independent influences can be quantified precisely for the recent past and selectively projected for more than a decade. A fourth factor, changed attitudes and preferences, has also been assessed as important but cannot be specified or its changes traced in comparable detail.

So while there are few problems in understanding the growth of retirement migration through the last three-quarters of the twentieth century, and indeed many of the details of the evolution of its patterns have been explained, some recent developments pose considerable puzzles, particularly the changing forms of and influences upon overseas retirement moves. It is not clear, for example, whether they supplement or substitute for internal migrations, nor whether older overseas migrants who select destinations for environmental and lifestyle reasons are drawn from the same age, income and social class groups as those who move to locations primarily for reasons associated with the presence of relatives and friends. It is therefore difficult to predict whether European 'sunbelt retirement' will continue to be the behaviour of a small minority or become much more widespread.

The most insistent finding is that our knowledge of international retirement migration is rudimentary – not even a basic taxonomy of its types is clear. Even the partial evidence we have shows multiple causes and forms and complex conditioning and operative processes. At present, these cannot be precisely specified so evaluation and projection have to be postponed, although a few general influences can be described. The number retiring abroad from any country is intricately linked firstly to the number who have worked abroad and who do and do not return, secondly to the number approaching retirement who originated from and have strong family connections with people in other countries, and thirdly to the number who have formed strong attractions to overseas destinations through holiday connections. The flows and transfers are affected by a host of social and demographic dynamics, such as changing age-specific economic activity rates and retirement ages, the rising work and career participation of women, growing affluence, levels of price inflation and sales activity in the housing markets at the origin and the competing destinations, and changes in the transferability of assets and of social security and health care benefits. They are also affected by the vagaries of political change and instability and, in some cases, reflect a country's colonial history. The British case may be more complex than most. Its climate produces a strong incentive to retire overseas; its imperial history has produced an exceptional range of family-related destination opportunities; it has achieved high levels of owner-occupation; and, in comparison to most other Western European countries, its early (and now remote) urbanisation means that relatively few people have strong ties to a rural or provincial region where generations of their ancestors lived.

While international migration attracts considerable academic and policy interest, and it is right that humanitarian agencies, governments and researchers are most concerned with the largest and most problematic flows of labour migrants, refugees and asylum seekers, this introductory review has identified sufficient questions about the influences upon and impact of international retirement migration to justify more attention. Research needs to be carried out because these moves exhibit several relatively unfamiliar and poorly understood motivations and controls, and current theory is found wanting. Policy interests are also engaged, most obviously by the fiscal and public expenditure impacts, but also because, at least in Europe, governments and EU institutions increasingly aspire to develop cross-national social security and health and social service frameworks. The increasingly active policy agenda is to raise the well-being and safety nets of care and support for older citizens, not only when resident in their own countries but wherever they choose to move. What is next required is a fuller appreciation of the factors underlying the emergence of a European international retirement realm and market, the theme of Chapter 2.

Notes

1. This assertion alludes to the concepts and literature of 'developmental psychology', which have recently contributed many valuable insights into adjustment to old age. Erik Erikson's discussion of 'generativity *versus* stagnation' is particularly apposite (Erikson, Erikson and Kivnick 1989: 73-6).

2. The statutory minimum age of leaving school in the United Kingdom was only 12 years until the Education Act of 1902, when it was raised to 14 years. In 1946 it was further raised to 15 years, and in 1960 to 16 years. Since the 1950s, the minimum leaving age has had less and less bearing on trends in the average years of full-time education.

3. Many detailed statistics and reviews are available. The average weekly gross income of pensioners (pensioner tax units) in the United Kingdom increased (in 1987 prices) from around £67 in 1971 to around £111 pounds in 1987 (Central Statistical Office 1991: Figure 5.6). According to a recent Family Expenditure Survey, households with a head aged between 65 and 74 years had an average disposable income of £197 per week, and those where the head was 75 or more years of age had an average of £153 (Hutton 1996).

4. Calculations of this measure are necessarily intricate and require multiple assumptions about (a) long series of economic-activity rates (which are particularly susceptible to error for 55-64 years of age), (b) future earnings and rates of inflation, and (c) the real value of future state benefits. The calculations were made around 1980, when the generous inaugural SERPS was in place but productivity growth in the British economy was low.

5. Among demographers and widely in America, *residential mobility* is often used to distinguish short-distance moves from long-distance *migration*. Sometimes the former is treated as synonymous with intrastate moves, reserving the latter for inter-state migration. As moves between New York and New Jersey, or from Washington DC to either Virginia or Maryland, can be short-distance suburbanisation moves, this usage has little merit.

6. Most of the fluctuations in the time series for the late working and the retirement age groups are similar, giving credence to their validity. Doubts must remain about the absolute level of the estimates, for these are a function of the responses given to the IPS surveyors, and these in turn depend not only on the honesty of the respondents but more importantly on their self-descriptions. Neither long-term outcomes nor demographers' interpretations always coincide with perceived or expressed intentions at the time of passage through a port.

7. These are grouped by the Department of Social Security (DSS) Benefits Agency according to whether there are reciprocal agreements with the nations concerned for the uprating of benefits through inflation adjustments and changed entitlements. There are three categories: Non-Reciprocal, Reciprocal (frozen rate) and Reciprocal EC/EEA countries. Detailed time series have been made available for only a small selection of the countries with relatively large numbers of UK pensioners.

International Retirement Migration and its Southern European Dimension

Introduction

The previous chapter disentangled some of the complex ways in which demography and the changing social and economic circumstances of employment and post-working lives have produced new ways of living and migrating in retirement. This chapter considers the growth of international retirement migration (IRM) in Europe, focusing especially on north-south moves – the flight to 'a place in the sun' (Williams, King and Warnes 1997).

The populations of retired northern Europeans living on the shores of the Mediterranean are the outcome of many different migrant pathways and processes. Among the most important are the reasons that led an individual to have experience of residence or visits abroad, the ages at which these experiences occurred, and the frequency, duration and diversity of foreign stays. These factors mould and interact with people's residential preferences, resources and migration decisions. Four life course differences have been most influential:

- First, there are major differences in the geographies of working lives. Whether individuals have worked abroad for any period of time is an important influence, as this provides both familiarity with living abroad, and knowledge of particular places, especially if they have retired *in situ*.
- Secondly, employment (and inheritance) differences influence the resources that individuals have at their disposal to fund their retirement abroad. They affect whether property is retained in the UK, and the type (if any) of health insurance held, as well as conditioning the type and location of the house at the destination. Given gender differences in employment and access to pensions, women generally tend to be disadvantaged.

- Thirdly, the age at which retirement and retirement migration take place influences not only the length of active old age, but also the like-lihood of having particular types of family connections with the UK (such as young grandchildren) and the possible engagement in part-time economic activity.
- Fourthly, there are differences in the knowledge and experiences that have been acquired in people's travel careers. Not only are there social class differences in the number and the destinations of holidays taken, but also differences in the types of experiences sought. These range from the adventurous traveller seeking out novelty and shunning other foreign tourists, to those who have tended to seek the 'familiar-ity' and 'safety' of tourist enclaves.

In addition to the various migration pathways, there are also many differ-ences in the places that become popular retirement destinations. While individual retirement migrants can be found in the remotest places, the more popular destinations have to meet certain minimum requirements. The first is an attractive climate and physical environment, closely fol-lowed by a minimum infrastructure in terms of roads, water and power supply, and a relatively secure and congenial social environment. A stock of suitable houses, or the means to provide these relatively quickly, is also important. Secondly, in order for a place to become a popular retirement migration destination, there have to be appropriate retailing, associations and mass media for the resident foreign communities. In this chapter we explore some of the broad determinants of the IRM flows to southern Europe. The literature on this topic is stronger on speculation than on empirical analysis, but nevertheless some similarities and differences are evident in the experiences of the main southern European destinations.

International Retirement Migration from Northern to Southern Europe

From enhanced mobility to international retirement migration in Europe

The growth of international retirement migration within Europe has been shaped by three major factors: knowledge of and familiarity with foreign destinations; transport and accessibility; and legal and institutional barri-ers. For British retirees, knowledge of the advantages and disadvantages of living outside the UK, as well as of specific destinations, can be obtained from several sources including the media, family members and friends. Here we focus on the role of working lives, tourism and 'travel careers'. The economic and military requirements of colonialism have, over sever-al centuries, created a significant group with experiences of living abroad. In the postwar period, despite the end of empire, the globalisation of eco-nomic activity has increased international skilled labour migration due to the skill interchanges required by firms in 'hierarchically organised glob-al systems of production' (Findlay 1995). Globalisation rather than

Europeanisation has characterised skilled labour markets, so that working abroad is as likely to involve time spent in the USA or the Middle East as in Europe. A general familiarisation with foreign lifestyles has probably been more important than the acquisition of direct knowledge of particular places in informing later-life migration decisions.

Despite the internationalisation of labour markets, most Europeans obtain direct experience of foreign countries from tourism. Since the 1960s, there has been remarkable growth in foreign holiday-taking. This has been fuelled by reductions in real prices, changes in the destinations preferred by tourists, and the increasing consumption of foreign holidays as 'positional goods' (Urry 1990; Williams 1995). The two dominant European source countries have been the UK and Germany. In 1965 the number of British people going abroad (for all purposes) was 5 million: the number increased by 140 per cent by 1980 and doubled again by 1995. Equally impressive are the statistics for the proportion of the UK population taking a holiday abroad – 13 per cent in 1971 and 35 per cent in 1995. Well over half the British population have taken a foreign vacation at some time in their travel careers. Those who holiday abroad tend to be younger, more prosperous and of higher socio-economic status than those who holiday in Britain. The growth in international tourism from Germany has been even more rapid: whereas only 5.8 million went abroad in 1962, this rose to 18.3 million in 1985 and to 40.7 million in 1995 (partly boosted by reunification). Similar patterns can be observed in other European countries (Williams and Shaw 1998). Moreover, foreign travel is becoming increasingly common amongst older people – there were an estimated 41 million tourists aged over 55 years in Europe in 1990 (Economist Intelligence Unit 1993).

The second factor in the growth of European IRM has been improved accessibility by both surface and air transport, as measured in cost and time. Technological developments and infrastructural investments, notably the introduction of the Boeing 707 in the late 1950s and the extension of the European motorway network, have significantly reduced travel times. The economies of scale of increased air traffic, linked to the competitive marketing of charter flights by international tour companies, have greatly reduced travel costs (Williams 1995). Over time the geographical extent and the frequency of low-cost fares have expanded, contributing to the effective internationalisation of the mental maps and search spaces of large sections of the population.

A third factor in the internationalisation of retirement within Europe has been the removal of legal and other institutional barriers to buying property and taking up residence in other member states of the EU. The democratisation of Greece, Portugal and Spain in the 1970s opened the door for pervasive changes in their legal and commercial practices; more recently, the Single European Act of 1986 removed many obstacles to freedom of movement, such as barriers to acquiring property rights. Article 8 of the Treaty on European Union has made further provisions in this respect, for example guaranteeing voting rights for all EU citizens in local and European Parliament elections wherever they reside within the Union. However, the importance of this factor should not be exaggerated; the scale of UK emigration to Cyprus (a non-EU member) exceeds that to Greece and Portugal which are member states, and retirement migration to Spain and Portugal from northern Europe was well established before these countries acceded to the Union.

The lure of the south

Southern Europe has long been esteemed as a tourist destination by northern Europeans, epitomised by the Grand Tour to Italy in the seventeenth and eighteenth centuries. By the late nineteenth and early twentieth centuries there had been a geographical extension of tourist destinations beyond Italy to other Mediterranean shores. There was also a social reconstruction of Mediterranean tourism in the form of repeated seasonal winter visits by Europe's wealthy élites. Reynolds-Ball (1899) saw the Mediterranean shores as the world's great winter playground – a 'pleasure periphery' and a healthy environment for northern invalids. While most visitors were transient, some northern Europeans became permanent residents in the Mediterranean region, particularly in Italy (Hamilton 1982). Since 1945, the early trickle of migrants has become a steady flow, forming one of the principal international retirement outflows originating in northern Europe. Four sets of reasons for the growth of retirement migration from northern to southern Europe can be suggested.

The first reason is grounded in personal finances. There were considerable house price differences between northern and southern Europe in the early postwar decades, as shown by Flower's (1988: 214) comments about the costs of buying properties in Tuscany in the mid-1960s: 'In those days for between six and ten million lire (or, say, the equivalent of £3,500-£6,000) you could pick up a good solid farmhouse with 20 or 30 acres of arable land and woods. And half of Chianti was for sale.' Property price differentials were accompanied by lower living costs: cheaper food, drinks and restaurant meals, and lower winter heating costs, at least in some Mediterranean regions. This attraction was stronger prior to the Mediterranean enlargement of the EU (in 1981 and 1986), for there has subsequently been a convergence in the costs of living within the Union. It is difficult now to assess the significance of these cost differentials, but Myklebost (1989) demonstrated their importance in the growth of long winter vacationing from Scandinavia to Spain. Valero Escandell (1992) for Alicante and Jurdao and Sánchez (1990) for the Costa del Sol also provide evidence of the importance of cost differentials in the attraction of northern European settlement migrants to Spain.

The climate is the second, and most obvious, attraction of southern Europe to retired migrants, based on the long-established reputation of the region as a winter resort (Premble 1987). Rodríguez, Fernández-Mayoralas and Rojo (1998) found that climate was by far the most highly rated locational factor by northern European retirees in the Costa del Sol. There is certainly a concentration of retirement migrants in those parts of Spain and Portugal with the mildest winter climates – the Algarve, the Costa del Sol and the Costa Blanca – as well as in Cyprus and Malta. The climate is attractive both in its own right and as enabling an active outdoor lifestyle. It should be noted, however, that the 'Mediterranean climate' is far from uniform, and winters can be cold and wet.

The third attraction of parts of the South – especially Tuscany, Provence, and the interior of Andalusia and the Algarve – is the cultures, landscapes and ways of life which match idealised middle-class myths of a lost rurality in northern Europe (Thrift 1987). Tuscany exemplifies this, and Hooper (1994) writes that there is 'a peculiar resemblance to parts of rural England before the arrival of electricity pylons and council estates'. Italy does not have a monopoly on such rural idylls. Robert Graves, for example, wrote that he had chosen to live in Majorca in the 1920s because 'I wanted to go where town was still town; and country, country; and where the horse plough was not yet an anachronism' (quoted in Burns 1994: 213). Buller and Hoggart (1994) record similar sentiments amongst British house purchasers in France.

The fourth factor lies in the increased familiarity with the Mediterranean regions, a familiarity – however superficial – born of the postwar mass tourism boom. This has played a key role in defining the search spaces of potential retirement migrants. For example, Serrano Martínez (1992: 84) explains the concentration of foreign residents on the coast rather than the interior of Murcia in terms, above all, of their previous knowledge of the area as tourists. Perhaps the most substantial evidence comes from Buller and Hoggart (1994) who found that only a quarter of British property purchasers in France had never had a holiday in that country.

The role of international tourism

Tourism influences IRM in two main ways: by informing individual search spaces and building familiarity with living abroad; and through the intertwining of tourism and retirement migration in the development of a resort, as generalised in Butler's (1980) resort cycle model of the successive stages of discovery, development, saturation and decline. It has been argued that the expansion of retirement migration is one of the strategies for responding to a downturn. There is certainly some logic in the proposition that tourist destinations are attractive to those intending to relocate when they retire, and Karn (1977) offers evidence of the tourism-retirement link in the UK. More specifically, Foster and Murphy (1991) provide North American evidence that retirement migration is more likely to be significant in the intermediate 'development' or 'consolidation' stages of a resort rather than in its decline. The reasons are that large-scale amenity retirement migration is based on landscape and climate attractions, and minimum infrastructural and social requirements. The attractions are shared in large measure with tourism, which also generates some of the infrastructure and social requirements of the retirees. These will be available by the intermediate stages of the resort life-cycle, whereas their quality may be in decline in the latter stages.

Given the key role of the evolution of tourism, it is worth a brief digression here to consider its historical evolution. The Grand Tour to Italy marks the beginning of modern tourism from northern Europe to the Mediterranean. By the nineteenth century, the international tourism maps of Europe were changing, with the attractions of Spain becoming more evident; for example, Málaga grew as a health resort in the 1830s and 1840s, drawing those who wished to escape the increasing crowds on the French Riviera (Barke and Towner 1996). Spas became a feature of most European countries, and examples range from Montecatini Terme in Tuscany to Geres in Portugal. While some of these resorts were poles of international attraction, most relied on the burgeoning local middle-class markets in the later nineteenth century. The French Riviera was probably the most prestigious and internationalised European holiday destination in this period. It developed initially as an upper-middle-class, winter-season tourism destination and this basic model remained little changed until the Second World War, although the summer season gradually became more important. After 1950 travel to the Mediterranean was profoundly transformed by international mass tourism, which was fundamentally different in terms of the social construction of the region as a tourism destination (Urry 1990). Mass Mediterranean tourism was constructed around sea, sand, sun and sex and paid scant attention to most of the indigenous cultural features of the destinations. Reduced costs enabled foreign holidays to be extended first to the lower middle class, and then to large sections of the working class; at the same time, the tour companies' pursuit of economies of scale made such an extension of the market an economic imperative (Williams 1995). In other words, there was cumulative causation in the expansion of mass tourism. The scale of this expansion was immense, and the Mediterranean region as a whole attracts approximately a third of all international tourists.

The emerging pattern can be studied in more detail by examining the evolution of tourism from the UK (Table 2.1). The most striking feature is the emergence of Spain's dominant market position even before the end of the 1960s. France and Italy both lost market share compared to 1951, but remained important destinations. By the 1990s the picture had changed again, with France regaining first position followed closely by Spain. Both France and Spain increased their market shares in the decade prior to 1995, while other southern European destinations lagged behind. The general message of Table 2.1 is clear, however: by the 1960s, mass tourism had firmly implanted southern Europe in the search spaces of potential British international retirement migrants.

Table 2.1 Main destinations of international tourists from the UK, 1951-95 (%)

Destination country	Visits of >1 night			Holidays of 4+ nights		% increase in total
	1951	1963	1968	1985	1995	1985-95
Spain	6	23	30	19	20	99
Italy	24	19	12	5	4	52
France	40	28	16	21	23	115
Greece				6	5	58
Portugal				3	3	74
Malta, Cyprus, Gib.				2	3	127
Other	30	30	42	43	43	92
Total	100	100	100	100	100	94

Source: BTA (1969: 29); BTA/ETB (1996: 50).
Note: Totals may not sum to 100 because of rounding.

Another relevant feature has been the growth of winter sun holidays. Some 10.6 million British holiday visits were made between October and March 1997. In general overseas winter holidays have been expanding at about twice the rate of the 'summer sun' market. Older people constituted an important element of this market, with 23 per cent being aged 55 and over (Mintel 1998). There have also been other changes in the Mediterranean tourism market, notably an increase in self-provisioning. Self-catering can be seen as a first step towards a later retirement migration; the experience of renting a villa or apartment may lead to the purchase of a holiday home, and some of these are later used for retirement.

Not all those retiring to southern Europe have habitually been 'mass tourists'; there are many types of tourists seeking different experiences from their travels. Tourists seek both novelty and familiarity, and this frames a continuum within which Cohen (1972) identifies four 'types' of tourist. He proposed the term 'environmental bubble' to indicate an area with a high score for familiarity, and which broadly equates to the notion of 'tourism enclave'. Cohen's four types are:

- The *organised mass tourist*, who takes an inclusive holiday which offers protection within an 'environmental bubble'. Familiarity dominates over novelty.
- The *individual mass tourist* is more autonomous and follows a flexible itinerary. Familiarity dominates but some novelty is sought.
- The *explorer* investigates new areas and tries to get off the beaten track.

Novelty is sought but if it becomes stressful, this tourist will retreat into the familiarity of the 'environmental bubble'.
- The *drifter* avoids any kind of commercial tourism establishment, seeks contact with the host culture and tries to live in the same way as locals.

Arguably, these different types of holiday behaviour reflect the tourist's tastes and underlying values, so that each group could be expected to seek out a particular type of experience or familiar/novel environment if retiring to southern Europe. As Chapter 3 will show, southern Europe is far from homogeneous and offers a range of environments for tourism and retirement.

Before leaving this topic, we note one further aspect of the research on tourism – that on host-guest encounters (Smith 1977). The literature on host-guest interaction often tends to be reduced to simplistic relationships, such as the notion that the greater the volume of tourists, the greater the cultural impact on the host community. Such over-generalisations are not always helpful: for example, there is evidence that tourism need not destroy cultural authenticity, but can be instrumental in gaining wider recognition of the existence of distinct cultures (McDonald 1987). To this we can add the additional complexity of the strong link between tourism and migration, for tourists may become in-migrants and, therefore, hosts. The fact that tourists and migrants may share a common language (different to that of the host nationality) and country of origin adds to the complexity of host-guest relations.

The Challenge of Quantification

Whilst the existence of large communities of northern retired populations in southern Europe has long been recognised, they are poorly enumerated. National and international bodies produce widely divergent estimates of the numbers of international migrants in particular countries. For example, according to Italian data for 1991, there were 3,162 and 10,733 British and German immigrants in that year (Williams *et al.* 1997: 119). These contrast with British and German estimates that there were, respectively, 7,000 and 39,207 emigrants to Italy! The difficulties lie as much in definitions as in the accuracy of data recording. The quantification of IRM is bedevilled by four main problems.

First, stocks and flows are inconsistently measured. Unfortunately, flow data rarely record ages and, moreover, five EU member states (Ireland, the UK, Portugal, France and Greece) do not maintain comprehensive population registers which would allow the detailed recording of such flows. Some countries, without population registers, record applications for 'permanent resident' status, but these are often retrospective and incomplete. Most comparative estimates of IRM rely on population stock data, usually derived from decennial censuses. However, the data on stocks are also flawed by high levels of non-inclusion, as a result of both deliberate avoidance and unintentional exclusion.

Table 2.2 European residents in Spain and Italy, 1983-95 (thousands)

Year	In Spain			In Italy		
	UK	Germany	France	UK	Germany	France
1983	31.9	25.3	16.2			
1985	39.1	28.5	17.8	27.9	37.2	23.7
1987	55.3	39.1	23.6	32.7	44.6	28.3
1989	46.1	27.8	17.4	23.0	36.6	21.1
1991	50.1	28.7	20.0	27.9	40.3	25.1
1993	58.2	34.1	25.5	29.1	39.9	27.0
1995	65.3	41.9	30.8	27.7	39.4	27.3

Source: SOPEMI (1995; 1997).
Note: Residence permit holders in Spain, population registers in Italy.

The second difficulty is the definition of an immigrant. Censuses and population registers may classify immigrants in terms of nationality, citizenship or last country of residence, all of which produce different estimates. The last definition is especially germane, given that many British retirees do not move directly from their 'home' country, but rather from another; they are, therefore, under-recorded in any classification based on this criterion. In addition, the criterion of the length of residence within any one year which differentiates residents from visitors is problematic because there is a continuum of resident/migrant types, ranging from the seasonal visitor to the permanent resident with no home in any other country (see pp. 43-4).

A third and linked problem concerns the classification of individuals with dual or changed nationality. This is especially problematic in the case of Malta, where many British immigrants have chosen to acquire Maltese citizenship following marriage. In addition, some retirement migrants acquire citizenship of the country where they worked abroad.

A fourth and particularly difficult problem is the under-recording of retirement migration. By its very nature, the scale of under-estimation is impossible to quantify, but Paniagua Mazzorra (1991: 265) has argued that official estimates of the numbers of foreign residents in Spain should be increased by a factor of 2.5 to 3 to allow for non-registration. While the Treaty of Rome and the Treaty on European Union enshrine the legal rights of EU citizens to reside in any member state, there are other reasons for non-registration. These include avoiding cumbersome and perhaps expensive (if they involve a professional translator) bureaucracy, and evasion of income and property taxes. Expatriates display both outright flaunting of registration and elaborate behaviour to achieve temporary absences.

Table 2.3 North Europeans resident in southern European countries, 1993

Country of origin	Italy		Greece		Portugal		Spain	
	no. ('000)	% Eur. total	no. ('000)	% Eur. total	no. ('000)	% Eur. total	no. ('000)	% Eur. total
UK	28.4	17.5	20.7	19.5	9.3	27.4	53.4	27.0
Germany	39.5	24.4	14.1	13.3	5.4	15.9	30.5	15.4
France	25.4	15.7	8.0	7.5	3.7	10.9	22.6	11.4
Netherlands	7.0	4.3	3.7	3.5	2.0	5.9	10.5	5.3
Switzerland	18.2	11.2	3.6	3.4	0.7	2.1	5.6	2.8
Sweden	3.2	2.0	2.3	2.2	0.7	2.1	5.3	2.7
Eur. total	162.0	100.0	106.0	100.0	34.0	100.0	198.0	100.0

Source: Eurostat (1996).

With these reservations in mind, we now examine the secondary statistics assembled by international agencies. Turning first to the SOPEMI data[1] on residence permit holders in Italy and Spain (Table 2.2), they show steady growth in the three main European groups of foreign residents – from the UK, Germany and France. In Spain, the UK is the largest northern European source of foreign residents, followed by Germany and France. Fluctuations in growth over time reflect both changes in data collection methods and, probably, the rate of registration, and so must be treated cautiously. Nevertheless, assuming that levels of error are constant across the three nationalities, the fastest rates of growth after 1985 were amongst the French and British, although by the 1990s the growth rates for Germans exceeded those for the British. In Italy, the obvious contrast is the far lower growth rates for all three foreign communities. British numbers are virtually static, while the French have the highest growth rates. As a result, the size of the British and French groups were virtually equalised, but both were smaller than the German group.

Eurostat provides broadly comparable estimates of the foreign population stocks in southern Europe in 1993. The largest numbers are non-European, reflecting recent immigration from the less-developed world (Misiti, Muscarà, Pumares, Rodríguez and White 1995). Table 2.3 presents data for immigrants from selected northern European countries; as with the SOPEMI figures, these data are not disaggregated by age and probably include more economically active than retired persons. Nevertheless, they demonstrate the importance of immigration from a few northern European countries, especially Germany, France and the UK. The UK accounted for an exceptionally large share of the foreign European populations of Spain (27 per cent) and Portugal (27 per cent), and held first

Table 2.4 North European populations in Portugal: age structure, nationalities and regional distribution, 1991 and 1996

Census, 1991 Age groups	Nationality (%) UK	Germany	France	Population Register, 1996	Nationality UK	Germany	France
0-9	9.9	10.9	13.6	Numbers			
10-19	11.2	37.4	59.6	1986	5,872	3,575	2,574
20-29	9.6	9.3	14.5	1991	8,912	5,133	3,399
30-39	12.2	12.6	3.8	1996	11,939	7,887	5,102
40-49	15.4	11.5	1.6				
50-59	16.5	8.8	2.1	Regional share (%)			
60-69	17.0	4.9	1.8	Algarve	50.3	26.5	10.5
70-79	6.4	2.5	0.7	Lisbon	31.3	36.6	49.3
80+	1.8	1.8	0.4	Rest of Portugal	18.4	36.9	40.2
Numbers	8,944	8,052	20,119				

Sources: Geoideia (1998: 77-80); Instituto Nacional de Estatística (1992).

place in Greece and second place in Italy. Germany held first place in Italy, and was second ranked in the other three countries. France took third place in all four countries. There were also significant numbers from the Netherlands, Sweden and Switzerland, with the Swiss being particularly numerous in Italy.

The above statistics point to the difficulties of international comparisons and the need to consider the various data sources for individual destination countries. Here we examine three of the four countries which are the focus of the case studies reported later in the book: Portugal, Spain and Italy. We lay particular stress on regional distributions within these countries. Discussion of the fourth, Malta, is deferred to Chapter 3; it is the only instance in which the entire country was studied, as opposed to a region or sub-region.

Portugal

Portugal's two main data sources are the registration of foreign nationals (staying in Portugal for more than six months of the year) and the census (Table 2.4). These provide divergent estimates of the sizes of the main European foreign resident communities in Portugal in 1991.[2] Whereas the figures are almost identical for the UK, which may be coincidental, the census enumerates 57 per cent more Germans and almost double the number of French than the registration data.[3] The British have a much older age profile, with more than a quarter aged over 60, compared to 9.2 per cent of the Germans and only 2.9 per cent of the French.

**Table 2.5 North European populations in Spain: age structure and
regional distribution, 1991 (%)**

Age groups	UK	Germany	France	Selected regions (& provinces)	UK	Germany	France
0-9	7.7	8.7	10.7	Andalusia	34.5	17.2	13.7
10-19	9.5	14.5	17.4	(Málaga)	27.9	12.0	6.9
20-29	11.3	15.1	21.6	Balearic Is.	8.6	10.0	6.4
30-39	11.7	11.7	12.9	Canaries	9.7	19.5	2.8
40-49	14.4	14.4	12.1	Catalonia	6.0	15.7	21.2
50-59	18.8	12.0	8.4	Valencia	30.5	19.0	22.2
60-69	11.7	8.9	9.3	(Alicante)	28.4	15.5	11.8
70+	11.7	8.9	7.5	Madrid	5.8	10.5	15.8

Source: Instituto Nacional de Estadística (1994).

The 1996 registration data collected by the *Serviço de Estrangeiros e Fronteiras*
suggest that the British are the largest of the three main European groups,
being more than half as numerous as the Germans, and more than twice
as many as the French. Distinct patterns of regional distribution are evident. Nearly half the French are concentrated in Lisbon. The Germans
have the most even geographical spread, although a quarter are found in
the Algarve (or more accurately in the *distrito* of Faro) and more than a
third in Lisbon. In contrast, half the British are concentrated in the
Algarve. These data confirm not only that the British are the largest of the
three legally resident communities but also that they are older than the
other national groups and the most concentrated in the Algarve.

Spain

Spain also has two main data sources for the enumeration of foreign residents. The first is the *padrón*, the municipal records of foreign residents
registered with local councils. As in Portugal, there is a legal requirement
that residents of more than six months duration must register with the
municipality, but in practice there is widespread evasion. Moreover, the
padrón is difficult to access. The 1991 Census is probably more useful; it
reveals that there were 238,503 EU nationals living in Spain in that year.
The largest national groups were the British (27.3 per cent of all EU foreign nationals), the French (20.5 per cent) and the Germans (19.3 per
cent). The British (30.5 per cent aged over 60) were markedly older than
the Germans (20.9 per cent), and especially the French (16.8 per cent),
indicating the large contribution of retirement migration from the UK

(Table 2.5). The British were also relatively more recent arrivals: 64.5 per cent had arrived in Spain between 1985 and 1991, compared to only 47.3 per cent of the French and 51.5 per cent of the Germans.

The regional distribution of foreign residents is highly uneven (Table 2.5). The most popular districts are the Mediterranean regions of Andalusia, Catalonia, Valencia and the Balearics, and also the Canaries and Madrid: 82 per cent of French nationals, 92 per cent of Germans and 95 per cent of the British lived in these regions in 1991. The British are particularly concentrated in Andalusia (especially Málaga province, which contains the Costa del Sol) and Valencia (especially Alicante province). These two provinces alone account for more than half the British residents in Spain. The Germans are more widespread but concentrate in Andalusia, Alicante and the Canary Islands. Finally, more than half the French live in the two Mediterranean regions closest to France – Catalonia and Valencia – and in Madrid.

Italy

Three sources provide quite different estimates of the numbers of foreign residents in Italy. The 1991 Census estimated Italy's foreign population at 625,034, made up of both *residenti* (with official resident status) as well as various non-officially resident groups. The largest European national groups were Germans (86,175), British (24,432) and French (23,393). The second data source are the *permessi di soggiorno*, the 'permits to stay' that foreign nationals should acquire within eight days of their arrival. These recorded 859,571 foreign nationals on 31 December 1991, and are more comprehensive than the census data for all European nationalities except the Germans (Table 2.6). Even these data are problematic: they depend on government policy with regard to regularising clandestine immigration, and there is some ambiguity as to whether EU citizens are legally obliged to acquire permits. The third source is the *anagrafe*, a register of population in each *comune*. These data, like the Spanish *padrón*, are based on the numbers of foreigners who have applied for and been granted *residente* status, which is essential for owning property, registering a car, and accessing local health services. The number of foreigners recorded on 31 December 1991 was 537,062, considerably higher than the 345,149 recorded in the census as having resident status, but much lower than the *soggiorno* total. Moreover, the *anagrafe* does not, of necessity, provide data on less permanent forms of immigration. It is also not possible to disaggregate the published data for individual nationalities (the British are included in the EU figure), although special tabulations can be acquired.

The regional distribution of foreign retirees in Italy can only be partially plotted because of the lack of age-specific data and, in some cases, of statistics for individual nationalities. For instance the regional data on *permessi di soggiorno* aggregate all EU countries together. In absolute terms the main regions of importance for EU immigrants are Latium, Lombardy,

Table 2.6 Europeans in Italy, 1991-2

Nationality	Holders of 'permits to stay' 31 December 1991	Enumerated by Census 20 October 1991	Census as % of permit-holders
UK	26,705	24,432	88.5
Germany	39,340	86,175	219.1
France	24,879	23,393	94.0

Regional distribution of EU nationals holding 'permits to stay', 31 December 1992

Region	EU 12 nationals	EU nationals per thou. popn.	Region	EU 12 nationals	EU nationals per thou. popn.
Piedmont	8,123	1.8	Latium	35,492	7.1
Valle d'Aosta	511	4.5	Abruzzo	2,047	1.7
Lombardy	25,362	2.8	Molise	162	0.5
Trentino	6,862	7.9	Campania	9,282	1.7
Veneto	8,140	1.9	Apulia	2,433	0.6
Friuli	3,212	2.6	Basilicata	174	0.3
Liguria	8,650	4.8	Calabria	927	0.5
Emilia-Romagna	9,411	2.4	Sicily	5,746	1.2
Tuscany	11,538	3.2	Sardinia	1,542	1.0
Umbria	4,617	5.8			
Marche	2,564	1.8	Italy	146,795	2.6

Sources: King (1993a: 286); Quirino and Leone (1993: 17).

Tuscany and Emilia-Romagna (Table 2.6). In relative terms, EU foreign residents are most important in Trentino-Alto Adige and Valle d'Aosta (northern border regions with Austria and France), Latium (containing Rome), and the environmentally-attractive retirement regions of Liguria, Tuscany and Umbria.

The general picture

The patterns of northern European residence in southern Europe are complex. Most sources indicate that the British are the largest group in all the main destinations, except Italy where the Germans are ranked first. The two most important destinations for the British are Italy and Spain but the SOPEMI data on legal residence show that, whereas in 1985 the numbers were similar in the two countries, by 1995 the British community in Spain was almost double that in Italy. Most of the data are not age-specific but, for example, the Spanish and Portuguese census data (Tables 2.4 and 2.5) and the British pension data (Table 1.4) reveal that these countries have been particularly attractive to older British people. All such comparisons, however, must be made in the light of reservations about the data series. The next section considers one of the principal sources of these statistical difficulties, that is the various residential models that can be adopted by the migrants.

Competing Models of Migration and Residence

The poor understanding of IRM is partly due to the problem of differentiating migrants from visitors. As Longino and Marshall (1990: 233) write, 'permanent migrants anchor the continuum on one end, vacationers on the other'. In practice, the continuum stretches from permanently-settled emigrants, through dual residence, seasonal migrants and second-home ownership to long-stay tourism. The difficulties are further exaggerated by the confused terminology for the various types of foreign residents. In this section, we provide a brief sketch of each of the main types of foreign older residents, focusing on the balance of time spent in the destination and elsewhere, and the forms of property rights. These are idealised types and they are empirically explored further in Chapters 5 and 6.

At one extreme of the retirement relocation continuum is the *long-stay international tourist*. Relieved of the constraints of paid work, retirees tend to take longer and more leisurely holidays than those in employment. The average number of foreign trips does decline with age, but the fall is far from precipitous, confirming the increase in active old age and the growing familiarity of older cohorts with foreign travel. The average number of trips per annum for those aged 55-59 is 0.8, and is 0.5 for those aged 70-74. There is no clear evidence as to the share of long-term stays within this total, but longer winter stays (in excess of one month) have been actively promoted to reduce the average unit costs of accommodation and transport suppliers. The long-stay tourist group does not generally have enduring property rights in the destination area, which increases their flexibility to vary the destinations of their winter holidays. However, there is a high degree of 'destination loyalty', as was shown in a study of older Norwegians who spent the 1987-8 winter in Spain as tourists. 'Lively scenes of reunion are enacted when people meet at the airport or in the hotel lobby for another season. Some may have as many as 10-15 winters in Spain behind them, most likely in the same place year after year' (Myklebost 1989: 211).

Second-home owners are primarily working-age tourists and tend to make occasional, relatively short visits to the destination. They are, however, different to long-stay tourists because property ownership involves legal and financial undertakings, and they are likely to be committed to regular visits to that particular property. The significance of this group is that many form the ambition for more extended and retirement residence in their chosen area, so that many second homes become retirement homes. International second-home ownership is a relatively neglected topic, with the exception of Buller and Hoggart's (1994) investigation of British property purchasers in France. Valenzuela (1998) suggests that in Spain large-scale foreign purchases of second homes began on the Mediterranean coast and in the Canary Islands in the 1970s, and that by the 1990s there were an estimated 1.5 million foreign-owned dwellings in Spanish coastal areas (some of which are owned by permanent migrants). Moreover, numbers are still increasing by an estimated 50,000 annually. The major concentrations are in the Costa del Sol, the Costa Blanca, the Balearic Islands and the Canary Islands. The majority of owners are British (30 per cent) or German (25 per cent).

Seasonal migrants are a diverse group of all ages but with many younger retirees: they are differentiated from second-home owners by the length of time they spend in their property in southern Europe. By definition, they will also have property rights elsewhere, usually in their country of origin, and they are probably more accurately conceptualised as being engaged in circulation than migration. The balance of time spent in the two (and occasionally three or more) homes is variable. At one seasonal extreme, such migrants may be 'snowbirds' escaping northern European winters, while a few are 'sunbirds' who move to northern Europe to escape the summer heat and peak tourism season. The amount of time spent at the destination ranges from a few winter months to virtually the full year. In Mijas (Costa del Sol), for example, Jurdao and Sánchez (1990) found that 44 per cent of foreign residents lived more than three months a year outside Spain. In most countries, those who remain more than six months face the legal requirement to register as residents.

The final group of retired migrants are the *permanent residents* who live all year round at the destination, excepting only the visits and holidays they take elsewhere. Most own their homes. They may or may not own property in the country of origin, and this is an important social differentiator in terms of assets and for the ease of returning to these countries. Retained property ownership is also a psychological barrier to long-term commitment to their new homes.

These are of course ideal types and the diversity of individual experience means that the categories overlap. Moreover, individuals may shift between these types over time, for while some migrants make a single, direct move to permanent settlement, others may make a more gradual transition from, say, second-home owner to seasonal migrant and then to permanent migrant. Although this typology is necessarily idealised, it does highlight important differences amongst those who have retired 'in the sun', not least with regard to property rights, whether individuals are 'on holiday' or 'at home', and their degree of long-term commitment to and contacts with the country of origin.[4]

Conclusions

The review of secondary statistics in this chapter has shown that substantial numbers of retired British persons live in Spain and Italy and, to a lesser extent, elsewhere in southern Europe. Given the vagaries of the sources, the presented numbers are minimum estimates, and it must be remembered that the counts of those of official retirement age exclude the early retired. The starting point for understanding the phenomenal growth of expatriate retirement is the ageing of the northern European populations, combined with the growth of wealth and income, which has created considerable potential demand for residence in the South. The conditions which enabled some of this demand to be channelled into international retirement migration include the reduction of the friction of distance, increasing familiarity with foreign destinations and spreading experience of living abroad. International retirement to the Mediterranean countries has been intricately associated with the evolution of tourism. The attractions of retirement moves are diverse but include the climate and outdoor lifestyle, the cost of living and, in some cases, the lure of imagined and idealised rural cultures. Individual migrants are faced with a potentially large choice of destinations, even within southern Europe. In the next chapter we explore some aspects of this place diversity, concentrating on the four regions where our field research was carried out.

Notes

1. SOPEMI is the OECD's monitoring unit for comparative international migration statistics. However, it should be stressed that in most cases SOPEMI presents data derived purely from respective national statistical sources: hence true comparability cannot be guaranteed.
2. The Spanish, an important migrant group in Portugal, are excluded from this analysis since they are not, for the most part, retirement migrants.
3. There is no definitive evidence as to why the French, compared to the British and Germans, should either be staying for shorter time periods or be less likely to register if resident for more than six months. One possible explanation may lie in the presence of 'second generation' naturalised Portuguese returning to the country – France was by far the most important destination for Portuguese migrants in the period of mass labour migration in the 1960s and 1970s. A second reason may be French students studying in Portugal, for which there is partial confirmation in the age distribution data.
4. The existence of competing typologies should be noted; perhaps the most important of these has been advocated by O'Reilly (1995a). Her five-fold classification is structured around five categories: expatriates, residents, seasonal visitors, returners and tourists. They are discussed

further in Chapter 6, but here we can note that her returners equate to our second-home owners, her expatriates to our permanent residents, and that she has divided our seasonal migrants into residents (in terms of legal status and orientation, and spending two to five summer months in the UK) and seasonal visitors (living in Britain but spending much of the winter abroad).

Three

The Importance of Place: Contrasting Areas for Retirement Migration in Southern Europe

Social, Legal and Environmental Contrasts Within the Mediterranean

Southern Europe contains a range of environments for tourism and retirement migration. Contrasting streams of migrants, at particular times, have sought to exploit these place differences. Moreover, place differences matter not only in shaping the scale and social selectivity of the new geography of international retirement migration, but also in conditioning how migrants are inserted into host communities, and the economic, cultural and social interrelationships which follow from this.

Processes of modernisation and development have been transforming Mediterranean Europe in the postwar period (King 1997). With the exception of Albania and much of the war-damaged former Yugoslavia, there has been a long political and economic convergence between southern Europe and northern Europe (Williams 1984). Living standards in southern Europe have risen towards the EU average and in some regions, such as Catalonia and most of central and northern Italy, have surpassed this (Dunford 1997). Liberal democracies have taken root where, until comparatively recently, there were dictatorial regimes. The trend to political and economic homogenisation has been institutionalised by the accession of large parts of southern Europe to the EU. Italy was a founding member of the EU, while Greece (in 1981) and Portugal and Spain (in 1986) joined just before a significant strengthening of the Union occurred. The Single European Act 1986, the Treaty on European Union 1991, and Economic and Monetary Union have all contributed to enhance economic and, to some extent, social convergence between

Table 3.1 Socio-economic indicators for selected southern European countries

Country	GNP per cap. 1993 $US	% employed in agriculture 1965	1992	Foreign tourist overnights 1994 (millions)
Cyprus	10,380	40	15	
Greece	7,480	47	23	41
Italy	19,840	25	9	102
Malta	7,970	8	3	
Portugal	8,950	38	17	21
Spain	13,580	34	11	104

Sources: Dunford (1997); Kliot (1997); World Bank (1997).

northern and southern Europe. Cyprus is also on the shortlist for the next accession to the Union, and Malta – although it initially decided in 1996 to defer its membership bid – is soon likely to join the leading applicants. And yet, despite these convergent tendencies, southern Europe remains a region of internal contrasts which is also sharply differentiated from its northern neighbours. Here we focus on three salient features of southern EU countries: their welfare states, levels of economic development, and experience of tourism and retirement migration.

Rhodes (1996: 14-15) provides a succinct summary of the welfare state model in southern Europe: 'The "southern model" has traditionally emphasised civil society solutions like church, family and private charity in combination with parallel residual public welfare institutions – providing, in other words, a rudimentary welfare state.' Other features of southern European welfare models include their relatively recent evolution, their fragmented social systems, and their weak tax bases and mechanisms for the distribution of benefits (Ferrera 1996). There are of course differences in the extent of welfare state coverage and in the development of these institutions. Thus in recent years the Italian model has been subject to cutbacks at the very time that the Spanish model is still in the expansion stage.

Secondly, although all the major economies of southern Europe have followed broadly similar development trends, there have been important differences in timing and detail. Italy was the first country to experience rapid economic transition in the 1950s, followed a decade later by Spain, Greece and Portugal. Despite some convergence amongst these economies (evident for example in life expectancy rates), especially since the Mediterranean enlargement of the European Union in the 1980s, significant differences remain in their levels of development (Table 3.1). GNP per capita in Italy, for example, is more than double that in all other southern European states except Spain. Another feature which has a bear-

ing on retirement migration to some parts of the Mediterranean region
has been the massive decline in agricultural employment in all these
countries, for rural depopulation releases a stock of dwellings for incoming migrants.

The third point to note is that tourism has had differential effects.
Extensive regions, such as the interior of Andalusia, much of central and
southern Italy, and most of the Greek mainland, have barely been touched
by mass tourism (Montanari 1995). Some of these regions have experienced a modest growth of rural tourism. Even where there has been mass
tourism development, the speed and timing of development have been
varied, so that the Mediterranean coast is peppered with resorts at different stages of evolution. Finally, the growth of tourism and retirement
migration have themselves, over time, transformed the types of environments that new migrants encounter.

Compared to those who arrived in the 1960s and 1970s, recent migrants
to southern Europe have found very different social, economic and political conditions. Much of the 'development gap' between northern and
southern Europe has narrowed, as we have already pointed out. Individual
destinations have also changed, following the growth of tourism and in-
migration, and of services and local populations to serve both these
groups. This has had two effects: the creation of cultural enclaves with
familiar, northern European types of services, where languages such as
English and German are widely understood; and the deterioration of the
quality of life in these enclaves as increased numbers result in congestion.

The Selection of Case Studies

Given the unreliability of most secondary sources on foreign populations,
combined with a lack of age-specific migration statistics, UK pensions data
(Table 1.4) probably provide the most reliable guide to the distribution of
retired British persons in southern Europe. There are seven countries in
southern Europe where significant numbers of UK pensions are received:
in rank order in 1997, they are Spain (34,225), Italy (24,536), France
(14,089), Cyprus (6,049), Portugal (3,801), Malta (2,365) and Greece
(1,686). Our research studies four of these; France, Cyprus and Greece
were not included. France was excluded because of Buller and Hoggart's
(1994) recent study of British property purchasers in which retirement
migrants were a feature (Hoggart and Buller 1995). Cyprus was omitted
because of a pending project on the island's British community (Damer
1997); and because many of its distinctive features – such as a long military and cultural association with the UK – were echoed in Malta. Finally,
Greece was left aside on the grounds of having the smallest numbers of
British pension recipients, although an offshoot project on Corfu has
been undertaken (Lazaridis, Poyago-Theotoky and King 1999).

There were several positive reasons for selecting Tuscany, Malta, the
Costa del Sol and the Algarve:

- Spain has the largest number of British pension holders, was the model for mass international tourism development in the 1960s, and looms large in media representations of British retirement abroad. The Costa del Sol was chosen because it has the largest concentration of British nationals (of all ages) living in Spain (see Table 2.5).
- Italy is the second largest destination for British pension recipients, and a country with strong historical and cultural associations for many British people. Within Italy, Tuscany with adjacent Umbria were chosen because they host important concentrations of British retirees.
- Portugal, which has the fifth largest number of pension recipients, was chosen because of its recent and relatively less intense tourism development, compared to Spain. The Algarve was chosen as the most 'Mediterranean' region in Portugal and as home to approximately one third of all British nationals living in that country (Table 2.4). Its retirement settlement has both coastal concentrations and a dispersed pattern in the rural areas stretching into the hills, and has similarities and contrasts with both the Italian and the Spanish experiences.
- Finally Malta was selected – despite having only the sixth largest number of holders of British pensions living in southern Europe – because of the island's historical association with the UK, its strong dependence on British mass tourism, the distinctiveness of an island destination, and for being outside the EU institutional framework.

The four case studies therefore represent places with differing levels of development, institutional affiliation to the EU, and histories of tourism and settlement. Their diverse experiences are now related individually.

Tuscany

A long British attachment

It has been written, somewhat inelegantly, that the British 'have always cherry picked the bits of Italy that please us' (Rees 1996). If this is so, then Tuscany has long been the ripest of the Italian cherries for both tourists and migrants. In the Grand Tour, Florence was the vital resting place in virtually all travel plans; the prime attraction was, of course, the artistic heritage and culture of the city, but the countryside was also admired and gazed upon in the eighteenth century. Kirby (1952: 2), for example, writes that the English 'footed it along the old roads in Tuscany as if they were in paradise' and alludes to their leasing many of the finest rural villas and castles.

In the nineteenth century, Tuscany became the home of a succession of English writers and poets, including Shelley, Byron, the Brownings and Trollope. Their writings contributed to the construction of Tuscany amongst the English upper and middle classes as a particularly divine and harmonious environment in which to be a visitor or a resident. During the course of the nineteenth century, the social composition of the flow of

British visitors to Tuscany changed. The young aristocrats of the Grand Tour gave way to more middle-class and intellectual travellers and settlers. For example, in 1863 Thomas Cook made his first exploratory visit to Italy. Brendon (1991: 80) writes that he 'crossed the Alps – in a *diligence* drawn by thirteen mules – and opened up northern Italy to mass tourism'. Increased tourism was followed by residence, and by 1900 the number of British living in Tuscany was estimated at 35,000 by the British Consul in Florence (Carmichael 1901).

After 1945, the social scene in Tuscany was to change in two ways which had a profound implication for British migration. The first affected the rural society which had produced the picturesque cultural landscapes so beloved by the British, particularly in the Chianti district (Flower 1988). Peasant share-croppers occupied the land under the *mezzadria* system. Their ancient tenancies had produced a dispersed pattern of settlement with substantial farmhouses (*case coloniche*) often attractively sited on hill-tops or hillsides. The *mezzadria* system collapsed with agrarian reform (King and Took 1983). Out-migration led to the *case coloniche* being abandoned, creating a supply of attractive properties for those seeking holiday or permanent homes.

The second major change was the intensification of tourism. Tuscany was always at the forefront of modern Italian tourism, along with the northern lakes and Rome, and it strengthened its position in the postwar years. By 1994 it was receiving more than 7 million tourists a year and 46 per cent were foreign; one of the largest contingents received by any Italian region (King and Montanari 1998). Within Tuscany, however, an important change had occurred. While Florence remained a pre-eminent attraction as a world tourist city, rural tourism expanded rapidly, especially from the 1970s (Loda 1994). By the 1990s, Tuscany and Umbria had the greatest density of farm-based 'agritourism' provision in Italy, with 40 per cent of the guests from abroad, especially Germany and the UK (Doccioli 1992). The importance of such rural tourism was twofold: it provided further incentives to renovate and convert farm buildings, and it extended the search spaces of tourists, creating a new potential migrant pool.

These changes opened the way for foreign buyers of *case coloniche* at initially exceptionally low prices. The largest group of purchasers was probably German, and Hooper (1994) wryly notes that 'Chiantishire' should really be known as 'Kiantiland'. But the British were also present in significant numbers. Their purchases in the 1960s foreshadowed a major shift in their geographical distribution, for the community in Florence declined and the new arrivals opted for the countryside. Writing from Villa La Pietra, his sumptuous home at Fiesole, Harold Acton (1986: 55) commented that 'the ancient farms of Greve and Castellina [in Chianti] have been converted to cosy cottages' and that 'the emigrants have imported an atmosphere of week-end Surrey'.

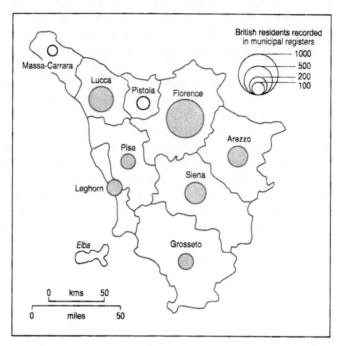

Figure 3.1 Distribution of British residents in Tuscany, 1992

Enumerating the British in Tuscany

Quantifying the size and distribution of the international retirement community in Italy poses significant data challenges even though there is a relative abundance of statistical sources. The three published sources are the census, records on sojourn permits for foreigners, and the *anagrafe* or local registers of foreigners (Quirino and Leone 1993; see also Chapter 2, pp. 41-2). The census is generally of limited value for our purposes, so only the other two sources are considered here. Special tabulations of sojourn permit data were obtained from ISTAT, the national statistical agency, and these confirm the relative importance of Tuscany for the British resident in Italy (King and Patterson 1998). In 1994, British citizens constituted 6.9 per 10,000 of the Tuscan population as compared to 4.7 of Italy's. While the data were not disaggregated by age, they reveal that 63 per cent of the 2,459 British permit-holders in Tuscany were women. Differential survival rates, the tendency for men to have married younger women, and the initial attraction of more women to Italy for study purposes may have all played a part in accounting for this. Turning to the municipal registers, special tabulations of these were also commissioned from ISTAT, yielding a total of 2,375 British residents in Tuscany at the end of 1992. As King and Patterson (1998: 162-4) demonstrate, the similarity of the two totals is deceptive, for both are under-enumerations. Interpolation of the data sets, information provided by the British Consul, and field knowledge lead us to estimate that there are about 4,000 British nationals living in Tuscany, and that around half are of retirement age.

The distribution of the British *within* Tuscany also differs slightly according to which data source is used, but here we employ the *anagrafe* data (see Figure 3.1). The map shows that the main provinces for British settlement are Florence, Lucca, Siena and Arezzo. The largest numbers are found in the province capitals and some other important towns such as the coastal resort of Viareggio, near Lucca. The two main rural concentrations are in Chianti (between Florence and Siena) and in the northern part of Lucca province, corresponding to the relatively isolated Garfagnana and Bagni di Lucca districts.[1]

The Tuscan environment: a harmonious balance

Florence is the recognised artistic and cultural heart of the region. It is the city which has been most touched by tourism, the pressures of which are well-documented (see King and Montanari 1998). But Florence is more than a tourist shrine, it is a city of almost half a million people with a diverse economic base. For these reasons, during the second half of the twentieth century it has ceased to be the principal home of the British in Tuscany. Many other historic cities adorn Tuscany and Umbria – there are well-established tourist itineraries through Assisi, Siena, Pisa and Lucca – as well as smaller architectural gems such as San Gimignano and Pienza, and quintessential villages by the score. While the cities and larger towns themselves are rarely attractive to British retirement migrants, the surrounding countryside, with its ancient villages and small towns, provides the setting for several clusters of foreign residents. The most renowned of Tuscany's sylvan landscapes is Chianti, the first major focus of rural British settlement after the Second World War. Its heart is the triangle formed by Greve, Radda and Castellina. There are also very attractive landscapes to the south of Siena, deep wooded valleys in the Garfagnana, the Casentino hills which form the border with Emilia-Romagna to the east, and the shores of Lago di Trasimeno in the south. Not all of the region conforms to the idealised view of a rural idyll, for there are major development corridors, especially in the Arno valley which is a heavily industrialised and urbanised sub-region, while seaside resorts have developed on the western coast around Viareggio. Tuscany therefore provides a rich variety of environments for incoming migrants, while the region has not experienced the cultural and landscape changes brought about by mass tourism in the other study areas.

Malta

From outpost of empire to independent state

Malta lies 93 km south of Sicily and some 300 km from the Tunisian coast. In terms of location, non-affiliation to the EU, politics and language, Malta is the most 'distant' from northern Europe of our four case studies.

But at the same time, a long historical association with the UK, provision for mass tourism, and the widespread use of English, make it a relatively familiar cultural environment for the British. Their settlement in Malta has been more complex and has been of longer duration than in other areas of European mass tourism. The roots of the affiliation lie in the strategic importance of Valletta's Grand Harbour for the expansion and control of the British empire. This importance was paramount during the Second World War, and the experiences of those years forged strong personal connections between the British armed forces and the Maltese. This was in many ways the peak of a British military presence on the island, around which had ebbed and flowed, over the previous one and a half centuries, a visible and highly self-confident British society. The islands were formally granted independence in 1964, and in 1974 became a Republic.

The closure of the Naval Dockyards in the 1960s was a major blow to the island economy. Large numbers of Maltese emigrated, both because of economic necessity and to escape what some saw as the social claustrophobia of life on the islands (Dench 1975a). Given their language skills, their destinations were the English-speaking countries of the empire and, of course, Britain itself. Maltese emigration statistics show that, between 1946 and 1976, over 140,000 left the islands through an assisted-passage scheme; of these, 58 per cent went to Australia, 22 per cent to the United Kingdom, and 20 per cent to the USA (King 1979). The emigrant streams to the various destination countries were to some extent differentiated and the UK was particularly attractive to young adults. The significance of this is that as early as the 1960s inter-marriage between the two communities was 'wholesale' (Dench 1975b: 137). By the early 1970s, British immigration controls had been strengthened and a new pattern emerged of reduced emigration and increasing levels of return (Lockhart and Mason 1988); in many instances the returnees were accompanied by British spouses and partners. The official statistics are not reliable in quantifying the return flows, but Dench (1975a) estimated that almost a third returned at this time .

The other consequence of the Dockyard's decline was the need to diversify the economy, and this led to the promotion of mass tourism after 1960. Malta, unlike Italy, had not featured in the romantic imagination of the British, and it had been seen as little more than a military outpost. Black (1996) writes that the marketing of Malta as a tourism destination was based on combining images of an unspoilt coastline with that of a 'home away from home', including fragments of information such as 'they drive on the left' and have 'English' telephone boxes (Black 1996: 120). Mass tourism familiarised a new group of British citizens with Malta. The expansion of tourism was, at times, startling. Whereas in 1960 there were only twenty-six, mostly small, hotels, by the mid-1960s the development of package tourism had opened up Malta to new mass markets. The take-off stage was during 1965-70, when there was a 257 per cent increase in visitors; this was partly the result of the British government's imposition of a £50 spending limit on holidays outside the sterling area in 1966, which made Malta more attractive. Tourism arrivals reached 728,700 by 1980 and although growth rates were less than spectacular during the 1980s, annual arrivals passed one million in 1992 (Beeley and Charlton 1994: 118). The mass tourism boom was fuelled above all by British visitors, and as late as 1992, three out of every five tourists still came from the UK (Beeley and Charlton 1994). This not only reflected good transport links and the attraction of an English-speaking environment, but also the way in which tourism had become intertwined with in-migration, which is the subject we now turn to.

By the twentieth century Malta had become accustomed to the presence of a permanent British community and the associated economic benefits. As early as the 1920s, one journalist was referring to the need to attract 'resident visitors', including pensioners (Casolani 1924). In 1964 a fiscal strategy was implemented to attract such wealthy British settlers: the offer of 6d in the pound income tax (2.5 per cent) to foreign residents with an annual income of at least £800. The income requirement was raised in 1968 to £1,400, but the tax rate remained a strong attraction to the 'sixpenny settlers'. With other concessions, Malta became the most attractive tax haven in southern Europe. Between 1963 and 1971, 4,443 took up residence in Malta (Libreri 1972: 15), including a large influx from Rhodesia after 1967.

The combined success of the tourism and settlement policies brought their own difficulties, notably a housing shortage as foreigners bid up house prices and house-building costs, and this contributed to the election success of Dom Mintoff's Labour Party in 1971 (Blouet 1993: 220). Mintoff's election campaign had been characterised by strong anti-British rhetoric and there were deep concerns that many of the resident foreign community would leave, but most government policies were relatively moderate, and they did not appropriate foreigners' property as some had feared. Paradoxically, those foreigners interested in buying found no shortage of cheap properties because of local political uncertainty and the worldwide recession following the 'oil shock'. According to one member of the British Residents' Association, the peak of British settlement was in 1976, two years *after* Malta became a Republic and five *after* Mintoff's election success. Migration has since continued but at relatively lower levels.

The migrants to the islands, both before and after the mid-1970s, have had one of three main associations with Malta: through the British colonial or armed services presence; through the country's enthusiastic fostering of mass tourism and retirement settlement; and through the labour migration to the UK (chiefly London) in the 1950s and 1960s. More than a century of close association between the British and Maltese on the islands and in England has produced many permutations of citizenship, of cultural and national affinities, and of economic and affective bonds in Anglo-Maltese families and households.

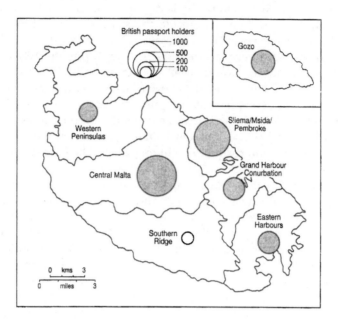

Figure 3.2 British passport holders registered as electors in Malta, 1995

Enumerating the British in Malta

As a small island state, Malta could be expected to have relatively reliable population registrations and enumerations, but there is considerable under-counting of foreigners. Moreover, a considerable number of inter-marriages between the Maltese and British populations leads to both unconscious and wilful mis-reporting of citizenship. And there is the perennial problem of the ambivalent status of visitors and temporary residents. The most useful, up-to-date and reliable data source is the electoral roll, which records the name, address, age, sex, marital status and nationality of the electors. The Maltese Electoral Commission made available to us on disc the 'aliens extract' of the 1995 roll. While it is certain that the roll is incomplete, there is no means of assessing the extent of under-enumeration.

The British are by far the largest group of foreign residents in Malta. The electors' list has 3,741 British citizens, nearly eight times the number of Australians, who are the second largest foreign group. The registration of 1,190 British citizens of UK pensionable age (60+ for females, and 65+ for males) contrasts with the contemporaneous figure that 2,177 UK pensions were being paid to residents of Malta in 1995. The discrepancy is large but can be accounted for by the receipt of pensions by Maltese who spent most of their working lives in the UK, and by those who were absent or evaded the electoral registration. Most key informants estimated a

Table 3.2 Age structure by sex of the major foreign citizen populations in Malta, 1995 (%)

Age group	United Kingdom			United States		Canada		Australia	
	f	m	f+m	f	m	f	m	f	m
15-29	17.9	15.9	17.1	26.6	20.9	43.1	44.9	57.4	46.7
30-49	32.5	25.9	29.8	48.2	40.9	39.2	30.6	33.5	34.3
50-59	17.8	17.3	17.6	9.4	10.9	10.5	12.2	1.9	4.7
60-69	15.7	18.9	17.1	8.6	11.8	2.0	7.1	4.5	5.9
70-79	10.1	15.1	12.2	6.5	10.9	3.3	3.1	1.9	5.3
80+	6.0	6.9	6.4	0.7	4.5	2.0	2.0	0.6	3.0
60+	31.8	40.9	35.6	15.8	27.3	7.2	12.2	7.1	14.2
No. 0+	2,193	1,547	3,740	139	110	153	98	310	169
No. 60+	698	633	1,331	22	30	11	12	22	24

Source: Malta Aliens Electoral Roll.

larger British retired population but they tended to include seasonal and temporary residents as well as permanent residents, and did not distinguish British by citizenship, nationality and place of birth. The British High Commission informally estimates the total British population on the island at around 5,000, based on necessarily incomplete – and sometimes out-of-date – voluntary registrations.

The electoral registers show that the British population is by far the oldest foreign group in Malta. A third of women (32 per cent) and 41 per cent of men were aged 60 years or more, while over a fifth of males (22 per cent) were aged at least 70 years (Table 3.2). Another important feature is the distinctive and substantial element found in Anglo-Maltese households. Their older British members are testimony to decades of friendships, inter-marriage, and close working connections in Malta *and* in England. These connections have encouraged intermarriage, both between Maltese natives and the British servicemen or women stationed on the islands (up to the early 1960s), and between Maltese labour migrants in England and British natives. One of the implications of these particular affiliations is that some argue that the choice of Malta for retirement by the British has passed its peak, given that the British military presence in Malta ceased in 1979.

Whatever the future of retirement migration to Malta, the electoral list does allow their present geographical distribution to be mapped, albeit crudely (Figure 3.2). Foreign retirees tend not to settle in Valletta and other high-density areas but rather seek apartments and villas at lower densities in resort and coastal areas. There are two main clusters – the largest lies along the north-east coast and consists of the modern settlement in San Pawl il Bahar (St Paul's Bay) and adjacent Mellieha; the next is the earlier twentieth-century concentration in and around Sliema. There is a tendency for the retired to select the most secluded areas, in northern Malta and in Gozo. For instance, 43.5 per cent of the British residents of Gozo are aged 50 years or more, in contrast to 25 per cent in Valletta.

Co-existence of tourism and migration on a small island

Malta's population has grown from 330,000 in 1960 to 376,335 by 1995, and inward migration has contributed to this (Markwick 1997). The distribution has been shaped first by nineteenth-century industrial and port expansion around the Grand Harbour and secondly by a spate of urban decentralisation since independence, linked to tourism growth and the need to remedy the shortage of low-cost housing. As a result, there has been a sharp reduction in living densities in the main conurbation, whilst residential developments have spread across the island of Malta, particularly in the north and centre. Valletta's population halved between 1957 and 1985, when it was 9,300, whilst Sliema's fell from 23,400 to 13,700. Tourism accommodation is clustered around Sliema and St Julians on the north-east side of the island. There are a few estates where the residents are non-Maltese, but dispersed settlement prevails and, as noted previously, retired British migrants have tended to seek out the more secluded parts.

These developments have brought about considerable environmental pressures that are only now being addressed. The area occupied by buildings expanded from 5 per cent of the islands in 1957 to 16 per cent in 1985 (Balm 1996: 83). There is concern about the loss of agricultural land, so that the 1990 *Structure Plan* proposes 'a dual policy of urban containment at the rural fringe and rehabilitation of the older urban areas'. This entails the reform of rent controls, ending 'home ownership' subsidies in undeveloped areas, and switching funds to existing built-up areas (Markwick 1997: 182). This will not necessarily deter retirement immigration, for renovated older apartments in the 'gentrifying areas' around Valletta's harbours may be more attractive to retired households than to young Maltese families. However, it can be argued that the densities of population and urban development are now so high that the islands' attractions to retirees have diminished. Malta has lost many of its rural and unspoiled coastal landscapes.

Costa del Sol

From fashionable resorts to mass tourism

Although Spain is a by-word for mass tourism, its rise to prominence has been relatively recent. In the course of the eighteenth century, Spain did

attract a few foreign tourists, informed by a new taste for wild and romantic scenery and exotic cultures, but it was the development of spa tourism
in the nineteenth century which brought the city of Málaga to the attention of northern European visitors (Barke and Towner 1996). By 1930
there was formal provision of hotel accommodation in Torremolinos, and
it was being visited regularly by foreigners – especially by English and
American painters (Pollard and Domínguez Rodríguez 1995). The Civil
War, and then the Second World War, devastated the emergent tourist
industry but by the late 1940s both Marbella and Torremolinos were competing as high-status destinations, attracting film stars amongst their
wealthy clientele. However, elsewhere there was little tourism provision in
the Costa del Sol outside of Málaga city. This scene was soon to be transformed.

In 1959 the Costa del Sol attracted 51,000 visitors, but this increased
more than twenty-fold over the next decade, reaching 925,000 in 1968 and
2.5 million in 1975 (Barke and France 1996). In 1995, 40.4 per cent of all
tourists to the area were from the UK (Valenzuela 1998), placing the
region firmly within the search spaces of large numbers of future potential migrants. It was inevitable that the arrival of mass tourism would be
accompanied by the loss of the region's previous status as an élite destination, although some resorts such as Marbella resisted the change. The
changing scene was caught by Michener (1971), writing after the onset of
the tourism boom:

> The trip from Málaga to Torremolinos took less than 20 minutes, but it repre-
> sented a journey from civilization to sandless golf links in the sun, small restau-
> rants with patios open to the sky, a Mediterranean more deeply coloured than
> sapphire, and, surprisingly, a cluster of 27 skyscrapers marking the official
> beginning of the town.

A wave of foreign purchases of property in the Costa del Sol also began
at this time. As early as 1963 there were reports of English estate agents
organising weekend flights to inspect properties (Barke and France 1996:
273). A further boost came in 1968-71 with German laws that allowed tax
relief on investments in Spain (classified as aid to less developed countries). The old village nuclei and the clusters of seafront hotels were soon
surrounded by modern *urbanizaciones*.[2] Jurdao and Sánchez (1990: 117)
estimate that there were 470 *urbanizaciones* in the Costa del Sol by 1969 –
including 120 in Mijas and 105 in Marbella. Most housed rapidly increasing foreign communities.

One extensive *urbanización* complex is Sitio de Calahonda, midway
between Fuengirola and Marbella. The development started in 1963, and
its most rapid growth occurred in the 1980s, coinciding with improved
communications, house-price inflation and the easing of UK exchange
control regulations. By the mid-1990s there were some 3,100 properties
divided into forty individual *urbanizaciones* of detached villas and low-rise
apartments, and with a mixture of permanent residents, seasonal migrants

Table 3.3 British and European nationals resident in Andalusia and Málaga, 1991

Andalusian provinces	Europeans no.	%	Málaga province	British no.	%	Other Europeans no.	%
			Age groups:				
Almería	2,337	5.3					
Cádiz	2,389	5.4	<50	7,305	49.1	16,435	50.0
Córdoba	511	1.2	50-59	2,601	17.5	5,320	16.2
Granada	2,756	6.2	60-69	2,995	20.1	6,473	19.7
Huelva	1,656	3.7	70-70	1,642	11.0	3,729	11.3
Jaen	287	0.6	80+	343	2.3	913	2.8
Málaga	32,269	73.0					
Seville	2,029	4.6	Total	14,886	100.0	32,870	100.0
Andalusia	44,234	100.0					

Source: Instituto Nacional de Estadística (1994).

and second homes. Calahonda has its own cluster of retail and leisure facilities. It is one of the largest complexes of *urbanizaciones* on the Costa, but in many ways is typical of the many that fringe the coast outside of the main towns.

The postwar tourism boom was sustained through to the late 1990s despite a blip at the start of the decade (Marchena Gómez and Vera Rebollo 1995). As a result, the Costa del Sol remains one of the leading tourism destinations in Europe: it is reputed to have more tourism beds than all of Portugal. It is, however, far from homogeneous, either socially or environmentally, and – despite the pressures of almost four decades of strong tourism growth – still presents a wide range of environments to incoming migrants.

Enumerating the British in the Costa del Sol

The main data source for quantifying foreign settlement is the census which records 44,234 Europeans as resident in Andalusia, over three quarters of them in the province of Málaga (Table 3.3). Amongst the other provinces the numbers are greatest in Granada, Cádiz and Almería, which have Mediterranean coastlines. As explained in Chapter 2, the census under-enumerates the actual population. It suggests that there are 14,888 British residents in Málaga province (Table 3.3), while the British Consul in Málaga estimates that there are approximately 50,000 British permanent residents in the Costa del Sol.[3] According to the census, 7,581 or 50.9 per cent of the British in Málaga province are aged 50 years or more, and 4,980 (33.4 per cent) are aged over 60. If the unofficial estimate of the Consul is correct, and if the census age structure is applied, there are

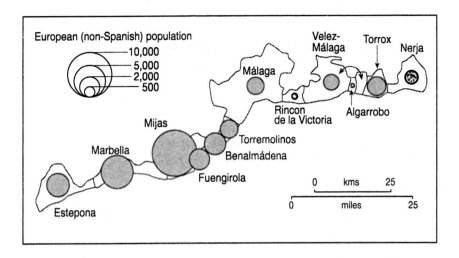

Figure 3.3 European population resident in the Costa del Sol, 1991

16,700 British older residents, a plausible total from our own field observations and key informant interviews.

Census data tend to underestimate those who are not full-time residents. This population may be indexed by records of second homes, of which there were an estimated 114,392 in the Costa del Sol in 1991 (Mellado 1996). According to a survey reported in the *Libro Blanco del Turismo de la Costa del Sol Occidental*, 52 per cent of second-home owners were aged 65 years or more in 1992; that is, some 57,000 second homes were owned by retirees. The proportion British-owned is around 15-20 per cent, so that we can estimate that 8,000-11,000 second homes were owned by older British people. These data reinforce the impression that the Costa del Sol is home to a substantial, perhaps the largest, concentration of British retired people living in southern Europe.

The distribution of foreign European residents is highly polarised within Málaga province (Figure 3.3). Not only is there heavy concentration in its coastal municipalities, but almost one third (32.5 per cent) of its foreign European population lives in a single municipality, Mijas. A further 15.9 per cent live in Marbella, 7.9 per cent in Estepona and 7.2 per cent in Benalmádena, so two-thirds live in just four municipalities. Note that the scale of the symbols in Figure 3.3 differs from that on the other maps by a factor of ten. The scale, clustering and visibility of the foreign populations in the Costa del Sol have received considerable research attention (see, for example, Eaton 1995; Jurdao and Sánchez 1990; Madden 1999; O'Reilly 1995a and 1995b; Rodríguez et al. 1998).

Residential enclaves and mass tourism infrastructures

Definitions of the Costa del Sol vary but perhaps the most widely accepted is that used by the region's *Patronato de Turismo*, the entire area from Gibraltar to Nerja (Barke and France 1996: 266). Most of our survey work was undertaken in a cluster of municipalities to the west of Málaga. Therefore, our comments on the environmental features of the area are limited to this smaller region which, nevertheless, extends more than 80 km along the coast.

The population of the province of Málaga increased from 775,000 to 1,161,000 between 1960 and 1991. This is above all a reflection of labour migration to the booming coastal strip, but there has also been leisure migration, including international retirement migration. The population growth rates in individual municipalities have been striking (López Carno 1995). Between 1950 and 1991 the population of Benalmádena increased more than twelve-fold to 25,747 while the population of Torremolinos increased nine-fold to 35,309, and that of Fuengirola increased six-fold to 43,048. The first two of these also serve as commuter dormitories for Málaga, indicating the way in which Málaga has been converted from a compact, high-density city to a linear metropolitan area. The travel writer Paul Theroux (1995: 29) commented on what he saw as 'a sort of cut price colonization, this stretch of coast, bungaloid in the extreme – bungalows and twee little chalets and monstrosities in all stages of construction, from earthworks and geometrically excavated foundations filled with mud puddles', which zigzagged – with occasional breaks – all the way up Spain's Mediterranean shoreline. Theroux's acerbic comments have value as an overall impression but conceal the area's diversity.

Torremolinos is perhaps the best-known resort of the Costa del Sol. It initially received day visitors from Málaga, and later became a high-status resort. Then with the opening of Málaga airport to foreign charters in the 1960s, it became the first mass tourism destination in the Costa. Development was high-rise to maximise access to the beach. While the early tourist facilities were hotels, apartments were also constructed for rent or sale. Of particular importance in this respect were the 6,000 apartments in the Playamar complex, which symbolised Torremolinos' destiny as a relatively low-cost destination for both short-stay and 'residential' tourists. Next along the coast is Benalmádena Costa, which has followed a similar cycle of development as Torremolinos, lagged by a decade or so. It remained relatively up-market until the 1970s but has subsequently acquired the mantle of a low-cost mass tourist resort. While the immediate coastal area is devoted to tourism, Spanish developers have been opening up new *urbanizaciones* in the immediate hinterland since 1970. A few kilometres inland lies Benalmádena Pueblo, which has maintained some of the features of an older Spanish village. The next settlement along the coast is Fuengirola which from an early stage was developed as a relatively low-cost tourist destination. Fuengirola has a high concentration of apartments and hence attracts relatively large numbers of long-stay tourists, including many older visitors and permanent and semi-permanent retirees (O'Reilly 1995a, 1995b).

West of Fuengirola, the character of the coastal development changes. The next municipality is Mijas with at its heart Mijas Pueblo, an old village nucleus whose vernacular character and physical separation from the mass tourism coast have made it particularly attractive to retired migrants (Jurdao and Sánchez 1990). Over time, residential development has spread into the surrounding rural areas, including the coastal strip of Mijas Costa, where there are relatively up-market hotels, golf courses and *urbanizaciones* (including Calahonda, described earlier).

The next municipality is Marbella, where growth was initially stimulated by the opening in 1954 of the exclusive Marbella Club. Despite rapid expansion – including massive foreign investment in the 1980s – the town has retained something of its reputation as a high-status resort through the development of luxury hotels, expensive *urbanizaciones* such as Andalusia Nueva, and the marina at Puerto Banus. Finally Estepona, much further to the west, developed later than the other destinations, and has a stronger orientation to residential tourism and settlement than to mass tourism.

Algarve

'An empire lost but a province gained'

Tourism in the Algarve barely existed at the start of the twentieth century, and the region was as little known to Portuguese as to foreign tourists. Foreign tourists, notably the British, started to arrive in the 1920s and the 1930s, staying at several small enclaves, defined as much by imperfect knowledge as by the existence of tourism infrastructures. The places mentioned in John Gibbons' *Playtime in Portugal* make clear just how few they were, being little more than Praia da Rocha, Sagres and Monchique (Gibbons 1936). Early tourism coincided with expatriate settlement, and by the 1920s and 1930s small seasonal British communities were identifiable, 'retired mostly from the ex-British colonies [and] attracted by the climate of the Algarve' (Pina 1988: 223). Monchique with its cooler summers was their favoured destination; here Gibbons (1936: 173) observed 'tiny colonies of exiles ... one could live like a prince down that way for very little money indeed'.

The growth of modern tourism in the Algarve dates from the late 1950s, when there was investment in new hotels and the construction of golf courses at Penina and Val do Lobo. Of particular significance was the opening of Faro airport in 1965, which ushered in the era of charter tourism. Tourism nights in Algarve hotels increased from a mere 232 in 1950 to 31,417 in 1960 and 1.1m in 1970 (Silva and da Silva 1991). Tourism facilities clustered first in proximity to the airport but then

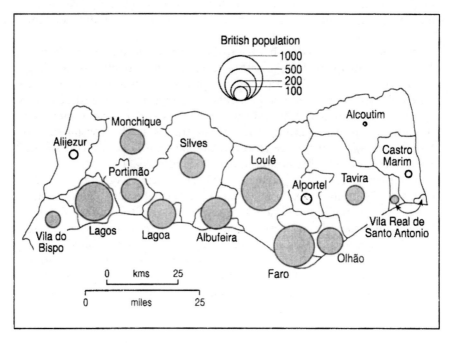

Figure 3.4 British population resident in the Algarve, 1991

spread to newly-fashionable Albufeira, patronised by film and pop stars such as Cliff Richard and Frank Ifield. Another cluster in the west centred on the resorts of Praia da Rocha and Praia da Luz, as well as the old town of Lagos. The four *concelhos* (municipalities) of Albufeira, Faro, Lagos and Portimão accounted for 70 per cent of all foreign tourist overnights in the Algarve in 1971 (Wuerpel 1974: 162).

Subsequently, tourism in the Algarve has been transformed, overnights rising to more than 10 million by 1994. Volume changes were accompanied by inverse shifts in the perceived 'quality' of tourism. There was mass construction of hotels in the coastal regions, and the area of major tourist development extended to Tavira in the east and beyond Lagos in the west. The Algarve market has remained dominated by British tourists, who in 1994 accounted for 41 per cent of all foreign bednights. In second place were German tourists (27 per cent); no other nationality had a significant presence. The Algarve, then, became firmly engraved into the circuits of mass tourism and hence into the migration fields of retired foreigners, but this happened much later than in many other parts of southern Europe.

The Algarve was a major destination for foreign settlement as early as 1970. Wuerpel (1974: 164) wrote that 'permanent residency is being established in the Algarve by foreigners in increasing numbers, the official record for 1970 listing 511 men and 469 women as holding residential permits'. More than half were from the UK, which led one local newspaper to comment that 'Great Britain may have lost an empire but she seems now to be gaining a province' (Wuerpel 1974: 164). The geography of settlement in the 1960s and the 1970s was moulded by a few entrepreneurs and property intermediaries who developed areas such as Praia da Luz. Meanwhile, in Monchique, 'Brigadier' Douglas Graham had started building holiday houses at Foia in 1963 and this gave birth to a small British colony whose members included ex-generals, masters of hounds and 'old cronies' from the City.[4] The one major interruption to the expanding inflows of tourism and migration came after the Portuguese military coup of April 1974 (Lewis and Williams 1998). A number of British residents did leave, and those who remained sometimes found the atmosphere tense and even intimidating. By 1976 democratic elections marked a return to more stable political conditions, and by 1978 there was renewed growth of tourism and inward migration, which was sustained in the 1980s and early 1990s (Williams and Patterson 1998).

Enumerating the British in the Algarve

There are few reliable data on retired British people living in the Algarve. According to the 1991 Portuguese Census, there were 3,080 British residents in the Algarve, by far the largest national group, followed by the Germans (862), Cape Verdeans (766), French (618) and Dutch (462). These numbers are probably gross under-estimations, and the British Honorary Consul estimated that there were at least 10,000 British residents in the Algarve in 1995.[5] According to the census, the British were significantly older than other foreign residents in the Algarve: 52 per cent compared to 32 per cent were aged at least 50. If the Consul's estimate is accurate, and the census does not under-record any particular age group, then there may be some 5,000 older British people in the Algarve aged over 50. Another indicator is provided by the 3,801 British pensions paid in Portugal in 1997 (Table 1.4), a number which excludes the early-retired, most seasonal migrants, and British persons not entitled to a state pension. The distribution of these between the Algarve and the rest of Portugal is not known; however there is little evidence of large numbers of British retirees living in regions other than the Algarve.

There are two main concentrations of foreigners in the Algarve: Loulé and Faro in the east and Lagos in the west (Figure 3.4). The British tend to cluster in and around Loulé, Faro and Lagos, the Germans in Lagos, Aljezur and Lagoa, and the French in Loulé, Faro and Olhão. Most permanent, and some seasonal residents, live in the rural hinterland, although this itself is divided into two sub-zones: north and south of the EN125 highway. The south is more densely settled although still largely rural, while the north is more agricultural, hilly and – in the far north – rather inaccessible. Amongst the older coastal settlements such as Carvoeiro and Praia da Luz there are signficant communities of British migrants, while the *urbanizações* (residential developments) on the coast consist mainly of second homes and investment properties let out to short-stay tourists.

A region of environmental contrasts

The net result of these changes is reflected in the population statistics for the Algarve. Whereas the population was in gradual decline through much of the twentieth century, and fell from 325,000 to 268,000 between 1950 and 1970, thereafter there was a reversal, and it climbed to 325,000 by 1980 and 340,000 in 1991. However, there has been a marked polarisation of population within the Algarve, with the interior municipalities suffering population losses during most decades since 1950, while there have been large gains on the coast (Cavaco 1980). This has gone hand-in-hand with urbanisation: by 1990, 64 per cent of the population lived in the eight main urban centres, and 70 per cent of the workforce were employed in the tertiary sector (Gaspar 1993: 180).

These population shifts have brought about significant environmental and landscape changes. Mass tourism, internal migration and growing foreign immigration have changed the face of the Algarve. There is now almost continuous coastal development from Tavira in the east to beyond Lagos in the west. It is densest between Faro and Albufeira where, in the words of Jorge Gaspar (1993: 185), 'urban overcrowding, the degeneration of certain parts of the coast, inter-sectoral disputes regarding the use of the land and a dispersed urbanization is on the way to covering every knoll and hillside of the coast'. The urbanisation pressures rarely extend more than 25 km from the coast so that the mountainous interior (the Serra de Monchique and the Serra do Caldeirão) remains relatively untouched by either tourism or settlement. The same is true of much of the area beyond Lagos, around Cape St Vincent and along the western Atlantic coast, large parts of which are now protected by an environmental management plan. While Portugal's 'other kingdom' may have become less socially distinctive and less isolated in recent decades, it still provides a variety of residential settings for would-be in-migrants.

Overview

The review of the four case-study areas has revealed considerable differences in the histories, geographies and impacts of tourism and retirement migration. Tuscany has had by far the longest history of international tourism and settlement, and it has long attracted the British. Whereas the original focus of settlement was Florence, in the postwar years the British have settled in the countryside. Malta presents a very different picture because, although long a place of military settlement by the British, only from the 1960s has it sought to attract tourists. Both in-migration and tourism are dominated by the British and they are now relatively dispersed throughout the islands. This is also the destination where language barriers between host and guest communities are least. The Costa del Sol and the Algarve both have more recent connections with the UK. The Costa del Sol received a handful of wealthy tourists in the 1960s, but there is now intense urbanisation along more than 80 km of a shore where tourism co-exists with one of the largest resident foreign populations in southern Europe. The scale effects are double-edged, for while the sheer numbers of expatriates support a range of specialised cultural and social services, they have also caused intense congestion and environmental pollution, particularly in the summer. The Algarve only became a significant international tourist destination in the 1970s. In contrast to the Costa del Sol, its European foreign populations extend more into the interior, although here too there are concentrations in coastal urbanisations.

Despite the scale and the impact of expatriate retiree settlement, it is under-researched in all four study areas. Most studies to date have examined retirement migration in individual and localised studies without reference to the general process that is affecting many areas in the Mediterranean basin. It is with this background in mind that we now turn to examine the diverse migrant origins, pathways and experiences of the individuals who constitute these foreign retired populations.

Notes

1. These remote hill districts of northern Tuscany have a long tradition of emigration to Britain; hence some of the British residents recorded here may be naturalised returnees and their descendants. For details see Farnocchia Petri (1995).
2. In the Costa del Sol, and elsewhere in coastal regions of Spain, the *urbanización* took the form of a residential development of villas and other dwelling units (studios, apartments etc.) often constructed in a self-contained estate.
3. Personal interview, March 1995.
4. *Algarve News*, 7 December 1984: 13.
5. Personal interview, May 1995. This figure may itself be an underestimate because of the discontinuity of the obligation to register with the embassy.

Four

Who Migrates? International Retirement Migration as a Socially Selective Process

Introduction to the Field Research

In this and subsequent chapters we present, analyse and discuss the results from our field research in Tuscany, Malta, the Costa del Sol and the Algarve. As indicated in the Preface, this field research had a number of interlocking components which need to be set out here in order to aid subsequent discussion and interpretation of the findings. Like many large research projects, ours employed multiple methods and generated both quantitative and qualitative data. Four main methodologies were used:

- A review of all published and unpublished literature and statistical data on the phenomenon of IRM in the four countries of study. Some of this material was assembled from standard library sources and data-bases available in the UK, and some from searches in libraries, statistical offices and town halls 'in the field'. Chapters 2 and 3 present a synthesis of this material.
- A self-completion questionnaire survey amongst older British residents in the four case-study regions. This survey yielded more than 1,000 responses and is described below.[1]
- In-depth interviews, most of which were taped and transcribed, with some 220 informants. Approximately 160 were with retired migrants, distributed equally between the four destinations. Second, about sixty key informants were interviewed, including clergy, medical and care personnel, property developers and estate agents, local administrators, teachers and academics (many of these interviews were with non-British people). The administration and targeting of these interviews are also discussed further below.
- Participant observation using flexible and ad hoc techniques such as attending meetings of residents' associations, participation in club meetings, luncheons, church services and outings, talking to people in shops, nursing homes, bars, pubs and at social gatherings.

Pilot visits to all four destinations were undertaken in 1995. The main fieldwork in the four countries comprised a virtually continuous research presence from September 1995 to December 1996. Approximately three months were spent in each of Tuscany, Malta and the Algarve; rather longer in the Costa del Sol where there is a greater British presence.

The questionnaire survey

The purpose of the self-completion questionnaire was to establish a broad comparative profile of the nature and evolution of IRM in the four study areas. An identical schedule (except for place-name changes) was used in all four areas. The questionnaire elicited quantitative and qualitative information on migrants' backgrounds (age, education, employment and migration history, holiday experience, households etc.); their aspirations for retirement and possession of relevant information and experiences (such as travel, tourism and second-home purchase); their reliance on UK or local health-care services; their lifestyles abroad, including overall satisfaction levels and particular problems faced; their ongoing links with the UK; and their plans for the future, including a possible return. The questionnaire was designed iteratively through an initial sift of themes and questions, focus-group discussions on a reconnaissance visit to the Costa del Sol, and successive testing of various drafts of the schedule on the other pilot visits. The final questionnaire fulfilled the pre-eminent criteria of workability and comprehensibility by the target population, and efficiency in terms of data collection to produce descriptive profiles and to test hypotheses. The questionnaire comprised thirty questions (some including subsidiaries) and took on average 30-45 minutes to complete.

Considerable initial thought was given to the question of sampling the target population. In the event, potential sample-frame lists (such as membership lists of expatriate and residents' associations, circulation lists of English-language newspapers, municipal registers, doctors' patient lists, telephone and other directories) often proved to be unavailable, or lacked the crucial filter of age. Only in two of the four destinations were lists that could serve as sample frames identified: the Electoral Roll in Malta and the membership list of AFPOP, the Association of Foreign Property Owners in Portugal (for details see Warnes and Patterson 1998; Williams and Patterson 1998). In Portugal useful lists were also provided by the Carvoeiro Residents' Association and other local associations. In the Costa del Sol a variety of questionnaire distribution techniques was followed, including the network of British Legion clubs, local residents' associations, church congregations and informal social networks and 'snowballing'. Given the high density of British residents 'on the ground' in the Costa del Sol, questionnaires were distributed and collected without much difficulty, especially within the Torremolinos-Mijas-Fuengirola triangle where we based most of our field survey. Tuscany presented a greater challenge both because the British older population are less numerous and more dispersed, and because no official (or unofficial) list was obtained except from the British Consulate in Florence; however, the Consulate's files were out of date and could only be used anonymously, with the Consulate staff sending out the questionnaires. The exceptional difficulties in Tuscany meant that, despite greater effort than elsewhere, the survey yielded fewer respondents (see King and Patterson 1998). For all four surveys, opinions on the comprehensiveness and representativeness of the lists we used were sought from local informants. Although our efforts to find detailed information on British residents from different sources have rarely produced definitive results, the imperfect triangulation that we achieved leads us to be relatively confident as regards the overall coverage of our questionnaire surveys.

Given the contested nature of concepts such as retirement, leisure, employment, (principal) residence and migration (O'Reilly 1995a), we adopted a flexible approach towards defining the target population. Potential respondents had to be living abroad for at least four months in the year, and either of 'retirement age' (over 60 years) or as young as 50 if they were actually 'retired'. However, as we shall see shortly, these concepts and criteria are by no means unproblematic. People living in institutional settings such as nursing homes were excluded from the survey.

Approximately half the questionnaires were distributed by post (with a stamped addressed envelope for return), and half by 'drop and collect' methods, which included both house-to-house visits and distributions and collections at society and group meetings. Some 2,980 questionnaires were distributed in the four locations and 1,066 returns received, 118 in Tuscany, 311 in Malta, 382 in the Costa del Sol and 255 in the Algarve. Whilst the rate of return (36 per cent) is close to the norm for postal and drop-and-collect surveys (Parfitt 1997: 100), in reality the response is somewhat higher, since we suspect that many questionnaires never reached their targets, owing to out-of-date addresses, the absence of addressees who were seasonal residents, and the failure of intermediaries to pass on questionnaires.

In-depth interviews

The final question on the self-completion questionnaires asked respondents if they would volunteer for a follow-up interview and, if so, they were invited to write in their telephone number. Overall, more than two-thirds offered to help the research in this way. Clearly, not all these offers could be taken up. Accordingly the in-depth interviews were set up following a pragmatic sample design which allowed us to capture diverse individuals, stratified according to the personal, household, locational and socio-economic profiles identified in the self-completion survey. Some interviews were conducted with people who had not (or did not want to) fill in questionnaires. Most interviews were with individual men or women; occasionally couples were interviewed together. The interviews took a semi-structured form, and were taped and subsequently transcribed. Typically such interviews lasted 1-1½ hours.

Most interviews with retirees took a life-history approach, but with close attention to the decision to migrate, experiences since migration, current housing and locational satisfaction, 'integration' and future intentions. The interview design was purposefully flexible to allow in-depth exploration of those topics about which the interviewee had particular insight – for instance, to enable a retired doctor to comment on the local health service, or an artist to speak about the attractions of the local landscape. Some interviews concentrated on property transactions and house moves, others on episodes of ill-health and experiences of local medical services. Future residential intentions were discussed in relation to the possibility of increasing frailty, the decision to enter supported homes or to seek extra help. The main purpose of the in-depth interviews was to explore such sensitive, even painful issues in a way not possible with the questionnaire survey and to capture some of the subjects' 'lived experiences'.

A second set of face-to-face interviews was conducted with key local informants – local political leaders, estate agents, planners and deliverers of health and welfare services, and leaders of various expatriate clubs and organisations. These interviews were also loosely structured around a common framework but varied considerably according to the respondent. Their overall aim was to identify the key issues in the growth and change of the IRM communities: the main problems encountered by retirees and by the local area in accommodating them, including house purchase and conveyancing; the degree of social and cultural integration both within the retirement communities and between them and the host society; and the economic impact on the area – both positive (e.g. support of local businesses) and negative (e.g. demands on local health services). These interviews were also taped and transcribed, except in a few cases where the key informant preferred to keep the conversation 'off the record'.

Who Are the Migrants?

Our first set of results presents basic profile data on the retired residents who have settled abroad in the study areas. As the analysis progresses we also subdivide the sample and cross-tabulate by destination region, year of arrival, social class, education and prior residential/mobility history. Table 4.1 sets out the sex, age, marital status and household characteristics of the questionnaire sample.[2] The total sample has a slight preponderance of males (56.2 per cent), probably because of the way in which the questionnaires were addressed (to households) combined with a tendency for males, as husbands, to take the responsibility for filling them in. Whether there is an excess of males amongst older British people in the destination regions remains unclear, because of the paucity of official data and the further problem of the unregistered status of some British residents – issues that were discussed in Chapter 3. On the other hand, there is some evidence from the Maltese Electoral Roll (Table 3.2) which shows a majority of males in the older age groups, and the Portuguese Census of 1991 gives

Table 4.1 Personal and household characteristics of survey respondents (%)

	Tuscany	Malta	Costa del Sol	Algarve	Total
Sex (n=1066)					
male	62.7	52.4	53.1	62.4	56.2
female	37.3	47.6	46.9	37.6	43.8
Age (n=957)					
50-59	19.3	20.3	19.1	25.8	21.0
60-69	28.4	34.2	50.0	43.9	41.5
70-79	33.0	29.5	25.7	24.4	27.4
80+	19.3	16.0	5.2	5.9	10.1
Marital status (n=956)					
never married	9.2	6.4	5.2	3.2	5.5
married	67.9	63.9	69.1	71.0	67.9
widowed	16.5	22.1	17.3	15.8	18.3
sep./divorced	6.4	7.5	8.4	10.0	8.3
Household size					
one person	23.9	29.9	25.4	20.9	25.5
two	63.3	60.8	70.8	72.3	67.4
three	8.3	6.5	2.6	4.5	4.8
four or more	4.6	2.9	1.2	2.4	2.3

Source: Authors' survey.

an excess of males for the British in the Algarve for all five-year cohorts between 55 and 80.

Table 4.1 shows that ages are widely distributed from 'young old' to 'old old', but that nearly 70 per cent were aged 60-79 years. In three of the four destinations the modal age band was 60-69; only in Tuscany was it older, with a third aged 70-79. The greatest differences are found in the 80+ category, with 19.3 per cent of Tuscany's respondents in this oldest category, compared to only 5-6 per cent in the Algarve and Costa del Sol. The oldest respondent, from Malta, was 100! Another measure of the inter-destination age differences are the mean ages of respondents: this shows a clear transition from Tuscany (69.1 years) through Malta (68.4) and the Costa del Sol (66.3) to the Algarve (65.6). Overall it is clear that we are dealing with a relatively young elderly population, with a whole-sample mean age of 67.1 years. This reflects the presence in the survey population of many 50-60 year olds, i.e. younger than the statutory retirement age. In all four areas, men tend to be slightly older than women respondents; this was most markedly the case in Malta where the male mean age of 70.6 years was significantly higher than the female mean of 65.4 years.[3]

More than two-thirds of the respondents were married (67.9 per cent) and a similar proportion (67.4 per cent) lived in two-person households (Table 4.1). These proportions are not dissimilar to the older British population as a whole. Men were more likely to be married than women, but less likely to be widowed, separated or divorced. Women predominated amongst the single-person households in all four case-study regions. Households of three or more persons were relatively rare (7.1 per cent): some involved a live-in carer but the majority contained either adult children or grandchildren. These larger, multi-generation households are more common in Tuscany and Malta which, as noted in Chapter 3, have a long and complex history of settlement of older British people.

These age and household characteristics hold few surprises. Overviews of northern Europeans retiring to Mediterranean countries such as Spain find that the typical retiree unit is a married or cohabiting couple without dependent children who move upon retirement in 'early old age' (Warnes 1991, 1994). It is particularly reassuring to note that the study by Rodríguez *et al.* (1998), which was carried out in tandem with ours in southern Spain, found similar profiles for the British in their survey: 54 per cent of their respondents were men; 23.2 per cent were aged 50-59, 49.3 per cent were aged 60-69, and 27.5 per cent were aged 70+; 75.7 per cent were married or living with a partner; and 73.7 per cent were in two-person households. These statistics (from Rodríguez *et al.* 1998: Table 2) can be compared to ours in the Costa del Sol column of Table 4.1.

Other parallels can be noted with studies of long-distance retirement migration between Canada and Florida, and within countries such as the UK, France and USA. Research carried out by Cribier and Kych (1993) on newly-retired people in Paris showed that outward migration was twice as likely for married couples as for single persons, whilst Parisians aged 50 years and more reach their maximum migration propensity at ages 60-64 years. In comparing these findings with London retirement migrants, Cribier and Kych noted similar trends except that retiring Londoners were most migration-prone at 65-69 and there was a much stronger wealth and social class filter: only the 'well-to-do' and middle classes had the financial means to migrate out of the British capital (Cribier and Kych 1993: 1408). Second, a major postal survey of anglophone Canadians in Florida (n = 2728) produced the following sample statistics: average age 69.2 years; 59.8 per cent of respondents were men; 89.5 per cent were married, 8.1 per cent widowed, and only 0.8 per cent separated/divorced and 1.1 per cent single or never married (Tucker, Marshall, Longino and Mullins 1988). Thirdly, a large telephone questionnaire survey (n = 814) of older people who had moved to western North Carolina (Haas and Serow 1993) generated sample characteristics which, again, were similar to those recorded by Table 4.1. This American study contained 54.9 per cent men and a mean respondent age of 69.4 years; 6.5 per cent of the

Table 4.2 Survey respondents' social class and employment characteristics (%)

	Tuscany	Malta	Costa del Sol	Algarve	Total
Social class (n=829)					
1 Professionals	12.9	7.3	14.3	11.2	11.5
2 Managers, intermediate professionals	58.1	47.6	53.4	61.2	54.2
3N Clerical, non-manual	19.4	24.9	24.4	18.4	22.6
3M Skilled manual	4.3	8.6	2.9	4.6	5.1
4 & 5 Intermediate and unskilled manual	0.0	6.5	1.6	2.0	2.9
Employment status (n=945)					
Employer	17.6	5.4	9.4	17.9	11.1
Self-employed	13.0	11.9	16.4	19.7	15.4
Employee	62.0	70.4	66.1	54.1	64.1
Never had a full-time job	7.4	12.3	8.2	8.3	9.3
Employment sector (n=796)					
Law, medicine, accountancy	11.2	20.9	22.8	14.9	19.2
Civil Service	13.5	11.7	8.6	13.1	11.1
Commerce	12.4	17.0	14.2	14.9	14.9
Manufacturing and sales	14.6	19.6	17.2	18.9	18.0
Teaching and higher education	16.9	9.1	14.9	12.6	12.9
Creative arts and media	13.5	4.8	6.6	6.3	6.8
Personal services	12.4	12.2	12.3	16.6	13.2
Armed services	5.6	4.8	3.3	2.9	3.9

Source: Authors' survey.
Note: Social class is the UK standard occupational classification based on last principal or full-time occupation of self or, for some wives, their (former) husbands.

sample were unmarried, 77.6 per cent married, 12.5 per cent widowed and 3.4 per cent divorced.

Builders or brokers? Employment and social class

Cribier and Kych's (1993) description of out-migrating retirement-age Londoners as 'well-to-do and middle class' provides us with a working hypothesis to examine the social and wealth characteristics of British international retirement migrants to southern Europe. The questionnaire did not ask about income or wealth, but it did elicit information on the 'last major employment' before retirement. This information was then categorised in three ways, corresponding to the three sections of Table 4.2:

employment sector, employment status (employer, self-employed, employee), and social class. The last of these categorisations was created by allocating previous main employment into the UK standard occupational classification.

As might be expected, social class is an important determinant of who becomes an international retirement migrant. For the whole sample (but excluding those who never worked – mainly women), we can see that nearly two-thirds were drawn from Social Classes 1 and 2 (professionals, managers and others with high educational qualifications), and only 8 per cent from manual occupations. This pattern is broadly uniform across the destinations, with one significant exception: Malta has only 55 per cent in Classes 1 and 2 and a much higher representation in the manual classes 3M, 4 and 5 – 15 per cent, more than three times the proportion in the other three destinations.

Two main mechanisms can be adduced to explain this lower-status Maltese pattern, which also includes the highest share of the clerical class. First the British naval presence in the island brought many working-class men to Malta during the war and in the early postwar decades, until the British withdrawal of the naval garrison and dockyards in the late 1970s. This experience of serving and working in Malta caused many to stay on for retirement or to come back for holidays and, ultimately, to retire there. Second, there are British women of retirement age living in Malta who are married to Maltese labour migrants who had moved to Britain in the 1950s and 1960s, and then returned to Malta with their British wives (Warnes and Patterson 1998).

The broad message of the social class analysis is clear: a large majority of retirement migrants are drawn from a professional and managerial background, more than 70 per cent in the cases of Tuscany and the Algarve. The 'clerical class' comprises a consistent minority of cases, reaching a quarter in Malta and Spain; only in Malta are the manual grades represented as a significant presence. Clear echoes of this social class pattern are seen in the middle section of Table 4.2, on employment status. Overall, 26.5 per cent of the respondents were employers or self-employed, this proportion rising to 37.6 per cent in the Algarve and 30.6 per cent in Tuscany, but falling to only 17.3 per cent in Malta. However, the usefulness of this section of the table is limited by the breadth of the 'employee' group which accounts for nearly two-thirds of the responses. This is remedied by the final part of Table 4.2 which gives more specific detail about the sectors and types of employment. The data show a wide spread of occupations across the mainly higher-status sectors of the employment spectrum. The main 'deviations' are Tuscany's extraordinary concentration (over 30 per cent) in teaching, higher education, the creative arts and media (compared to Malta, 13.9 per cent); Malta's relatively high concentration in commerce, manufacturing and sales; and the Costa del Sol's over-representation in law, medicine and accountancy. With these examples in mind, we can begin to make a distinction, partly

Table 4.3 Age left full-time education (%)

Age (years)	Tuscany	Malta	Costa del Sol	Algarve	Male	Female	Total
below 14	4.9	19.9	16.3	8.7	16.8	11.2	14.3
14-16	15.5	35.3	39.3	34.8	32.2	37.1	34.4
17-18	30.1	28.6	22.7	33.8	26.6	29.4	27.8
19-21	14.6	10.2	12.6	12.6	9.4	15.4	12.1
22 and older	35.0	6.0	9.2	10.1	15.0	7.0	11.4
mean age	19.6	16.7	17.1	17.5	17.5	17.2	17.4
n=	103	266	326	207	500	402	902

Source: Authors' survey.
Note: Extreme cases – e.g. one of 7 years and 19 of over 30 years – have been removed from this table.

on the basis of destination, between those retirees who possess intellectual as opposed to material capital.

Cultural capital: education

Further light on the retirement migrants' social background is shed by Table 4.3 on the age at which full-time education terminated. For the total sample we see that 62.2 per cent finished their education at the school-leaving ages of 14-18 years, 23.5 per cent continued beyond 19, which implies some kind of further or higher education, and 14.3 per cent had minimal formal educational qualifications, having left school before the age of 14. Bearing in mind the age of the sample, and the contemporary pattern of school leaving in the pre-war, war or early postwar years, the profile of responses once again indicates a higher-than-average status for the retirees.

Examining the individual destinations, the Costa del Sol and the Algarve conform fairly closely to the total-sample distribution, except that the Costa del Sol has almost twice the Algarve proportion in the below-14-years category and the Algarve figure for 17-18 years is much higher than the Costa del Sol's. The more distinctive educational backgrounds are found in Tuscany and Malta. The Tuscany respondents possess significantly higher educational levels than all the other groups. The average age of finishing full-time education for the Tuscan respondents is three years higher than the Malta respondents, two and a half years higher than those in the Costa del Sol and two years higher than the Algarve sample. More than a third of the Tuscan respondents finished their education at 22+ and a half at 19+; compared in Malta to 6 per cent and 16 per cent respectively. Moreover, one fifth of Maltese respondents left school before the age of 14 – consistent with the comments on social class and employment made above. For the Tuscany respondents, it is possible to see a clear relationship between their very high levels of education, their high levels of participation in the arts and teaching profession, and their attraction to Tuscany as a retirement destination. In other words, we can again distinguish between retirees (and destinations) who possess intellectual or cultural capital and those with material capital.

Table 4.3 also demonstrates that there are gender differences in the distribution of ages of leaving full-time education. On average, women had slightly less full-time education than men and, in particular, much lower participation rates in higher education. On the other hand, the female respondents generally had a more complete school education – only 11 per cent left school before 14 years compared to 17 per cent for men. These gender differences are common across all four destinations.

The diverse educational and class backgrounds of the respondents can be elaborated upon by reference to a small selection of the in-depth interviews. Box 4.1 presents the case of Victoria, who lives in Florence. Her account explains how her educational experience was intertwined both with her father's colonial career and with her own subsequently mobile lifestyle.

Box 4.1 Victoria's story: a cosmopolitan itinerary to Tuscany

Well, I first started school in Bombay. Father was in the Army and I was born out there. Then he returned to live in Lewes and I schooled in Sussex, after which I went to Brighton Technical College and did commercial and secretarial studies for three years... From this I joined the Foreign Office and they sent me to Egypt and from then on I started working and moving abroad... I met my husband, who is Italian, in Egypt ... we came to live in Milan for six months and I started learning Italian: I had been speaking to my husband in French before that. We then moved to Genoa for five years. Both my daughters were born there and when my second daughter was 10 months, we were transferred to Peru. My husband is a banker and is also Spanish-speaking, which is why he was sent there. We were in Peru for three years and I learnt Spanish. We came back to Milan after Peru and my children started school in the Italian system. After another two years we were transferred through my husband's job to Venezuela and the children went to local schools which were half Italian and half Spanish. They spoke English with me at home though. My Spanish got better but my friends were mainly Italian since there was a huge Italian colony living in Venezuela. Then the country went to pot and the government in Venezuela got into debt... We had to decide where to settle in Italy. My husband is from Tuscany and had a beach property to come back to... He found a job in finance here in Florence and that was the deciding factor.

The contrast between retirees whose educational backgrounds distinguished their trajectories towards material or intellectual capital is clear in the next two interview extracts. First, Bertram, interviewed in the Calahonda estate on the Costa del Sol:

> I left school at 15 to join the family building business. Then I went into the Army for two years... My father died in 1963 and I took over the business, employing 130 people. I eventually sold out because I had a triple by-pass operation in 1983 and was advised by the doctor to get out of the business. By that time I owned a small apartment on Calahonda Beach and another in Marbella, bought as an investment.

Contrast this with Jeremy, who lives in Chianti:

> I was 16 when I first visited Italy on holiday with my parents. We crossed the border from Menton to Ventimiglia on a hot day... Love at first sight! I decided that this was the country I wanted to live in... At school, I studied Greek and Latin and the Classics to equip myself for finding a job here one day. I studied archaeology at university and was soon offered a job at an American university which had a study centre in Florence. In 1973 I started work on an archaeological excavation halfway between here and Siena.

These interview extracts exemplify the diversity of educational patterns and the way these patterns differentiate between retirees with mainly intellectual as opposed to material capital. The cases cited also demonstrate how education is bound up with family history, British colonialism and (often within the colonial framework) cosmopolitanism – features which, as we will see later, shape retired migrants' attitudes and behaviours in later life.

Comparison with other studies

At this point we digress from the presentation of our survey results to make brief comparisons with other studies of IRM. The most directly comparable study to ours is by Rodríguez *et al.* (1998) on north Europeans retiring to the Costa del Sol. Their survey covered 300 respondents, most of whom were British (189), with smaller groups from Germany (45), the Nordic (38) and Benelux (28) countries. Given the small size of these non-British samples, their results for other north European countries must be regarded as no more than indicative. For their total sample Rodríguez *et al.* (1998: Table 3) found that 41 per cent of respondents had university education, 51 per cent had a maximum of secondary education and 7 per cent had only primary education. Respective figures for their British sample were 38 per cent, 57 per cent and 5 per cent. The Nordics and Benelux had most experience of university education (nearly 60 per cent), whilst the Germans had much lower qualifications (only 28 per cent had university education, and 21 per cent had only primary schooling). By and large, these data indicate a higher educational standard than that recorded by our Costa del Sol sample; this is probably because their survey area included high-status areas at the extreme eastern and western ends of the Costa del Sol (Nerja and Salobreña to the east, Marbella and Estepona to the west).

In terms of employment, Rodríguez *et al.* (1998: Table 3) found similar patterns to those of our survey, namely (for their British sample) a predominance of entrepreneurs and employers (27 per cent), senior managers and executives (18.6 per cent), professionals (16.5 per cent) and middle managers (14.9 per cent). Eight per cent were self-employed, 5.3 per cent were non-manual employees, and only 6.9 per cent were manual workers. Although these categories do not exactly match those in Table 4.3, the broad pattern of high-status and financially-rewarding pre-retirement work is obvious. The Nordic and Benelux retirees had, if anything, a higher status profile (more professionals, executives and senior managers), whilst the Germans had a lower social profile – 17.8 per cent were former manual workers, 11.1 per cent non-manual employees and 17.8 per cent middle managers.

Buller and Hoggart's (1994) research on British home-owners in rural France was not specifically about retired Britons although 85 of their 406 respondents were of retirement age and this subgroup was discussed in a separate paper (Hoggart and Buller 1995). These authors, too, found an overwhelming middle-class origin for their retired respondents – 24.8 per cent were former teachers and lecturers, 22.2 per cent were former company directors, and 20.5 per cent were managers.

Thirdly, we can briefly report and compare the results of a major North American study of older Canadians in Florida, based on a mail survey of 2,728 anglophones in 1986 (Tucker *et al.* 1988) and a follow-up survey of 1,028 francophone Canadians in 1988 (Tucker, Mullins, Béland, Longino and Marshall 1992). Although these Canadians were predominantly seasonal migrants or 'snowbirds', their profiles were remarkably similar to the European case studies and, for that matter, to those of United States internal migrants and snowbirds. For instance, the Canadian snowbird population was found to be predominantly upper or middle class, with high levels of education – 38 per cent of anglophones and 21 per cent of francophones had tertiary education. The modal income for both groups was $20-40,000; relatively high given that the surveys were taken more than ten years ago. Regarding employment, a concentration was noted in professional, managerial, business-owner and civil-service categories. Although the similarities were more important than the differences between the anglophone and francophone groups, the latter tended to have slightly lower education and employment status. French- and English-speaking retirement migrants also tended to settle in different parts of Florida. These differences indicate interesting cultural influences on retirement migration which have some parallel with those noted for the south of Spain.

Table 4.4 Year of arrival in destination country (%)

	Tuscany	Malta	Costa del Sol	Algarve	Total
before 1965	8.5	5.8	2.3	1.8	3.9
1965-9	9.4	14.7	1.7	4.1	7.0
1970-4	17.9	10.4	3.5	7.3	8.0
1975-9	8.5	3.2	6.9	3.2	5.2
1980-4	6.6	11.5	24.6	12.3	15.9
1985-9	24.5	21.6	36.7	36.5	30.9
after 1990	24.5	32.7	24.3	34.7	29.2
n=	106	278	346	219	949

Source: Authors' survey.

Timing of Migration and Pathways to Retirement

International retirement migration can be seen, at least in part, as a progression from the mass tourism boom which transformed international travel and holiday-making in Europe from the 1960s (King, Warnes and Williams 1998; Williams *et al.* 1997). Given that those who participated in this sun-seeking tourist boom were young and middle-aged adults in the 1960s and 1970s, we might expect retirement migration to have grown during the 1980s and 1990s. Moreover the marketing of some Mediterranean coastal resorts as retirement destinations might be seen as a strategy for them to maintain a market role after losing their competitive edge in the global tourism market. However the addition of a retirement role to regions of mass tourism has not been synchronous in the various Mediterranean tourism destinations – insights into the phasing of both tourism and retirement development in different regions of southern Europe were given in Chapter 2. The differential age distributions of the survey respondents in Table 4.1 also suggested a phasing of arrival times in the various destinations: younger retirees imply a more recent development of retirement migration.

Table 4.4 clearly supports the notion of a differential development of retirement migration according to destination. In the Costa del Sol the great majority of the respondents (85.6 per cent) arrived after 1980, whereas the main boom in retirement settlement to the Algarve appears to have come only after 1985, 60.1 per cent of respondents arriving after that date. Tuscany and Malta have significant numbers of much earlier settlers. Overall, 35.8 per cent of Tuscan respondents arrived before 1975 and 30.9 per cent for Malta, but only 13.2 per cent in the Algarve and 7.5 per cent in the Costa del Sol. Calculation of the 'mean year of arrival' produces a revealing sequence: 1980 in Tuscany, 1982 in Malta, 1985 in the Costa del Sol, and 1986 in the Algarve.

Interpreting Table 4.4 is not entirely straightforward. Differential rates of survival and return, and subsequent trends in new arrivals, undoubtedly complicate the picture. Moreover, by no means all respondents arrived at or after retirement age: many, especially in Malta and Tuscany, were already there because of work or family links and 'aged in place'. Other local circumstances impinge on the temporal pattern: for instance a sharp drop in arrivals in Malta in the late 1970s corresponds to a period of discouragement of British settlers when the government's priority was to house the Maltese (Warnes and Patterson 1998). As for the aggregate demand for foreign retirement migration, supply-side factors have been influential, such as the British recessions of the mid-1970s and early 1980s, and the British housing boom of the late 1980s which made it particularly advantageous to convert housing assets into foreign property. This last factor was considered pre-eminent by Buller and Hoggart (1994) in their research on British property-owners in rural France.

Timing of arrival and socio-economic background of migrants

With the above analysis and caveats in mind, we now examine further the relationship between the timing of migration and the characteristics of the migrants. The underlying hypothesis is that, following the development of tourism as initially an élite and later a mass phenomenon, retirement migration has progressed analogously. The analysis is carried out for the various measures of socio-economic status discussed above in the context of Tables 4.2 and 4.3 – social class, economic background (employment status and sector), and education. The bare bones of the analysis are presented in Table 4.5. In comparison to previous tables, both rows and columns have been amalgamated to simplify the presentation and achieve row and column totals which are of a similar magnitude.

We start with social class. The social class array of Table 4.2 has been dichotomised to two groups: professionals and managers; and clerical and manual workers. At first sight little change over time is apparent: the ratio of approximately two-thirds in the upper-status group and one-third in the lower-class group remains fairly constant from the 1960s to the 1990s. Closer inspection and interpretation of the data does however reveal a trend. If we discount the pre-1970 column (as probably being people who did not move upon retirement but were already living in the destination through ties of work, family or marriage), then there is a transition from the highest proportion of Classes 1 and 2 in the 1970s (over 70 per cent) to lower proportions in the 1980s and 1990s. This pattern is consistent with higher-status pioneer retirees arriving in the 1970s (when IRM first started to become significant in southern Europe), and lower-status arrivals in the 1980s and 1990s.

The social class analysis is far from convincing. However, the trend suggested above is backed up by a shift in employment status with 1980 (or thereabouts) again a turning-point. Before that year employers and the

Table 4.5 Year of arrival by social and economic status (%)

	before 1970	1970-9	1980-4	1985-9	1990 and later	Total
Social Class (n=823)						
1 and 2	61.0	70.2	63.4	67.8	64.3	65.6
3, 4 and 5	39.0	29.8	36.6	32.2	35.7	34.4
Employment status (n=850)						
Employer, self-employed	33.7	36.6	27.0	29.6	26.3	29.4
Employee	66.3	63.4	73.0	70.4	73.7	70.6
Employment sector (n=761)						
Professions, civil service	24.3	27.9	39.2	30.6	32.3	31.5
Production, business, services	50.0	41.9	45.8	46.4	52.8	48.1
Creative, intellectual	25.7	30.2	15.0	23.0	14.9	20.4
Age left education (n=896)						
before 17	33.7	32.8	57.7	50.0	54.8	48.7
17-18	41.0	31.0	26.8	28.2	22.0	27.9
19+	25.3	36.2	15.5	21.8	23.2	23.4

Source: Authors' survey.

self-employed constituted more than 35 per cent of arrivals, whereas afterwards the proportion slips to less than 28 per cent. Again the highest-status arrival decade seems to be the 1970s. The same evolutionary sequence is produced by the data on age at which full-time education ended. The population leaving school before 17 years of age increases quite sharply from less than one third before 1980 to well over one half after 1980, indicating a downward shift in the level of 'intellectual capital'. The same pattern is evident in the proportion leaving school after the age of 19 – 36.2 per cent in the 1970s, only 15.5 per cent in the early 1980s, but then recovering somewhat to 23.2 per cent by the 1990s.

Another perspective on this evolutionary pattern is seen in the change in the migrants' employment types. Table 4.5 collapses the detailed employment sectors listed in Table 4.2 to provide more coherent categories. 'Professions and civil service' includes civil servants and persons employed in law, medicine and accountancy; 'production, business and services' includes manufacturing and sales, commerce and personal services; and 'creative and intellectual' contains lecturers, teachers and those involved in the media and creative arts. This last category almost exactly mirrors the sequence of percentages for 19+ education: a peak of 30.5 per cent in the 1970s, falling abruptly to 15.0 per cent in the 1980s when professionals and civil servants seem to take over. The production and business group remains fairly constant over time, except for a trough in the 1970s.

This evidence on the emerging social profile of retirement migrants to the four destinations can be set alongside other information – more qualitative but in some respects more precise – from the interviews. Some of the interviewees were amongst the early pioneers as settlers and retirees and had a keen perspective on how both the areas and the expatriate populations had changed. Here are two extracts which refer to two stages in the British settlement in Torremolinos, which the first interviewee began to visit in the late 1950s:

> It was a small village, not many people and rather a bohemian crowd. Augustus John was living here at one time. There were a few writers and artists and well-known upper-crust names that were living out here quietly. The minute you arrived everyone knew there was somebody new and you were automatically introduced and taken up... San Miguel was just a little street of cottages with an old butcher's shop run by a gypsy. I had a friend who bought one of the cottages for £300... When you got to the bottom of the street there was a tiny church and some steps and then a sort of goat track down to the beach... There was a tremendous amount of poverty here in those days ... but for us things were very cheap.

The contrast with Torremolinos today could hardly be greater! Calle San Miguel is now a frenetically busy tourist thoroughfare. The second interviewee, a writer now living just inland from the coast, described the social scene amongst the British residents in Torremolinos in the early 1970s:

> They were mostly professional people at that time – army officers, doctors, barristers. Some were retired but others had come out before retirement. There was a good British society at the Villa Luisa, and through that we made friends... We were a small but close group, adventurous and worldly.

A similar story emerges from the early-arrived interviewees in the Algarve, bearing in mind that the main phases of tourism and retirement settlement came about ten years later than in the Costa del Sol. Many interviewees referred to the 'colonial set' who were settled in villas in the hills around Monchique by the early 1970s, and to the contrast between those who arrived before and after the Portuguese revolution of 1974. Barry, a property developer who came in 1964 with his Portuguese wife, commented on the 'backwardness' of the Algarve and on the different groups of British settlers:

> There was a great opportunity here, I could see... The place was totally undeveloped with no hotels and no airport. I found it extraordinary that this beautiful place was not developed at all... As a property man, it was a unique opportunity for me, plus I had a built-in translator with my wife. Her parents, who came from Estoríl, were appalled that I was bringing her to the Algarve,

which they regarded as Africa!... Tourism only really began here in the late 1960s, after they opened the airport. There was no accommodation for tourists before that. We had been building villas for retired ex-colonials, who needed land with their property. Many of those who came in the early days had been used to living abroad in places like Tanganyika ... it was a bit like the days of the Raj down here then... Servants were a-plenty, booze was cheap and the climate was good... Then the revolution came and the market stopped totally... Things didn't really recover until 1981... Now the typical profile of a Brit. buying property is a middle-aged couple taking two or three holidays here who then decide to buy in the Algarve. They have children of married age who can come out here and share the house for a holiday... They are not the colonial type now of course – mostly they're professional or small company businessmen.

Although the evidence is fragmentary, there is some support for a social class change in IRM to southern Europe. The settlement was pioneered by people of unusually high education in the 1960s and 1970s, with 'intellectuals' (lecturers, teachers, artists etc.) and, especially in the Algarve, retired people from the colonies. Since the 1980s the phenomenon has become socially more broadly based, with higher proportions of employees in production and services.

'Pathways to Paradise': spatial mobility prior to retirement

It has already become apparent that by no means all British older people living in southern Europe migrated there at or soon after retirement age following a prior experience of holidaying in the chosen destination. This 'taken for granted' pattern is useful as a model only insofar as it acts as a normative yardstick to examine the much more complex reality of different pathways and experiences of living and working abroad prior to the situation in which the survey 'captured' the respondents as 'retired British migrants' in one of the four destinations.

The questionnaire elicited much information on international spatial mobility prior to retirement. Four key attributes are analysed in this section: whether respondents had ever lived abroad for more than three months; where they had lived during the five years prior to arriving in their 'retirement country'; what kind of links they previously had to the destination country; and whether they had acquired a second home in the destination country prior to moving there. These four variables are set out in Table 4.6 by the five 'arrival cohorts' used previously.

Many respondents had considerable experience of international mobility and migration prior to the retirement phase of their lives. One half had lived abroad for at least three months, and well over one third had lived at least partly (22 per cent entirely) abroad during the five years preceding their arrival in the retirement destination. These experiences were most common amongst the earliest arrivals. For instance, 45 per cent of those who arrived before 1970 had lived exclusively abroad in the previous five years, compared to only 17 per cent for the post-1980 arrivals. And

Table 4.6 Year of arrival by prior spatial mobility (%)

	before 1970	1970-9	1980-4	1985-9	1990 and after	Total
Had you ever lived abroad for > 3 months? (n=946)						
Yes	59.2	22.2	45.0	47.1	48.9	49.7
No	40.8	44.8	55.0	52.9	51.1	50.3
Where did you live in the 5 years prior to moving to current destination? (n=918)						
Exclusively abroad	45.3	30.9	20.9	13.9	18.8	22.0
Abroad and UK	17.9	17.9	18.2	14.6	12.2	15.3
Exclusively UK	36.8	51.2	60.8	71.5	69.0	62.7
What were your prior connections to the area? (n=816)						
Mainly family/childhood	23.2	19.6	12.7	13.8	15.8	15.9
Mainly work	29.3	11.8	11.1	9.4	8.1	11.5
Holidays only	47.6	68.6	76.2	76.8	76.2	72.5
Owned second home in destination area prior to moving? (n=896)						
Yes	26.3	33.6	43.0	32.1	49.4	38.5
No	73.7	66.4	57.0	67.9	50.6	61.5

Source. Authors' survey.

while only 45 per cent of those who arrived in their destination prior to 1980 had lived exclusively in the UK, among the post-1985 arrivals the proportion was over 70 per cent. These trajectories underscore the complexity of IRM: by no means is it simply a case of emigration from the UK at the time of retirement.

This leads to the question of which countries the survey respondents had resided in, and whether these countries might have changed over time. Key informants had suggested that some of the earliest retiree arrivals were 'ex-colonials', particularly in the Algarve. Of course the terms 'colonials' or 'ex-colonials' are imprecise and are often ascribed to particular lifestyles and attitudes rather than strictly to employment in the administration of the (ex-)colonies. Given the dismantling of the British colonial system after 1945, and the more recent rise of multinational companies, one might expect a change in the countries in which the latest cohorts of expatriates had lived and worked, with Britain's colonies and traditional trading partners receding, and more experience of living in North America and EU countries.

More than 100 of the in-depth interviews provided biographical details of various patterns of living and working abroad prior to the retirement in southern Europe. We select a few cases which typify common paths. The case of Victoria, whose birth and early educational background in India were recounted earlier, is our first case, because her own life history spans the transition between the colonial era and the more recent 'internationalist' experience of many expatriates we interviewed. Reference back to her account in Box 4.1 shows how, from her childhood in the 'colonial' locations of Bombay and Sussex, Victoria moved into the 'international set' of the banking world of her Italian husband, learning languages along the way, eventually coming to settle in Tuscany in middle age.

The more 'traditional' career in the colonial territories is represented by Anthony, who settled at Praia da Luz in the Algarve in 1991, having first visited on holiday in 1988 when he had just retired from a military and business career, latterly in Nigeria and Cyprus:

> I have lived abroad all my life, I have literally been all round the world. Cyprus was my last but one posting and ... I bought an apartment on the island for my eventual retirement. It was intended to be a bolt-hole while we looked around for a more permanent place... I retired [at] 56 and was attracted to Cyprus by the climate and the tax advantages. It was a happy place to have a base... We had two years retired in Cyprus before coming here... We did find Cyprus a bit constricting because it is an island. You had to jump on a ferry each time you wanted to go somewhere. People from the UK didn't come visiting as the air fare was too high. And it is a divided society, of course. We thought we wanted to see more of Europe as I hadn't worked in Europe as such... We didn't fancy France or Spain, I think we would have liked Italy but we didn't know anyone there and we had friends in Portugal.

Typical of the slightly younger retiree with a multinational life history was Brian, who retired at 55 from a career as an international advertising director, and now lives in a Tuscan hill-town with his Australian wife. He describes his mobile career and his links with Italy:

> I was asked by a prestigious American advertising agency to go to Australia... I liked Australia, settled down, and eventually became director of the company... I got sent to our office in Milan to do a specific job there. That's what started the Italian thing... Then I spent a spell in New York but I used to come back to Australia through Italy... I'd hire a car and drive all over the place... The last few years of my time in the East were in Hong Kong. I was sent there by the company and I ran the Art Department there. When I got back to Australia I felt I didn't fit in very well any more... I was getting on and advertising is a young man's job... We decided to retire to Tuscany because this was the part of Italy we liked best in terms of its landscape.

The remaining two sections of data on Table 4.6 refer to specific prior connections to the retirement destination. Answers to the question about prior connections to the destination area were distilled into three mutually exclusive groups (for a tabulation presenting multiple linkages see King *et al.* 1998: Table 6): respondents whose primary connection was through family, marriage or childhood; those whose key link was through work; and those whose only link was through previous holidays. Overall it can be seen that tourism functioned as the primary channel for acquiring information and experience of the chosen destination area, accounting for 72.5 per cent of the responses. Once again a clear temporal pattern is evident: family linkages played a significant role for pre-1980 arrivals, while work linkages were more important for those who settled before 1970. In fact for the earliest cohort of arrivals, family and work connections outweighed the influence of holidays. A breakdown of the gender differential in family and work connections (King *et al.* 1998: Table 6) shows that women were approximately twice as likely as men to have family connections or to have married a native of the retirement destination country, whilst work connections were more important for men – except for Tuscany where many retired women had previously worked as language teachers, art historians etc. (King and Patterson 1998).

Prior second-home ownership in the retirement country constitutes another powerful linkage to the intended destination, not least by providing practical experience of house purchase and day-to-day living. Table 4.6 confirms that second-home ownership has been a steadily increasing conduit and antecedent for retirement migration, from about a quarter of arrivals in the 1960s to a half in the 1990s, reflecting the pattern of development of mass tourism in the Mediterranean.

It is also important to realise that these experiences of living abroad and linkages to retirement destinations not only vary through time but also vary by destination and by socio-economic background. For instance, three-quarters of the retirees in Tuscany had experience of living abroad compared to about a half in Malta and the Algarve and only 41 per cent in the Costa del Sol. Nearly two-thirds of the respondents in Tuscany had lived exclusively or partly abroad in the five years prior to coming to Italy; whereas for the other three destinations two-thirds had lived exclusively in the UK. 'Prior connections to the area' shows an obvious split between the two Iberian areas, where around 87 per cent of respondents had had only holiday experiences, and Tuscany and Malta, where half the prior linkages were through family or work.

Conclusion

This chapter has addressed the basic question: who migrates for retirement abroad? In a generalised sense the answer is relatively clear: British retirees in southern Europe are predominantly well-off, with above-average levels of education and an employment background mainly in business, management and the professions. In this regard they are similar to other European international retirement migrants (Buller and Hoggart 1994; Rodríguez *et al.* 1998), and they are similar to some groups of long-range internal older migrants, especially those who migrate for amenity reasons to regions like the south coast of England and the French Midi (Warnes 1996).

Several interesting and significant variations emerged from the survey. Respondents ranged in age from 50 (our imposed minimum) to 100 years. Respondents in Tuscany were on average the oldest, those in the Algarve the youngest: the contrast corresponds to the historical phasing of retirement migration in different parts of southern Europe. Two-person households, comprising a married couple, were the norm, although one-person households accounted for 30 per cent of the Malta sample. In the great majority of cases, retirement abroad is a shared enterprise, undertaken predominantly by couples that are 'close' and expect to pursue activities together. Other characteristics were also differentiated by destination: retirement-age people in Tuscany enjoy a significantly higher social and cultural status than those in Malta, the only destination to have a sizeable presence of manual employment retirees. Particularly striking was the high level of education of the Tuscany respondents and the disproportionately large number who had had careers in teaching and the arts. This enabled us to make a distinction between retirees possessing 'intellectual' versus 'material' capital.

The final part of the chapter examined IRM more explicitly as a 'time-space' phenomenon (Malmberg 1997) with distinctive phases. The crucial temporal link between IRM and the prior development of international mass tourism was re-emphasised, but it was also discovered that significant numbers did not become international retirement migrants mainly through a prior experience of holidaying in the area. These 'alternative paths' to IRM were particularly important in the earlier phases of IRM settlement, and constituted a majority of respondents in Tuscany. Malta also has a complicated history of inter-communal links with the British. In both Malta and Tuscany significant numbers of older British residents arrived before retirement age. Year-of-arrival analysis supports the hypothesis that IRM started in the 1960s and 1970s as an élite phenomenon and in the 1980s and 1990s acquired a broader social base. A partial recording of geographical mobility prior to retirement reveals that our subjects had considerable migration and travel experience prior to settling in their chosen destinations. These earlier migration paths were moulded by both former 'colonial' links and participation in the skilled international migration flows of the modern global economy. Whilst these diverse experiences of travel, work and residence overseas are important, the findings confirm that for the majority the key link with the destination is previous holidays, for some through the purchase of a second home prior to and in anticipation of retirement. In saying this we imply the motivations for migration: the subject of the next chapter.

Notes

1. A full description of the methodology is given in the final report of the project to the ESRC. Copies of this and of the survey questionnaire are available from the authors.

2. The incomplete nature of a small fraction of the questionnaires returned, with some answers missing, means that the totals across the different variables are usually below 1,000. For instance, about a tenth of the sample did not fill in their age. Although we excluded under-50s from the analysis, we left in those 'ageless' respondents who, from their answers to other parts of the questionnaire, clearly satisfied our age criterion. Contrary to popular convention, men were twice as likely not to reveal their age as women.

3. Too much should not be read into this male-female age difference since it probably relates partly to how the sample was taken. Whilst on the one hand it can be pointed out that, in most marriages, the husband is older than the wife, it also has to be borne in mind that our survey, by and large, did not receive two separate responses from married couples. Hence female respondents are more likely to be widowed. On the other hand it also became clear from some of the questionnaires (and from the in-depth interviews) that many respondents were in their second marriages, with perhaps an even greater chance of a significant male-female spousal age gap. For more details on the age differences in the Malta sample see Warnes and Patterson (1998).

Five

The Siren's Call: The Migration Decision

Introduction

In this chapter we analyse the apparently straightforward question: why do people migrate for retirement? The deceptive simplicity of this question hides a range of nuances in terms of how the question is posed, disaggregated, perceived and interpreted, both by researchers and above all by the migrants themselves. The chapter is structured around three different perspectives on the migration decision: the reasons expressed by the survey respondents for the move; a more specific examination of their residential strategies; and their evaluations of their decisions to retire abroad. Before we commence this analysis, we need to identify the key points in the literature on this subject.

Explaining Retirement Migration: A Recapitulation

The 'decision to move' is a central part of the etiology of migration. Yet generalisations are difficult – and dangerous – to make because of the diversity and complexity of the phenomenon of migration. Hence standard models or typologies of migration decision-making – for instance those based on rural-urban migration or international migration from poor to rich countries – may have little or no relevance for IRM. It is significant that most general overviews of 'why people move' in Europe or globally (e.g. Fischer, Martin and Straubhaar 1997; Hammar and Tamas 1997; King 1993b) have absolutely nothing to say about IRM.

A more promising approach is to start with the literature on migration in later life, but – as we saw in Chapter 1 – most of this refers to North America and internal moves, with variable relevance to IRM. For instance, in Wiseman and Roseman's (1979) typology of retirement migration – based on kinship, return to place of origin, or amenity – only the last approaches IRM, as studied in this book.[1] Another more 'commonsensical' approach was taken by O'Reilly (1995a: 31): 'British people are migrating to Spain for various reasons, the obvious ones being sun, sea, scenery and leisure opportunities.' She then mentions some less obvious motives such as benefits to health and a lower cost of living. This analysis of attractions is summed up in the title of another review of elderly migration: 'for sun and money' (Fournier, Rasmussen and Serow 1988). Such generalisations have their limitations, as when inflation turns a lower cost of living into a higher one. Health, too, may be a double-edged sword: on the one hand the seaside, a warmer climate or country air might be thought of as healthy environments for older bodies; but a migration may also remove a person from established health-care structures (Daciuk and Marshall 1990).

Another important recapitulation is that 'amenity-led' retirement migration comprises two distinct if sometimes overlapping streams: that towards sunny coastal locations, and another towards rural areas which are attractive havens of tranquillity or valued cultural landscapes (Williams *et al.* 1997). In our study, the Costa del Sol and rural Tuscany are the relevant respective examples, but there are many others in other parts of the world. As Buller and Hoggart (1994) have shown, the purchase of homes in France by the British middle classes is essentially the pursuit of a rural idyll.

There are several ways in which the retirement migration decision has been conceptualised and modelled. One separates the decision to move from the subsequent decision of where to go. But an inverse sequence can also operate, whereby repeated holiday visits to a favoured destination generates a decision to retire there (Cuba 1991). Another version of the staged model concerns the retirement/migration sequence: normally retirement is followed by migration, especially over long distances, but the reverse can also happen.

A further dimension for discussion is the pre-planned or spontaneous nature of the decision to migrate on retirement. 'Remote thoughts' or 'distant visions' of a future retirement in a more attractive environment may start quite early in life; for others the decision to leave may be sudden, perhaps triggered by a particular experience or life event (Wiseman 1980). Such a trigger may constitute the final push that makes the move a reality rather than a nebulous concept. Generally, however, environmental preference retirement migration is patterned more by 'pull factors' emanating from the destination than 'pushes' from the origin since, at an aggregate level, destinations are more spatially concentrated than the origins of the migrants (Haas and Serow 1993).

Other research in the United States has suggested a different two-stage model of elderly migration: a first stage, amenity-driven, by which younger, affluent early-retired tend to move in search of those features of a better quality of life which are important for them (warm weather, safe environment, pleasant landscape etc.); and a later stage where dependent, often widowed, elders tend to move in search of care and support to localities near their children and other relatives (Choi 1996; Haas and Serow 1993). According to Longino (1992), older people who are most likely to relocate for retirement are: those who have the fewest 'moorings' (ties to home); those whose desired lifestyle in retirement is incompatible with their existing place of residence; those who hear the 'siren's song' from other places; and those with the health, economic and psychic resources to move.

These factors form a useful framework of general conditions for IRM and will be used to inform our own analysis of migration reasons in this chapter. In the previous chapter we noted that retirement migrants to southern Europe over-represent those with prior experience of international mobility, and we have presented data to show how the migrants are, in general, an educated and well-to-do population.

Reasons for Migration to Southern Europe

The decision to spend part or all of one's retirement life abroad is an aggregate of several linked considerations including when to retire and when to migrate; which country, region and locality to move to; what kind of property to invest in; whether or not to retain one or more properties elsewhere and how to divide time between them; and what the formation of the retirement household might be. Another highly relevant question is *when* the decision to retire abroad was first made or considered. The self-completion questionnaire sought information on most of these dimensions, while the in-depth interviews provided nuanced case examples. We should also recognise that migration decisions are often difficult to 'explain' in retrospect: the answers to standard questions may be *post hoc* rationalisations, hiding motives, meanings and contingent factors. We acknowledge all these weaknesses, but the uniquely large data-set on international retirement migrants that has been assembled has its own riches and strengths.

Selection of destination country

When asked about the reasons for their initial move to the retirement destination, the respondents gave a wealth of information. Of the total sample, 925 gave a first, most important reason, and each respondent gave on average over three reasons. The responses have been collapsed around nine principal reasons in the following analysis. For reasons of space, they are somewhat abbreviated in the tables; therefore it is useful to spell out the nine categories:

- climate and other aspects of the natural environment such as landscape and clean air;
- pace of life, feel healthier, relaxation, opportunities for golf, sailing and so on;
- lower living costs – housing, food, heating, lower taxes;

Table 5.1 Reasons given for residence in the retirement destination (%)

Reason	All listed reasons	Main reason	Second reason	3rd - 9th reasons
Climate, environment	27.6	40.4	29.6	15.5
Pace of life, health	16.8	15.7	17.8	17.0
Lower living costs	14.1	6.7	17.4	17.9
Social advantages	9.4	2.7	7.7	16.1
Admiration of the country	9.0	6.3	8.7	11.5
Childhood, family links	7.5	11.8	5.7	5.2
Antipathy to UK	6.2	7.6	5.3	5.7
Practical advantages	6.1	2.1	6.1	9.4
Work or business	3.3	6.8	1.6	1.5
n =	2802	925	768	1109

Source: Authors' survey.

Table 5.2 Reasons given for residence in the four destinations (%)

Reason	Tuscany		Malta		Costa de Sol		Algarve	
	1st	2nd	1st	2nd	1st	2nd	1st	2nd
Climate, environment	15.4	28.8	37.5	29.8	48.1	28.8	44.2	30.9
Pace of life, health	10.6	8.8	14.6	11.2	18.4	24.6	15.2	19.1
Lower living costs	2.9	1.3	8.6	20.0	6.2	17.2	6.9	21.8
Social advantages	4.8	1.3	4.1	12.1	2.1	7.7	0.9	5.3
Admiration of the country	11.5	28.8	7.9	7.0	5.0	4.9	3.7	8.0
Childhood, family links	19.2	13.8	15.0	5.6	8.9	5.6	8.8	2.7
Antipathy to UK	14.4	3.8	15.0	5.6	8.9	5.6	8.8	2.7
Practical advantages	2.9	6.3	3.4	9.8	1.8	4.2	0.5	4.8
Work or business	18.3	7.5	6.0	0.9	2.7	1.1	8.8	0.5
n =	104	80	267	215	337	285	217	188

Source: Authors' survey.

- social advantages: presence of a British community, many friends, good social life, opportunity for relatives to visit, friendly local population;
- admiration of destination country's society, culture, low crime rate;
- childhood or family links, including marriage to a local person;
- antipathy to the UK, often referring to high crime or poor social values; general wish to live abroad; long-term expatriate with no wish to return to the UK;
- practical advantages: English widely spoken; good travel to UK; already possessed second home in destination;
- work or business links to country before retirement.

Table 5.1 displays the nine collapsed reasons.[2] Although the aggregate frequencies in the first column of the table give the broad comparative picture, more revealing are the first and second nominated reasons. Climate (40 per cent) clearly outstrips all other reasons as the main nominated reason; only pace of life and family links also exceed 10 per cent amongst first reasons. For the second and lower-order reasons, climate is far less prominent, whereas the relevance of secondary reasons such as living costs, social advantages, admiration of destination country and practical considerations emerges clearly. In a relative sense, climate and family and work links are far more important as primary than as subsidiary reasons.

Table 5.2 examines the ranked contrasts by destination, for first and second nominated reasons only. The Costa del Sol and the Algarve have remarkably similar weightings of both first and second reasons; unsurprisingly they also conform most closely to the whole-sample distribution set out in the middle two columns of Table 5.1. Tuscany shows the most difference from the total sample: here climate descends into third place as a first factor after family and work motives, whilst the obviously linked factors of 'admiration for Italy' and 'antipathy to the UK' are much more important than for any other destination. The expressed reasons in Malta stand somewhere between the Tuscan and Iberian cases: they show higher scores for living costs and social and practical advantages, especially as second nominated reasons. It is also interesting to note that climate scores a constant 30 per cent as a second factor across all four countries, but varies from 15 per cent (Tuscany) to 48 per cent (Costa del Sol) as a first factor. Among the four destinations, the Costa del Sol's climate is the warmest, sunniest and driest, and Tuscany's the coolest, cloudiest and wettest, but there are also contrasting *social* evaluations of climate, as we see in the next table.

Table 5.3 sets the nine main reasons for migrating against two variables which formed part of the background analysis in Chapter 4, namely year of arrival and the age at which respondents finished their full-time education. The year of arrival analysis shows clear contrasts between the pre-1980 and post-1980 arrivals. Climate was a prime reason for less than a third of the pre-1980 cohort, compared to 40-45 per cent for the post-1980

Table 5.3 Main reason given for residence in retirement destination matched against year of arrival and education (%)

Reason	Year of arrival				Age left education		
	before 1980	1980-9	1985-9	after 1990	<17	17-18	19+
Climate, environment	32.7	44.2	40.1	45.1	42.8	40.1	36.7
Pace of life, health	10.9	15.0	20.9	14.8	19.5	14.0	8.8
Lower living costs	5.9	10.2	4.7	7.6	7.5	6.6	6.2
Social advantages	2.3	2.7	2.8	3.0	2.1	2.5	4.0
Admiration of the country	6.4	3.4	4.2	9.8	3.3	8.3	10.2
Childhood, family links	18.2	12.2	10.4	7.6	12.5	9.9	11.9
Antipathy to UK	5.9	6.1	9.1	8.0	5.4	9.5	9.7
Practical advantages	2.7	1.4	2.8	1.1	2.1	2.1	2.2
Work or business	15.0	4.8	4.9	3.0	4.7	7.0	10.2
n =	220	147	287	264	425	242	226

Source: Authors' survey.

groups. Similarly, 'pace of life' was the main reason for less than 11 per cent of pre-1980 settlers, but for 15-20 per cent of the post-1980 group. Family and work links show steady diminution as retirement migration factors across the successive cohorts from pre-1980 to post-1990. These findings are internally consistent since it has been shown that the earlier arrivals came disproportionately for work and family reasons (Table 4.6). The second half of Table 5.3 shows the relationship between expressed migration factors and the respondents' educational background. Previous analysis had suggested that the education measure was a more sensitive discriminator of social status than our social class or employment indicators (see Chapter 4). Table 5.3 shows that the higher the educational status, the lower the importance of climate, lifestyle (pace of life, health etc.) and living cost motives. Positive correlations, on the other hand, are observed between education and social advantages, admiration of destination country, antipathy to UK, and work links as reasons for migration.

One path amongst many

The received wisdom amongst some professionals who work with older people tends to be that 'the best place to retire is the neighborhood where you spent your life... Like boats to a mooring, people are tied to their environments by investments in their property, by the many community contexts in which they find meaning, by friends and family whose proximity they value, by the experiences of the past, and by life-styles that weave these strands together into patterns of satisfying activity' (Longino 1994:

Table 5.4 Other options for retirement (%)

	Tuscany	Malta	Costa del Sol	Algarve	Total
Stay in former home in UK	21.4	16.8	21.2	17.7	19.2
Move to new home in UK	22.9	23.6	20.4	21.5	21.8
Move elsewhere in Europe	35.7	36.1	34.3	42.0	37.0
Move to another continent	11.4	13.1	15.1	10.2	12.8
Other	8.6	11.3	9.0	8.6	9.2
n =	70	161	245	186	662

Source: Authors' survey.

405). Retirement migrants to southern Europe have clearly broken their moorings; or maybe their moorings were never that strong anyway. Mixed residential strategies based for instance on two homes and seasonal migration are an attempt to preserve some ties whilst responding to the 'siren's call' of a more exotic lifestyle. Clearly, the decision 'to go or to stay' is complex, and many actual and potential retirement migrants will have carefully considered various residential and migration options. In Haas and Serow's study in western North Carolina, respondents were asked: 'how seriously did you consider staying in your home county after you retired?' One-third replied that they had seriously considered staying put, but of course the answers to this question are biased because the survey only concerned actual migrants (Haas and Serow 1993: 216). The same problem is present in our survey, but we are only concerned, for the moment, with the behaviour and characteristics of those who *did* move, and now turn to the various options considered by the respondents.

The questionnaire asked whether the following options were considered: stay in former home in the UK, stay in former home abroad, move elsewhere in the UK, move elsewhere in Europe (other than the country actually chosen), or move to another part of the world. For the 'move elsewhere' options, respondents were asked to name their preferred counties (in the UK) or countries (in Europe or elsewhere in the world). Almost exactly half the respondents had considered one or more of these options: of the valid responses, 471 stated that none were considered, whilst 470 stipulated one or more (153 gave two and 39 listed three). Table 5.4 shows that, for the total sample, 37 per cent considered a move to another European country, 13 per cent a move to another part of the world, 22 per cent considered relocation within the UK, and 19 per cent thought of staying in their existing UK home. Of the 'other' category, the options were 'stay in former home abroad' (4.4 per cent), move to some other unspecified destination (2.7 per cent) and 'touring' (caravanning, sailing etc., 2.1 per cent).

The pattern of responses differed little among the destination regions, although respondents in Malta were less likely to think of staying in their former UK home, and the Algarve group were the most likely to have considered alternative European destinations. Where the differences are more revealing is when individual countries are named. In Tuscany, France was overwhelmingly the most favoured alternative destination; in Malta, the most popular alternatives were Spain, Cyprus and Portugal; in the Algarve, Spain, France and Italy were the most frequently mentioned; and in the Costa del Sol, France was the most popular alternative, followed by North America, Italy and Cyprus. In these responses, one may infer the perceived similarities between Tuscany and France (with appealing rural landscapes and 'ways of life'), between Malta and Cyprus (as English-speaking ex-British colonies with military connections), and between Spain and Portugal (being Iberian countries with strong holiday and climatic attractions).[3]

The interviews revealed in more detail the reasons why the chosen country was preferred over its 'competitors' and some clear consistencies emerged. In Malta, language was often the clinching factor; in Tuscany it was the quality of the landscape; whilst interviewees in the Algarve often commented rather negatively on neighbouring Spain to justify their choice.

Let us first look at a few cases from Malta. Emily and her husband had both had army careers. Their search proceeded through a sequence of carefully considered options before they finally settled on a flat in Sliema:

> He was keen on Gibraltar because he'd been there before the war, but there was still the barrier with Spain. We went to Guernsey to look but we didn't like it. Then we went to Cyprus but there were political problems, so eventually we decided to look here. We came here after reading an advertisement from an estate agent in London. They arranged a weekend preview ... the flight was paid for. That was it!

For some retired migrants the choice between rival destinations was finely balanced. Mr and Mrs Green settled in Qawra in Malta in 1989, but Portugal ran a close second:

> We had been on holiday to ... different areas of Portugal and we liked the people. And it was a little nearer to where our son lives in France. We had to weigh up the advantages between there and Malta, where we had been on holiday on and off for twenty years. We did know Malta better than Portugal, and there wasn't the problem of language here.

For the Benningtons it was a toss-up between Malta and France:

> We had first thought about France. I had business connections in Grenoble, and we had numerous friends in that area and in the South of France. We were thinking specifically of Languedoc – we even knew the mayor of Montpellier personally... I knew Malta from my time in the Navy... My wife wondered if we

really shouldn't have gone to France, we did know more people there. Now we know more people here in Malta than we would have done there. There is no language barrier and my wife is happier driving here than she would have been in France.

We have seen that those who settled in Spain had usually done so because of their prior holidays (Table 5.2). Their decision to choose Spain had generally been fairly straightforward and not many weighed up alternative destinations; where mentioned, they were usually France, Cyprus or the United States. Cost and climate were commonly the decisive factors, as the following extracts show:

> Initially we were thinking of America and we went out there for a few months and looked around. Then my husband changed his mind ... we opted for a holiday home in Spain, so people could come and visit us.

> In our industry we had a lot of ups and downs. I tried to find work overseas - Nigeria and the Middle East. When things were not going well with the business, my wife suggested I should retire. I was only 56 then and didn't know if we could afford it. We had thought of Cyprus but it was too far and too expensive... Spain was cheap and we could manage.

Many of the interviewees in the Algarve drew unfavourable comparisons with Spain and the Spanish. Here is one interviewee, a retired engineer from Birmingham, who expressed strongly negative views:

> I've also been several times to Italy and looked at the Adriatic as a possible place to settle, as well as Malta. But Malta is very insular and here we are on the mainland of Europe ... we could drive home from here. In Italy I didn't like the undercurrents... We don't like Spain at all. So many parts are congested and the Mediterranean Sea is filthy. Here we are on the Atlantic and it's much better... Some parts of inland Spain are very nice, of course, but frankly I don't like the Spanish. They pile on the taxes... I find the Portuguese are very friendly and helpful people.

Whilst some of the Algarve interviewees stressed the unique quality of the landscape, this element was more prominent among the retirees in Tuscany. Derek, a retired surgeon who bought in Chianti in 1966, retiring in 1970, had considered other options, but was captivated by the countryside:

> We had looked at Corfu and France, but [some friends] were here and we came to see them – I was on a medical conference in Florence and [they] had just bought a house in Chianti... We had ideas of finding a place in France but we fell in love with the countryside here and started looking around. At that time houses were very cheap. We found this ruin, with some land around it, and my wife came out again a few weeks later and signed the deeds.

Choice of region of destination

Although one can hypothesise that the selection of a retirement destination is a decision-making process that moves progressively from macro- to micro-scale, identifying first the desired country, then the desired region, then the location and the property, in practice these stages may be elided. The questions that asked the reasons for moving *to this area of* Italy/Spain/Malta/Portugal did not generate a set of responses that could be distinguished from the expressed reasons for selecting the country or the property. The reasons that were given were specific to the region and could not be easily cross-tabulated. More insights were gained from the in-depth interviews, many of which probed the locational decision-making process in more detail.

Sometimes the selection of the region was based not on a comparison of regions within the same country but on a choice between specific regions internationally. Thus, for example, Peter, who had grown up in Paris and worked mostly away from England, including a spell in Florence, made his choice between Chianti and the South of France:

> By the early eighties most of the South of France had become suburbia, unless you moved out into the sticks. We knew this part of Chianti from being in Florence ... we came here at weekends... We moved here because we had more friends in the area.

For Bernard the choice of location had been quite precisely worked out, taking into consideration the criteria of landscape, closeness to the sea, and cost of property. He and his wife had bought a small, modern villa in the terraced olive groves behind Viareggio, with a spectacular view of the urbanised coast. Like Peter, Bernard had connections both to France, where he had spent part of his childhood, and Italy, which he had often visited to purchase machinery for his hosiery business in Leicester:

> It was my original intention to be near the Côte d'Azur ... but then I saw the price of property in that neck of the woods... So we started working our way down, taking holidays in different places in Liguria ... looking at houses on the sea because we both adore the sea and swimming. But in Liguria it either meant you took an expensive villa or there was nothing else... So we started coming down a bit more, then a bit more and we reached Viareggio. Some estate agents told us that there were some pretty villas not right on the seaside but if you go up into the hills you'll find something that costs a lot less. We saw this place, and fell in love with it.

As those who have settled in this region often stressed, Tuscany is one of the most beautiful parts of Italy, even of Europe. Brian, whom we have already met in the previous chapter, chose Tuscany essentially because of the landscape, believing that 'there are other beautiful landscapes but this is one of the best ... you get wonderful light here – it's changing all the time ... that absorbs me'. Sir Julian, a retired judge, chose Chianti for a mix of reasons related to landscape and the way of life:

> When I first started travelling to Italy in the 1950s, I used to go down to the east coast, south of Ancona, and I got to know that part of the country pretty well. Later on, when the children grew up, I started to do motoring tours of Italy and a good deal of that was spent in Tuscany. I got to know all the towns here and the countryside, it became my favourite part of Italy... I decided that when I retired I would live in Chianti. I find it an agreeable part of the country and I like the people here. Siena is very beautiful and we are also in easy reach of Florence. Also in reach of the sea, and it's wine country.

Within Spain, whilst there was some acknowledgement of the scenic attractiveness of inland areas, most people's residential choices were restricted to the well-known tourist coasts and islands. Generally the Costa del Sol was preferred to the other Mediterranean coastal regions because of familiarity and its warmer and sunnier winter climate, while many perceived the Canaries and Balearics as isolated. According to one interviewee:

> The Costa Brava winters are not good; it's a bit like the South of France climatically... You need to go further south... The Costa del Sol climate, we think, is the best in Europe. Even now, in February, we are wearing summer clothes.

Cyril, a retired mental health worker from Sheffield, living on a hill inland from Torremolinos, agreed:

> We had looked first at the Costa Brava but didn't like it; then down to the Benidorm area, but that seemed like Blackpool. I liked Tenerife – that was a possibility. But there you are stuck on an island, plus it is expensive to keep flying out of an island. The same with Majorca, which was too touristy for me. But here it is so quiet and the Spanish people are very nice. We had visited Fuengirola and Marbella on holiday, so we knew the area well, including inland. Also you get more sunshine here – the temperature is marvellous.

In Portugal, almost no respondent or interviewee considered any Portuguese regions other than the Algarve for retirement, although there was some differentiation within the Algarve, for instance between west, centre and east, or between the coast and inland. Malta, of course, is the smallest of the study regions, although there is a clear division between the main island and Gozo. The latter is a quieter, more picturesque and more agricultural island, and it tends to attract higher income and status retirees, rather like rural Tuscany. Abigail, widow of a famous writer, lives in a small village and was attracted by a love of small islands and by the special qualities of the Gozitan landscape. She described how she and her husband chose Gozo in 1968:

> We realised how much we liked islands. We thought of the West Indies for a bit and then decided to look at the Channel Islands... We sold up everything and

Table 5.5 Reasons for choice of property (%)

Reason	Main reason given for choice of property					Other reasons (all destinations)
	Tuscany	Malta	Costa del Sol	Algarve	Total	
Size	7.8	19.4	12.2	9.6	13.1	7.3
Price, rent	7.8	12.9	14.4	10.1	12.2	8.0
Layout, condition, fittings etc.	11.8	23.0	17.7	12.4	17.2	18.0
Setting (view, residential area)	11.8	14.5	17.7	15.6	15.6	16.6
Location (access to facilities)	14.7	7.7	18.7	19.3	15.3	16.4
In the countryside	16.7	6.0	6.7	11.9	8.9	8.9
Period House	7.8	4.4	1.2	4.6	3.7	3.1
Already owned, second home	7.8	2.0	1.8	12.4	5.1	1.7
Garden	2.0	1.6	3.4	0.0	1.9	5.3
Near friends, relatives	4.9	0.0	0.3	0.5	0.8	3.4
Other	6.9	8.5	5.9	3.6	6.2	11.3
n =	102	248	327	218	895	1400

Source: Authors' survey.

we settled on Guernsey, but as soon as we arrived we heard a lot about Malta. Another author lived on Guernsey and he was building a holiday home in Malta. He told us about Gozo and we came to look at the island. We were definitely looking for somewhere warm to live... We only came for a week at first, and in those days there were no estate agents so a moonlighting teacher showed us around. We had heard about the empty farmhouses so we wanted to look at them. We liked the island and found the shapes of the hills which rise out of the valleys rather fascinating. At that time there were more donkeys than cars and great herds of sheep and goats wandering around. It was almost biblical. Very simple. This appealed to us... He told us about one farmhouse he knew [and] brought us there when it was getting dark. We saw a courtyard ... but there was no electricity. Then we saw that the only lighthouse in the two islands beamed right into the house... All around were marvellous coastal views and cliff walks... Warren decided to take it! It was awfully cheap too.

Choice of property

The choice of a place to retire is often a spatially staged process by which the country is first selected, then the region or district, and finally the property itself. For some people the region may be more important than the property; for others the nature or environs of the property – a penthouse flat with a sea view, or a *casa colonica* with an olive grove – may be the overriding concern. The choice of property is often a highly personal and intuitive decision. Some can vividly articulate their rationale, but others cannot elaborate beyond reporting an intuitive or spontaneous feeling that the chosen property was the 'right one'.

In the questionnaire, respondents were asked what was the most important reason for their choice of property, and they were also invited to add up to three further reasons in order of importance. Notable contrasts are found between destination regions and between the first-ranked and other reasons (Table 5.5). For instance, compared to the other regions, retirees in Tuscany were more influenced by countryside location, the availability of historic and vernacular properties, and nearness of friends.[4] Respondents in Malta and the Costa del Sol were more interested in the size, price, layout and internal amenities of the dwelling and in the nature of the surrounding residential neighbourhood; they were less concerned about a countryside location, a period house, or nearness to family and friends (although the presence of a garden, including a roof garden, had some importance on the Costa del Sol). The pattern of response in the Algarve, broadly speaking, was between the two described: only the reason 'already owned prior to retirement' scored significantly higher than in the other three destination areas.

Many of the reasons are more subtly intertwined than the stark categorisation of Table 5.5 indicates. Combinations of reasons reflect not only the different characteristics of the destinations and individual properties but also the class, wealth and lifetime travel and work attributes of the respondents. From the in-depth interviews, we first explore the often close connection between choice of property and prior holidaying in the area. Louis, a former public relations officer, retired to the Algarve in 1990. His account of selecting a modern property was typical of many others who had settled in this region:

> I'd been to Portugal several times on holiday. I wanted to live in a sunny climate and I like the people... The key to us coming here was for me to sell my bungalow in order to buy this. But it was an awkward time to sell in England, in 1990. It wasn't a great sale but we managed to buy this... We must have looked at about twenty properties. We saw most of them very quickly but this one we kept coming back to... It was ideal for us, being so near the airport, and elevated but not too high. If we had been any higher we might have been affected by damp during the winter time and my wife has a bad back... We knew what sort of accommodation we were looking for and also we didn't want something that needed a lot of maintaining... We also wanted a pool ... it gets terribly hot out here in the summer.

Some retirees have quite specific needs when looking for a property, often because of health problems. Andrew had worked for the BBC for nearly thirty years but had been forced to retire early because of spinal problems. His surgeon advised a move to a warmer climate:

> I spent half of the winter in bed, I was in a steel corset and couldn't walk far, especially in winter... I needed a warm climate and the south of Spain seemed

ideal... We contacted some estate agents, and when we saw Calahonda we liked it straight away... We had special considerations – a ground-floor flat or a place with a lift... we'd also asked for a south-facing view. This apartment fitted the bill. The bedroom was large and that was important for me as I spent so much time in bed... Calahonda was clean, neat and tidy. It had amenities close at hand – three supermarkets, DIY shops and lots of restaurants ... also a bus service to larger places.

Even in rural Tuscany, nearness to basic amenities is an important factor for those whose mobility becomes more restricted. Sir Julian, whose rationale for choosing the Chianti region has been considered, also explained why living close to a small village is important for him:

When you get to be a man of my age, it is very convenient to be able to walk to the shops ... there are three grocers, a doctor and a chemist ... there's also an excellent restaurant in the village. The doctor is a real advantage: local surgery twice a week.

In Malta, unlike Tuscany, there are relatively few secluded rural properties and living near or in a village has different connotations. In this next extract, Susan sets out her reasons for choosing a new house built over its own garage on the edge of a Gozitan village:

I had various criteria. I had about £25,000 sterling from the sale of our bunga-low in Yorkshire. I wanted a house, not a flat, I fancied living on the outskirts of a village and to be in a place where my husband could play with his tools in a garage. I wanted somewhere near where a boat could be moored and also have a garden... Then we found this place ... it was a brand new, totally empty house with archways. To me it was huge. It was also cheap – only £10,000! I decided it was for me.

In contrast to the carefully-reasoned accounts in these cases, other interviewees expressed mainly intuitive or emotional reasons, leading to a sudden, snap decision to 'go for it'. Often this reaction applied to a prop-erty which was old, even a ruin. Vanessa and her husband bought a derelict country property in the Algarve in 1986:

Well, when I walked into the rooms, I felt I had been born here! It was quite habitable though in a primitive way – there was no sanitation or running water or electricity... All the foundations of the house were there and almost all the little windows ... the foundations were dug out of bedrock, worn away because of use over the years. We have restored the place to how it was 300 years ago ... it has been a labour of love.

Clearly, in rural areas such as Tuscany and the sparsely-populated parts of the interior Algarve, the 'search and selection' process tends to be based on finding a 'character property', usually one in a secluded setting with good views. Even in Tuscany, however, where many retirees are very wealthy, cost is rarely irrelevant. Many buyers acquired properties that were in need of substantial repair because they were cheap (though not necessarily in the long run) and because of the challenge of restoration. Such restoration generally has one of two objectives: to return the property more or less exactly to its former state, as with Vanessa above; or to make an imaginative conversion, turning a pigsty into a kitchen, or a cow-shed into a bedroom. The following case exemplifies various of these points. Lloyd retired at the age of 47 after a career in the Army, spent almost entirely abroad. His property was a Tuscan farmhouse nestling under the battlements of a castle near the Umbrian border:

> We had holidayed here for a number of years and loved the area. We didn't have enough money to buy a house with land in England... We came here for a long weekend to see houses ... an agent showed us properties on his book ... when we saw the photo of the tower we decided to take a look at it. It was more expensive than we could really afford ... but when we actually saw the property we thought 'that's it!'... It was unlike any other property we saw ... about £20,000 for a tower, a not completely derelict farmhouse and about two acres of land. But it was value for money – we could have found nothing like that back in England... Of course, we paid out a lot for restoration on top of the price of the property ... we took eight years to do it and it has been drip-feeding all the way.

In Malta some of the character properties selected by retirees are in urban areas – for instance, in Senglea overlooking the Grand Harbour, or in one of the inland towns such as Mosta. Such places are away from the traditional 'expat' areas and are chosen by some retirees for precisely this reason. Here Kate recounts her experience of renovating an old house in the small town of Mosta:

> I already knew the expat areas because I had been coming on holiday here for years... The agent showed me here; it was a ruin but I fell in love with it. They were selling it very cheaply, it cost me 5000 Maltese pounds in 1989. I restored it over the next two years. It cost me 16,000 Maltese all told, which was about £27,000 sterling... I put in two bathrooms, restored the floor downstairs, rebuilt some walls and I had to put in drainage and electricity. Some windows and doors had to be put in as well... This is a typical Maltese house, which is Moorish... There's a lovely courtyard with arches. The walls are very thick slab with the centre filled with rubble. The windows are small as you need to keep the light and the heat out in Malta... I also liked this house because of its shape and the fact that it is tucked away in an alley, a long way from the road, so it's very quiet...

The final theme we wish to draw out of the in-depth interview material on property selection is the local geography of the regions of retirement settlement, in particular the variations in the perceived desirability of different districts, and the contrasting changes over time. Our first example comes from southern Spain. Frank, a retired engineer, drew a clear distinction between his chosen retirement location near Estepona, and the overcrowded resorts which have been densely settled by British residents.

We had the house built the way we wanted it, on the side of the hill. We could see the possibilities when we first drove up here. You can see Gibraltar and North Africa, the mountains stretch all the way round, and the view is wonderful. The location really appealed to us... Estepona is still a typical Spanish town in its centre, and although there are blocks of flats and urbanisations on the outside, it hasn't been taken over by the Brits. Here there is a lovely beach which is never full. Nine out of ten people on that beach are Spanish. Not like Torremolinos and Fuengirola, with their mass-market buildings along the coast.

British residents in the Algarve also precisely differentiated the relative attractions of the various districts. As with the above quotation, there was a strong element of self-justification: a property regarded as central and convenient by one commentator may be regarded as overcrowded and inauthentic by another. The general view seemed to be that little remained unspoilt in the central Algarve south of the EN125, that the west was damp and windy, the east flat and remote, and the Monchique area hilly and misty with vestiges of the 'colonial, cocktail set' who settled in the 1960s and 1970s. Here is the view of a retired couple living in a valley near Silves:

When we took the decision to come to the Algarve, well, we didn't want to live in an urbanisation or be near one. We wanted to be north of the EN125, for peace and quiet. Also we wanted a decent garden and there was plenty of water down here ... we have a well beside the river... We are in the Arade valley here. In Moorish times the river was navigable to Silves.

This rather bucolic setting was then compared with other parts of the Algarve:

The eastern Algarve – Tavira for example – is too flat for us. We went into the back of Tavira, up in the hills there, but we weren't impressed, the access was bad and water was difficult. Then we looked at the western Algarve but that was really too far away from the airport and we didn't like the land west of Portimão... We didn't want to be too far inland up in the Monchique – in that area there are many expensive developments and English-speaking people who are not interested in mixing with the Portuguese. They just have cocktail parties every night!

Sometimes the factors about a property and its immediate environs which attracted a British settler change over the time the individual has been resident there. Michael married a Maltese woman at the end of the war. Now a widower living in St Julians, he describes how the area has changed:

We came here in 1977 ... it was so quiet and select... But there have been tremendous changes, especially in the last ten years. [It's] become the hive of night-life. It's where the young Maltese come by coach-loads and there are discos and fish-and-chips here now. The one-way traffic is chaotic and the streets are crowded... Why don't I move on? Well, it's too much of an effort and I'm 72 now. I am resigned to a flat I like in a changed area.

Michael's case provides a link to the next major theme, residential mobility in the destination regions, and patterns of mobility between first and second homes in the UK and abroad.

Residential strategies

We have noted that there are many deviations away from the 'taken for granted' model of retirement migration – from the situation where the retirement coincides with the migratory move and with the simultaneous selling of the UK property and purchase of the retirement home abroad. In this section we examine the associations between the sequencing of migration and retirement and the retention or sale of properties in the UK and abroad.

Acquisition of property abroad before retirement

First, let us regroup the scattered information we have already presented on pre-retirement property acquisition abroad. Pages 85-8 described the frequency of international mobility and foreign residence prior to retirement. Table 4.6 showed that half of the respondents had lived abroad for at least three months, and that more than one-third had lived exclusively or partly abroad during the five years prior to arriving at the current destination. The same table showed that 38 per cent had owned a home in the destination country. The pre-retirement experience of foreign residence and property ownership was found to be highest in Tuscany and the Algarve. The association with the prior acquisition of a second home was also brought out in Table 5.5.

These various indicators of foreign residential strategies contain ambiguity and imprecision. For instance, prior ownership of a home in a particular destination country may be linked to earlier employment and may not indicate the purchase of a holiday home to be used subsequently as a retirement residence; indeed it may be in an entirely different region.[5] In other cases the purchase of a foreign residence was not as a second home: it was the owners' only home. This occurred for several people with few residential or work links to the UK. Another element of imprecision concerns the distinction between ownership (with or without a mortgage) and the degree of access to property given by renting, time-share or joint purchases with friends or family members.

Rather than complicate this issue further, and given the fact that some respondents had difficulty in answering the questions about multiple property ownership, so that the data given on residential options may not be very accurate, we simply report that for a significant number of retirement migrants the purchase of their foreign retirement home took place some time before retirement. The purchase was often with future retirement in mind, but in other cases a more immediate objective, commonly to acquire a holiday home, was paramount, and the decision to occupy it as a retirement home came later. In southern Spain, the acquisition of a holiday flat or villa correlated well with frequent pre-retirement holidaying in the region. Gary, a retired chemical engineer, is a typical case:

> We knew Mijas well from holidays ... We started talking to estate agents and we got the impression that Mijas was a good place to live... So we bought this apartment as a second home for holidays... A few years later, in 1991, we moved out here and this is now our main base.

The following account from Percy and Sue, who had run their own business in Derby and who 'wanted to retire while we had plenty of time to enjoy ourselves', is more complex. It illustrates some details about how properties in the Costa del Sol are marketed and acquired, and shows that, for retired persons with no occupational pension, a local income may be essential to finance the retirement stay. The couple live on the Calahonda estate and their account starts with the inspection flight promoted by the property company:

> The flight was reasonably cheap... We were put up in a hotel when we got here, and we were taken out for meals in the evening. So many properties were shown to us that we got a bit boggle-eyed with what we had seen. In the end we didn't know which area we had bought in! This particular place had been a holiday home owned by a couple from Madrid ... we bought it for £14,000, just within our price range ... of course, this is quite a few years ago, in 1982... We used to use it to come out on holidays and we rented it out to friends... We started to live here permanently in 1986... Then the peseta became weak and we bought a studio in Torremolinos which we still have. We have been renting that out. Now we have another four studios for rental. We knew we would need a peseta income when we lived here. It was a matter of thinking ahead ... using the money from the sale of our business.

Several of the Algarve respondents had also bought properties in this region prior to their retirement, though often for different sets of reasons. Reflecting its early involvement with the 'ex-colonial set', the Algarve became popular for British expats who preferred not to buy property in the UK. Typical of this group was Hamish, who had been managing plantations in Malaysia:

> We came here first in 1970 with three young children ... decided we liked the area and we explored around ... at the end of three weeks we decided to put roots down here with retirement in mind. Having a place here was for speculative reasons at the beginning, and for holidays. The girls were at boarding school in Scotland and this was handy for them on visits... We liked this place from the beginning, and the climate. We knew we would never return to Scotland when we retired – we couldn't take all those grey skies again.

The most complex pre-retirement residential strategies were found amongst the respondents living in Malta. This is undoubtedly because of the multifaceted connections between Britain and Malta. Many of our informants had been in Malta long before their retirement. Some had worked in the British armed forces establishments or had been connected to Anglo-Maltese civil ventures such as airlines or industrial companies. Others had come to the island through marriage to a Maltese – some British women had married Maltese migrants in London and then migrated to Malta with their husbands, whilst many British service personnel had taken Maltese wives. Like Hamish, in the Algarve, others had chosen Malta as a conveniently located and climatically benign 'half-way house' between the UK and their expatriate work-places in the Middle East or Africa – a place where they could 'perch' for a while between foreign assignments, and a place which was sufficiently 'British' to remind them of 'home'.

Keeping a foothold in the UK

In contrast to the previous subsection, which looked at acquisition of foreign property prior to retirement abroad, this one examines decisions about the respondents' properties in the UK – not forgetting that some 'lifetime expatriates' never owned a property in the UK. In many cases, disposal of the UK property was necessary to finance the purchase of the retirement home in southern Europe. Others had sufficient wealth to purchase a foreign property whilst retaining their UK residence. Those who retained a UK property had diverse strategies. Some explicitly retained it out of a lack of commitment to or confidence about living permanently abroad. Some said they wanted a base for visits to see relatives and friends, whilst others established a regular pattern of seasonal migration, wintering in southern Europe and returning to the UK for the summer. Some explained that the property was retained as an insurance against a possible return forced by ill-health or a family problem.

About 40 per cent of the survey respondents retained their UK property at the time of their move to their first retirement home abroad. The share is similar across the four destinations, but a little lower in Spain. The interviews provide insights into some of the reasons behind the retention and subsequent use and disposal of UK property. Gary, a retired engineer living in Mijas Pueblo, was expansive about the process of 'letting go':

> You always wonder how things will turn out when you make an overseas move. I don't think you should leave a place solely because you are disaffected with where you live. I didn't have a chip on my shoulder about England. We were worried about the contact with our son and daughter, although they had been at university for some time before we left and we knew they wouldn't be living at home any more ... [but] ... we are a close family and are always on the telephone to each other. They find it inexpensive to come out and see us, which is fortunate. You do give up some of your friends and colleagues, of course, but we didn't feel we were cutting any real cords... We kept our house in England because the property market was depressed when we tried to sell in 1990. We have good tenants there on rental ... our property in the UK, we feel, is safe... We have not considered going back to England. Mind you, if things were to change dramatically here, we probably would go back but we'll burn that bridge when we get to it!

Unlike Gary, many kept a UK property for a while and then sold it. Sir Julian, from Tuscany, said:

> When I came to live here, I thought it might be useful to keep a flat in London. Useful for the children and also when I went on a visit to London. But it was expensive and after a couple of years I gave it up.

Several explained why they had *not* retained properties in the UK. One exceptional case involved a London flat which had been wrecked by tenants who proved to have diplomatic immunity and could not be sued for damages. Another case concerned a retired couple in Portugal who retained a house in Sussex which was rented out: when the couple returned for visits to the UK they stayed in a hotel to avoid disturbing the model tenants.

Clearly, then, UK properties were kept on for a variety of reasons: unwillingness to pull up roots, at least initially; as a hedge against things not working out; for use by adult children; as a source of rental income; and of the difficulties of selling in a depressed market in the early to mid-1990s. Interestingly, very few cases were found where retention of the UK property was due to a specific *intention* to return one day. Most of the interviewees we have quoted were exercised only by their ability to reside in either or both the UK and their chosen retirement region, but there were also more complex situations. These were of two main types: 'lifetime expats' with no property in the UK but perhaps with property elsewhere (Cyprus, Bermuda and France were cases in point); and people who had owned or rented property in another region of the country in which they retired. A few respondents in Spain and Portugal had worked in Madrid or Lisbon, while in Tuscany several informants had lived in places as diverse as Milan, Rome and Capri as well as those making more localised moves, from a working life in Florence out to the countryside for retirement (see King and Patterson 1998). Finally, we encountered a few people with multiple homes, some in more than two countries.

Movement back and forth

A substantial minority of respondents maintained two or more residences, enabling the option of dividing their time between different places to achieve 'residential amenity maximisation' (King *et al.* 1998: 92). However, the study of retirement migration can easily slip into a simple dichotomy of seasonal versus permanent migration. As we pointed out on pp. 43-4, several refinements need to be made to this too-simple typology.

First, for any given individual, the type of movement may change over time. Repeat holiday visits can act as a stepping-stone, via purchase of a second home, to seasonal movement and then to permanent emigration, the last stage often coinciding with retirement. Even this sequential typology is an oversimplification, for 'seasonal emigrants' spend variable amounts of time at different times of the year in their countries of origin and 'abroad' (Williams *et al.* 1997: 116-17, 129). Even the attribution of

Table 5.6 Number of weeks spent at present address last year (%)

	< 26	27-39	40-49	>50	n
Destination:					
Tuscany	10.4	7.5	36.8	45.3	106
Malta	6.5	14.5	41.1	37.8	275
Costa del Sol	14.0	14.0	41.1	30.8	328
Algarve	10.9	15.4	42.1	31.7	221
Total	10.6	13.8	40.9	34.7	930

Source: Authors' survey.

'home' and 'abroad' can change once retirement migration takes place.

In her paper on British migration to Fuengirola, Karen O'Reilly (1995a) distinguishes between several categories of residents, tourists and travellers and refutes the mutual exclusivity of 'visitor' and 'resident'. She proposes a fivefold terminology:

- *expatriates* have no intention of ever returning to their home country;
- *residents* live more or less permanently in Spain, but return to Britain for 2-6 months each year usually to escape the heat and crowds of summer; many are retired;
- *seasonal* visitors live more or less permanently in the UK but visit Spain each winter, attracted by the mild climate, the low cost of renting accommodation, and the social/leisure activities;
- *returners* own second homes in Spain to which they return periodically but irregularly, to fit in with work and other commitments;
- *tourists* come to Spain specifically for holidays of short duration.

O'Reilly's typology is based on the 'individual's sense of commitment or orientation to one or other place of residence'. She argues that 'the grey area between residence and visiting, migration and sojourning ... needs to be conceptualised if research can progress in this area' (O'Reilly 1995a: 29). It certainly highlights the various ways in which British people 'engage with' the Costa del Sol. Its relevance for this research is partial, however, since our survey respondents were defined (by us) as those who spend on average at least four months per year in southern Europe. Hence we are dealing with 'expatriates', 'residents' and various types of seasonal migrants and not with tourists and occasional visitors. Moreover, in Chapter 2, we argued that any such typology also needs to take into account the rights and responsibilities pertaining to property ownership and legal registration.

Table 5.6 shows that practically nine-tenths of our respondents spend at least half the year in southern Europe, and three-quarters at least forty weeks. Substantial numbers do spend several weeks a year out of the area, and a quarter are away for at least three months a year.[6]

Table 5.6 cross-tabulates time spent in the retirement property with the destination region. The share who were away from their retirement region for at least three months of the previous year ranged from the Costa del Sol (28 per cent) and the Algarve (26 per cent), to Malta (21 per cent) and Tuscany (18 per cent). The same sequence is evident among the longest stayers: around 30 per cent in the Costa del Sol were away for less than two weeks in the previous year, compared with 31 per cent for the Algarve, 38 per cent for Malta and 45 per cent for Tuscany.

As the in-depth interviews revealed, a seasonal pattern of residence generally involved a movement to the UK during the summer. For those with weak ties to the UK, the weeks spent away from the retirement base might be spent touring, sailing, or holidaying in other countries or continents. It should also be noted here that seasonal or extended visits to Britain are not necessarily dependent on retention of a property, for many retirees stayed with children, other relatives or friends. The 'return for the summer' was much less evident for the respondents in Tuscany; here summer is less hot, and the winters can be severe, especially inland. In the Algarve and the Costa del Sol, many respondents did however remark on the unbearable heat of high summer. Another factor is that frequent and inexpensive charter flights from Málaga and Faro facilitate frequent returns from the Algarve and the Costa del Sol in comparison to Malta (where many retirees complained of the high cost of air fares) or Tuscany (where fares are higher than from Spain and many retired settlers are a long way from the airports of Pisa and Florence).

Residential mobility after retirement

Nearly half (44 per cent) of the survey respondents had moved at least once within the destination region. Whilst a simplistic perception of a retirement move is that it is 'final', to be succeeded only by a forced move into some kind of sheltered accommodation, migrants moving abroad in their late fifties or early sixties can expect another twenty years or so of active life, but also for their circumstances to change, sometimes in ways that encourage further residential moves. Amongst the reasons for later moves that were reported to us were changing household structure, decreased income and personal mobility, and unpleasant changes in the neighbourhood, many associated with the impact of mass tourism or the loss of a view.

Table 5.7 presents the quantitative data on the residential behaviour of the survey respondents. Judged by the share who made two or more moves, the greatest mobility was in Tuscany (22.6 per cent) and Malta (19.5 per cent); the lowest in the Algarve (10.4 per cent). On the other hand, the Tuscan sample also contained the greatest share of non-movers – 60.4 per cent.[7] Overall, the respondents in Malta had made the highest average of onward moves (0.83), followed by Tuscany (0.72), the Costa del Sol (0.66) and Algarve (0.57). These differentials are however partly

Table 5.7 Residential behaviour since first or retirement move to destination country: number of moves and tenure of property (%)

	Tuscany	Malta	Costa del Sol	Algarve	Total
Moves since arrival					
0	60.4	48.6	59.4	59.1	56.3
1	17.0	32.0	26.1	30.5	27.8
2	15.1	11.2	8.4	6.8	9.6
3+	7.5	8.3	6.1	3.6	6.3
average no. of moves	0.72	0.83	0.66	0.57	0.69
n =	106	278	345	220	949
Tenure of first property					
Owned	65.7	63.5	86.6	81.0	76.3
Rented	24.8	32.3	11.3	16.6	20.1
Other (loaned, tied)	9.5	4.2	2.1	2.4	3.6
n =	105	260	335	211	911
Tenure of present address					
Owned	83.8	64.9	91.6	94.3	83.5
Rented	10.5	33.2	7.5	4.2	14.7
Other (loaned, tied)	5.7	1.9	0.9	1.4	1.9
n =	105	268	322	212	907

Source: Authors' survey.

'explained' by the fact that respondents in the destinations with the highest residential mobility have, on average, tended to be there longest (see Table 4.4). The average number of moves per year of residence in the destination region shows less variation: 0.059 moves per year in Malta, 0.057 in the Algarve, 0.050 in the Costa del Sol, and 0.045 in Tuscany. If these probabilities were unchanged over 15 years, in Malta 60 per cent of the population would make at least one move, whereas in Tuscany the same would apply to exactly one half of the retirees.

The first detailed case study of residential mobility comes from Tuscany, and is set in Box 5.1. It provides an excellent account of the main residential options in Tuscany and Umbria: town or country living. The interviewee, Douglas, had been a lawyer and a university administrator. Like most retirees to Tuscany, he had settled in a rural property, but after several years in the countryside he and his wife decided to move to a local town to be near amenities and to avoid the problems of rural isolation in later life.

Box 5.1 Residential mobility in Tuscany

On retirement at 63 years of age, Douglas bought a large derelict farmhouse and an acre of land on the Tuscan-Umbrian border in 1987. He describes this house and its restoration:

> We had a study, three bedrooms, two bathrooms and a kitchen. It was not like that at the beginning – we had to put in the bathrooms. We had to replaster and rewire all the rooms, we had to put down floors, put in water and install drainage, plus electricity. We had to strip the roof and replace the beams, and new windows and doors too. It only cost us £15,000 to buy but the work cost us another £100,000. There were some old olive trees, and we planted some more olives. We had a croquet lawn and a herb garden. We intended to see our lives out there... Well, the problem was that we had six kids and they kept coming out on visits.

Douglas was asked what made him subsequently sell up and move:

> The spark was a letter from the Swansea vehicle licensing place to say that my licence had expired. I was over 70. We were dependent, living in the country, on a motor car and my wife doesn't drive. It made us think what would happen if we couldn't drive the car. As you get older you must be more sensible. Instead of slogging around mowing the grass, cleaning the bathrooms and entertaining what seemed to be the whole of England, we thought it would be better to live in a town centre with less vast premises so that could be our last move before the cemetery!

After searching in several local towns they found a suitable old house in an historic town about 20 km away.

> We wanted to live in the centre of an historic town in this immediate area where we had made lots of friends... We were lucky to find this place. The origins of the house are fifteenth-century, I think ... there are frescoes, and a chapel behind the library... The whole house was empty and the roof needed re-doing ... but we liked the garden here. It is difficult to find a place with a garden in a walled city centre... It wasn't very expensive. We paid 190 million lire; about £80,000. We spent another £35,000 on re-wiring, a new bathroom etc.... This is the only construction work we had done. Living in town has many advantages... When we run out of something, we can get it in seconds from the shops. I can walk to the bank and the restaurants are nearby... We have achieved what we wanted to do, namely comfortable and spacious accommodation within walking distance of everything. And this town is excellent because it has good administration and all through the winter there are free film shows, music and concerts.

The relatively high degree of residential mobility amongst British retirees in Malta is partly related to the variety of housing options available within a small place (urban, rural, coastal, interior, village, Gozo etc.) and partly to the relatively large rental sector. The lower part of Table 5.7

shows that renting accounted for one-third of respondents' dwellings for both the first and the current residence in Malta. In the other three destinations ownership is not only much higher at the first property, but also increases at the expense of the rental sector as subsequent moves are made. The obvious implication is that, in Tuscany, the Costa del Sol and the Algarve, a significant number of retirees start off by renting and then move into ownership afterwards. From the interviews clear reasons for this pattern emerge: the idea of 'testing the water' before a major financial commitment to house purchase is made; the delay in selling the UK house; or the need to rent whilst a new property is built or an older property restored.

In an earlier interview extract, Michael described how a flat he had bought in 1977 in St Julians had become surrounded by traffic and nightlife over the past twenty years. Too old to move on, he had resigned himself to living in 'a flat I like in a changed area'. Michael's account provides a good example of the phenomenon of 'static displacement' (Bhabha 1994: 217), which occurs when places that were once familiar and comfortable become utterly changed so that residents feel 'displaced' even though they have not moved (see also Rowles 1978). Many other respondents, especially in Malta and the Costa del Sol, bemoaned the changes which had occurred in the areas where they had invested in their retirement properties. Whilst some, like Michael, had decided to 'stick it out', for others a move was triggered to a more favourable location. In the next extract Terry describes a move from a township on the fringes of Málaga to Mijas Pueblo. At the same time he expresses a British expatriate's views of the local 'place geography' and some rather inconsistent perceptions of the Spanish population:

> One of the reasons why we moved out from the other side of Málaga was that it was developing rapidly with many high-rise apartments going up. The countryside was being gobbled up. Car parking became a problem. Although we like the Spanish, they were crowding in with their weekend apartments. It wasn't the little village we once knew and we decided to move. This is the less Spanish side and there are a lot of expats here... We were quite taken by this apartment and we loved the view... We like the Spanish residents of Mijas – we find them very friendly. They seem to accept us. You feel more in the Spanish environment on this side. It is also a very handy place to live in. There are a mass of shops nearby and some marvellous attractions. We are also on the level here and that is important as you get older.

Moving to a quieter, less touristic location was also a common theme in Malta. For Deirdre it was mainly to do with new building taking place immediately in front of her first property. Deirdre came to Malta in 1988 after she had been widowed and her mother had died. She had been brought up in East Africa and had chosen Malta because many of her friends had bought property there and 'Malta was the nearest to the tropics I could get!'

I bought the flat at Xemxija which was a mistake. Three months after, time-share units went up in front of my flat ... blocking the wonderful view over St Paul's Bay. I now realise you should rent for a year before buying... I sold that flat ... this one is much better and I have all the shops nearby. All the area in front is a green area. I went to the Planning Department in Valletta about it and they confirmed it was a green area. I wish I had checked more carefully with my first place.

Residential moves in Malta took place for other reasons. Several British retirees who initially invested in traditional farm and village properties decided to move to smaller dwellings which are easier to manage. Daphne was widowed before she came to Malta. Retiring from a career as a school matron in Sussex, she bought a farmhouse in an inland village in 1989.

I went through an agent... I asked to see old places... I was interested in the architectural features, solid walls, high ceilings... The house I bought had been converted but most of the features had been kept. It had two courtyards – I made a garden in one of them... But when you retire, well you don't realise that you are getting old ... it dawns on you that there will be certain things in the house you can't do. That's why I sold that house – it became too much for me... Quite a few English people ... bought big farmhouses, sold them and then moved on. They found the same problem as me – they were difficult to keep up as you grow older.

Daphne then moved to Qawra, a coastal residential area popular both with Maltese, who had holiday flats there, and with British residents. In this next extract she offers a different set of perspectives on her present flat:

I am only renting here and would not buy again ... if you buy anything new, they ask for 17.5 per cent tax, and I am not prepared to pay that to the government... Since I left England my daughter got married there and my son is now planning to get married at home. My family will grow up over there and I think in two years time I will go home... I will miss Malta but I miss my children more.

The evidence presented here shows that retirees change their residential location or property type for various reasons, but a few recurring themes stand out. First there are adjustments to changes in the locality. Sometimes the changes were unforeseen, in other cases the move is impelled by poor 'market research' into the advantages and disadvantages of different locations and property types, as with Daphne. A second type of onward move anticipates the future, when the individual or couple become more reliant on local amenities, as with Douglas. Finally there is the possibility of a return to Britain, hinted at by Daphne.

Evaluating the Migration Decision

This final section of the chapter examines our informants' *post hoc* evaluations of their moves abroad. The analysis is built around a cluster of questions which first asked respondents to list the three greatest advantages they perceived of living in the destination region in retirement, followed by the three greatest disadvantages; then followed the questions: in what ways have respondents' expectations about living abroad in retirement been disappointed, or surpassed?

The overall finding is that the overwhelming majority of our respondents see retirement abroad in a positive light: the advantages consistently outweigh the disadvantages, and disappointments are relatively few. However, we must acknowledge the possibility of two potential sources of bias. The first is familiar to all retrospective accounts, the problem of *post hoc* rationalisation. Having retired abroad, informants may be keen to convince themselves that it was the right decision and unwilling to admit to themselves (let alone to others) that it was a mistake. Secondly, people who have become unhappy, disenchanted, frail or sick will have returned to Britain, thereby removing themselves from the field survey; or, if still resident in southern Europe, will be reluctant to answer a questionnaire or to be interviewed. We did not interview people who were very sick or in hospital or nursing homes.

The 'burnt bridges' syndrome – the need to make the best of a problematic situation given that there is no turning back (or that to turn back would be to admit failure) – probably applied to some of the respondents. In interviews it was rarely admitted personally but often attributed to others. While acknowledging that some of the retirees rationalised their decision in this over-positive way, the fact that there was no clear evidence of widespread unhappiness or disappointment leads us to reaffirm the positive overall finding.

Second, it is undeniable that our survey population was selective of 'successes'. The sick, the frail and the poor and disaffected are the most likely to have returned. It is also true that retirees in difficulty – in poor physical and/or mental health, or on very low incomes – are less likely to have responded to our questionnaire. In Tuscany, where the questionnaire survey was administered from the British Consulate, it is known that persons in difficult circumstances were deliberately *not* sent questionnaires to avoid disturbance and distress. In all destinations, key informants confirmed that there were elderly British residents who were isolated, vulnerable and in poor health. We made special efforts to seek out isolated and low-income retirees. Such cases appeared to be more numerous in Florence, Malta and Torremolinos, where British retirement occurred earliest and where, therefore, there were more very old people. People in distress clearly 'escaped' our data capture, but we have no evidence from our key informants that they are numerous, and it should be remembered that many of their problems cannot be 'blamed' on migration abroad.

Tables 5.8 and 5.9 present the respondents' answers to the questions about advantages and disadvantages. For most advantages and problems, the destination region appears to be the main discriminator; thus in the tables the regional dimension is presented. Cross-tabulations of each named advantage or problem by age, education, social class or length of

Table 5.8 Ranked advantages of having retired to destination region (%)

	Tuscany	Malta	Costa del Sol	Algarve	Total
1st advantage					
Climate	52.0	52.8	69.0	70.2	62.8
Pace of life	21.6	12.6	15.0	19.5	16.2
Lower living costs	1.0	14.6	6.1	2.3	7.0
Social advantages	5.9	7.5	6.4	3.3	5.9
Admiration of country	8.8	5.5	0.9	2.3	3.5
Practical advantages	1.0	3.5	1.2	0.9	1.8
Other advantages	9.7	3.5	1.4	1.5	2.8
n =	102	254	326	215	897
2nd advantage					
Climate	31.3	24.4	22.6	20.9	23.6
Pace of life	17.7	16.7	29.0	34.5	25.7
Lower living costs	2.1	14.1	16.8	15.0	13.9
Social advantages	20.8	26.1	21.3	17.0	21.5
Admiration of country	22.9	9.0	4.2	7.3	8.4
Practical advantages	0.0	7.7	5.5	2.9	4.8
Other advantages	5.2	2.0	0.6	2.4	2.1
n =	96	234	310	206	846
3rd advantage					
Climate	32.1	19.0	11.4	16.7	17.3
Pace of life	8.6	15.2	27.0	25.9	21.3
Lower living costs	3.7	20.7	14.8	19.5	16.3
Social advantages	22.2	26.1	26.6	23.0	25.0
Admiration of country	19.8	4.3	5.9	5.2	7.0
Practical advantages	3.7	12.0	11.4	8.0	9.6
Other advantages	9.9	2.7	2.9	1.7	3.5
n =	81	184	237	174	676

Source. Authors' survey.

stay yielded few significant results. There is however some evidence that respondents with higher educational standards and professional backgrounds have a greater tendency to stress advantages and surpassed expectations in the social, cultural and environmental spheres, whilst the lower-status groups mention financial problems more frequently.

Advantages and surpassed expectations

The prevalence of various advantages correlates almost exactly (as one might expect) with the rank ordering of reasons given for the original migration decision (see Tables 5.1 and 5.2 and pp. 93-6). Not only is the aggregate listing of ranked factors/advantages identical, but also both the inter-regional contrasts and the differences between first and subsequent reasons/advantages show great similarity (Table 5.8). Climate emerges as by far the most important of the first-ranked advantages; precisely because of this, its weighting diminishes as a second- and third-ranked advantage. It was most important in Spain and Portugal, where it scores around 70 per cent as a first-ranked factor. As we repeatedly heard during the in-depth interviews, the advantages of the climate are less the warm temperatures and hot sun (few respondents spent a great deal of time sunbathing) than the opportunities the climate facilitated for a more varied, relaxed (but often more active), and healthy lifestyle. In Malta, Godfrey was adamant that:

> climate plays a part. The dampness in England is terrible and that makes you old. Most of my friends in England are not healthy – they seem lifeless, they walk around like real old men! I feel much fitter than them and remain active. I swim a lot here, even though there are very few beaches.

One of the most remarkable accounts came from Cyril in Torremolinos. A widower, he had had two heart attacks twenty years ago, but since moving to Spain he had taken up dancing, jogging, weight-lifting and completed three marathons! His physical jerks were combined with a relaxed attitude to life:

> If I am not working in the flat, I can sit outside in the sun, go for a jog or a swim, or wander down to the front and sit with a coffee... You live longer in Spain. Life is easier all round ... no stress and strain. You don't fret if people are late or arrangements are changed – that's how it is here. The longer you are here, the more you take life in a relaxed manner. I don't even wear a watch any more.

'Pace of life' was consistently the second most important first-ranked advantage. 'Lower living costs' scores high for Malta as a first-ranked factor, and its importance is also maintained among second and third advantages. The most destination-specific advantage – subsumed under the heading 'admiration of country' – scores highest for Tuscany, consistent with our earlier discussion of how the 'Italian way of life' was an exceptionally strong attraction factor in the region.

It is important to appreciate, however, that by their answers and behaviours many respondents perceived the advantages as interrelated rather than discrete. Hence the climate favours an outdoor life which in turn leads to greater health advantages, a more relaxed and sociable lifestyle, and lower living costs through reduced heating bills. Some of these interconnections were elucidated well by the respondents.

Among the positive expectations which were actually exceeded, climate and lifestyle do not feature prominently, largely because these were essentially 'known' factors inherent in the original migration decision. Instead the most common answer is the pleasure felt by the respondents at the friendly and welcoming nature of the local people, indigenous and expatriate. In Tuscany there was a notable expression of satisfaction at the environmental attractiveness of the region – again consistent with the qualities of the Tuscan landscape and architectural scene noted earlier.

Many interviewees linked the relaxed way of life in southern Europe with issues of safety and security, making comparisons with what they saw as an increasingly crime-ridden society in the UK. Family values, young people's behaviour and respect for the elderly were frequent themes. Here are two examples from Malta where the safety argument was often stressed:

> The Maltese get on fine with the British, and it gets better as you get older. In England you are ostracised if you are old, you are reduced to the TV and the garden. Here there is respect for the elderly... I am impressed by the young generation here. By and large they are very respectful and life revolves around the family, unlike in the UK (Michael, St Julians).

> When we go back to England, we don't go out in the evenings. You even have to be careful with your purse when you go shopping in the day time! It's not like that here... Also, we don't get scroungers in Malta. In Bristol, on every street corner, there are young people with begging bowls. You don't feel harassed like that out here (Stan and Edith, Qawra).

On the other hand the discourse of 'safety' is also tempered by fear of growing insecurity locally. Crime levels are perceived to be rising and were often linked to 'outsiders' and to problems of drugs, especially on the Costa del Sol.

> The thefts are minor and can happen at any time of day – often when people are having a siesta. As regards violence against a person, there is little of that. It is fairly safe here, I feel ... ladies can walk around safely at night. I must also say that as far as burglaries are concerned, the miscreants are just as likely to be non-Spanish! Perhaps non-local people, if they are Spanish (Gary, Mijas Pueblo).

We noted earlier that the chief 'surpassed expectation' of living abroad in retirement was the friendliness of the local people. As Buller and Hoggart (1994: 105) found in France, the 'bonus' of discovering how friendly the locals are may be a reaction from an initial fear that the locals might *not* be welcoming, and so expresses a sense of relief. It may also be the case that the friendliness of the local people is mainly communicated in a superficial way through simple greetings, or dealings with shopkeepers: friendliness might be guaged by whether the locals speak English! Another possibility is that the 'welcome' is not specifically directed towards the 'colonising' British but is simply a reflection of the sociability of Mediterranean or rural people, whose own views of the retired settlers may be quite ambivalent. The notion of the 'friendly local' is part of the imagination of a 'rural idyll' or arcadia that some retired British possess: evidence to confirm these notions may be unconsciously privileged over contrary indications.

Dick, from Mijas Costa, gave a typical reaction which was repeated consistently across the four destinations:

> I must say the Spanish around here have been marvellous to us... We haven't come up against any resentment, personally. A lot depends on your attitude to them, of course.

Stan and Edith were very impressed by their Maltese neighbours' generosity:

> The Maltese like to have British friends and introduce them to their families... We visited our neighbour's relatives and happened to tell them, in passing, that our daughter was expecting a baby. The next time we went back and saw them, they had crocheted a matinée coat for the baby! It reminds me of the time when people used to be happy to do things for one another.

The final set of advantages we wish briefly to elaborate on are cultural attractions. The cultural and environmental attractions of Tuscany have already emerged strongly but similar factors were quite frequently recognised in other destinations (Table 5.8). Duncan and Iris had written 'cultural attractions' in the section of the questionnaire on surpassed expectations. In the follow-up interview they enlarged on this:

> Since we have been here, we have found more cultural activities than anywhere. Beginning in May, we have the Algarve Music Festival which is sponsored by the Gulbenkian Foundation. We have top musicians coming here and a wonderful Cultural Centre in Lagos. Tickets are 500 escudos [about £2] and there is something musical on every night for six solid weeks. We belong to an archaeology association also. They have two meetings a month and we get speakers from England – brilliant speakers. Usually there are slide shows and we have field trips.

Erica lives in a flat in a converted hotel in Malta and contrasted Malta's cultural attractions with those of Lanzarote where she previously had a time-share:

> Lanzarote is just a volcanic place. Malta is steeped in history; it is very cultural. I have Maltese friends here and we go the Russian ballets and operas which come every year... I do love the history here and I regard this place as a home from home.

The use of the term 'home from home' is interesting since it reveals a certain ambiguity as regards the question: where exactly *is* home? We shall analyse this rather fundamental question of retired migrants' place identity more fully in the next chapter.

Table 5.9 Main disadvantages of living in retirement abroad (%)

	Tuscany	Malta	Costa del Sol	Algarve	Total
Language	7.9	2.9	34.3	15.1	17.9
Bureaucracy, red tape	31.5	2.9	12.1	30.2	16.5
Separated from family	16.9	9.6	17.9	9.0	13.3
Poor medical/hospital services	11.2	5.3	3.2	16.6	8.1
Exchange rate/banking difficulties	1.1	20.1	6.4	0.5	8.0
Lack of mental stimulation	3.4	3.3	7.9	5.5	5.5
High cost of air travel	0.0	13.4	1.1	2.5	4.6
Rising cost of living	6.7	5.7	3.6	2.5	4.2
Other disadvantages	21.3	36.8	13.5	18.1	21.9
n =	89	209	280	199	777

Source: Authors' survey.

Note: Other disadvantages include poor roads, dangerous driving (especially Malta, Portugal); summer heat (especially Malta, Spain); winter cold (Tuscany); poor quality utilities/public services (all destinations).

Disadvantages and disappointments

Table 5.9 displays the most commonly-expressed disappointments of living a life of retirement in the southern European destinations. Overall, language was felt to be the biggest problem, and a disappointment in that relatively few respondents had progressed in learning the local language. In Malta language was understandably less of a barrier, whereas in Tuscany many respondents had some knowledge of Italian before they reached retirement age. Since language is a key factor in the process of integration, we postpone further discussion to the next chapter.

Bureaucracy was the next most frequently expressed major disadvantage: most important in Italy and Portugal, least important in Malta where the public sector, modelled on the British case, was generally seen to function well and in a familiar way. For many respondents, this disadvantage was a real frustration, even exasperation, and there is no doubt that it reached such a high complaint level partly because of the inevitable bureaucratic procedures encountered during the process of settlement: buying a property, getting a telephone installed, registering a car, importing furniture, sorting out tax liabilities, and so on. Virtually every interviewee had their own story to tell about the 'red tape' they had encountered. The following examples illustrate the variety of bureaucratic problems and the way in which the more percipient observers linked bureaucracy to the wider social and political context. Three quotes from Italy cover issues as diverse as buying a house, claiming back tax, and treating a pet dog:

I detest the bureaucracy ... the sheer amount of paperwork when you buy a house for example... Anything to do with the state is terrible. The people who work for the state are arrogant (Ken, Montepulciano).

Tax-wise you never feel secure... I earnt some money teaching English in Florence. They paid me, less tax. But the money wasn't high enough to pay tax on. But to claim any tax owed to you, the average time takes five years ... this is legalised state robbery! (Richard, Montepulciano).

The bureaucracy is terrible here ... it means you can't move without bits of paper. For example, I took my dog to the vet to be treated. He gave me some papers and told me to carry those papers with me every time I took the dog for a walk! There are rules for everything here ... bureaucracy is endemic, and the locals complain too, of course – it's part of their society and political system. But the locals know how to take short cuts through bureaucracy. You therefore need Italian friends when you live here (Colin, Umbria).

Views on bureaucracy were equally vehement in Portugal, as suggested by Table 5.9, but Leonard had found a solution:

Portugal is a third world country ... the bureaucracy is terrible. You wait ages to queue in a bank... They tell you to pay car tax, then they change it and don't tell you. They stop you on the road and you get fined... Now we have our 'Mr. Fixit'. He deals with the villa management, has been here eight years and speaks the language. He is helping us out with our car MOT. He charges, which is fair enough.

The third most important disappointment listed on Table 5.9 is separation from family. We have no clear understanding of why this was twice as important for respondents in Tuscany and Spain as for those in Malta and the Algarve but offer two suggestions. In Malta, many British retirees live with or proximate to their families, for reasons that have been explained. In the Algarve, a high proportion of the respondents were high-status retired expatriates, for whom separation from family has been a more or less constant condition throughout their lives.

Amongst the other prevalent complaints, lack of mental stimulation relates to questions of social life and integration, dealt with in Chapter 6, whilst medical issues are dealt with in Chapter 7. The high cost of air travel is a specifically Maltese problem, as are exchange rate problems, for the Maltese pound has doubled its value from its former parity with Sterling, eroding the very low cost of living of the 1960s and 1970s. Rising cost of living is also mentioned by a significant minority of respondents in the other three destinations as a major problem. Persons on modest and fixed incomes are particularly vulnerable, and some have had to 'trade down' in the housing market or contemplate a return to Britain.

Conclusion

This has been a long chapter, so the conclusion will be brief, building links to the next chapter. We started the chapter by posing the simple but broad question: why do people migrate abroad for retirement? We have found that many different routes and mechanisms bring older British people to live in southern Europe in their retirement, including marriage to a local person, prior work experience in the country, purchase of a holiday home before retirement, and expatriate life-paths across the world. These biographical pathways produce a correspondingly diverse range of residential motivations and strategies. Some people divide time between two (occasionally more) residential sites, implying different relationships with the host environment (the subject of the next chapter). Those who migrate 'for sun and money' (Fournier *et al.* 1998) have a different set of relationships to the locale than those for whom the cultural and visual attractions of the destination are paramount. We have shown that, to some extent, the sun-soaked resorts of the Costa del Sol and the Algarve attract a different type of retiree than the rural charm of Tuscany or Gozo, and we have certainly found evidence of retirees who 'hear the siren's song' and who have 'few moorings' to Britain (Longino 1992). People who have not lived in Britain very much, who have had mobile international careers and who have biographical backgrounds in the former British colonies were well represented in the survey population. For others, repeated holiday-making was the common channel which formed the aspiration for the eventual retirement move.

Notes

1. Return to origin and to kin do have powerful meaning for IRM where the migrants are returning labour migrants – for instance Portuguese returning from France (Cavaco 1993) or long-term Italian migrants returning from the United States (Cerase 1974); and we recognise that movements to join kin who have previously emigrated comprise another class of international moves by older people.
2. It should be stressed that the separation of these individual factors may simplify or confuse their real meaning or interpretation. Terms like 'climate' or 'environment' have variable significances; to some people they have as much a social as a physical or natural significance. As an illustration, Myklebost (1989: 210) points out from his interviews with Norwegian retirees in Benidorm that, in many cases, the factor of climate operates indirectly – less through the warm and sunny climate *per se* than through the effect on people's health.
3. It is interesting to compare these country choices with Buller and Hoggart's questionnaire data from their survey of 406 British housebuyers in rural France: 9.8 per cent considered Spain as an alternative country, 5.3 per cent considered Italy and 5.0 per cent Portugal

(Buller and Hoggart 1994: 72). Whilst these data indicate similar preferences, there is a major difference. Only 20 per cent of those relocating to France considered another continental European country, compared to 37 per cent in our South European survey, suggesting that France offers something that it is particular to that country.

4. The Tuscan responses were remarkably similar to those given by British home-owners in France where 'rural area', 'scenery', and 'character property' were the three most frequently-cited reasons (Buller and Hoggart 1994: 81).

5. Buller and Hoggart (1994: 65) report that, of the quarter of their respondents who had already lived in France prior to buying their present French property, the vast majority had lived in other parts of France than the department in which their current French home was located. Among our study countries, similar displacements are most likely in Italy, from Rome and the commercial cities of the North.

6. The proportions would be biased if the survey differentially under-represented those most likely to be away. The fieldwork was timed to avoid the periods (high summer, Christmas) when non-permanently resident respondents are most likely to be away.

7. This complex picture for Tuscany relates to the different types of residential mobility within the region, notably as between Florence, the Chianti district and the more outlying areas of southern Tuscany and Umbria. See King and Patterson (1998: 168-9, especially Table 6).

Six

Living Abroad: Language, Social Activities and Integration

Introduction

This chapter explores some of the comparative differences between and within places in terms of how people live in retirement abroad. It examines issues of integration, language as a social barrier, and the creation and maintenance of networks of friends and family. It also touches on the practicalities of running a home in a foreign land, and identifies some of the cultural barriers encountered in the everyday life of older persons resident abroad. We will also re-visit some important points noted earlier: that, for some people, retirement is not a 'clean break'; that many people continue to work, either for income or in a voluntary capacity; and that the distinctions between 'retirement', 'work' and 'leisure' are often very blurred.

One pervasive theme is the comparative geographical dimension. Knowledge of language, the nature (and lack) of integration, and the characteristics of intra-group social life will all be shown to vary by destination and, indeed, within them. Different integration dynamics will be shown to exist between the distinct streams: the seekers of the rural idyll, and those drawn by the warm climate and relaxed lifestyles of coastal holiday settlements.

This chapter has four main sections. First we examine language, a key requirement for integration since it mediates communication between the expatriate population and the host society. Lack of competence in the local language constitutes a major barrier to cross-cultural communication and contact with the local population, although Malta is a partial exception. In the second part of the chapter we look at the nature and process of integration, recognising the multifaced nature of this notion. We examine some of the inhibiting factors of the host environment, and

those which derive from the social, cultural and psychological characteristics of the British residents. Two themes are most thoroughly explored:
adaptation to the host societies of Tuscany, Malta, the Algarve and the
Costa del Sol, and social integration within the expatriate societies, characterised perhaps by their enduring 'Britishness'. The third section of the
chapter turns to the retirees' social activities within their national and residential communities, with special attention to the memberships of clubs
and other aspects of associative life. This analysis of intra-group social
activity enables us to provide some answers to questions about the extent
to which British retirees abroad take with them their home culture and
values, and perhaps use these to construct communities with a predominantly introverted and even enclave mentality. The final section of the
chapter will focus on the frequency and nature of the links to 'home', and
concludes by addressing the question, 'where is home?'

Tongue-Tied: Language as a Barrier to Communication

> I have a lot of respect for Phil, an electrician who spoke not a word of French.
> On his first visit to France – his first holiday abroad ever – Phil marched into an
> estate agent (*sic*) and bought an old barn in the Dordogne. That takes a lot of
> courage.[1]

This quote indicates that language is not an insuperable barrier to settling
abroad, although we can only speculate about how Phil's conversion of the
barn proceeded, how he dealt with local suppliers, and how he managed
to communicate with his new neighbours. And as an electrician speaking
no French, he clearly contrasts with the social background of most British
residents, retirees and second-home owners living in rural France.
Language competence varies widely, and this section of the chapter will
explore this variation, relate it to the wider issues of adaptation and integration, and analyse its correlations with social class, education, length of
time in the destination country and other relevant features. The underlying hypothesis is that language ability is the most significant indicator of
the ability to integrate with the local indigenous community and to come
to terms with the local culture.

There were two self-completion survey questions on language experience. One asked the respondents to assess their own knowledge of the
local language as 'very fluent', 'quite fluent', 'some knowledge', 'a few
words' or 'none', and was followed by subsidiary questions on ability to
read newspapers, restaurant menus and official forms in the local language. The other asked whether the local language was 'a great problem',
'an irritant', 'no problem' or 'a challenge full of interest'. Although the
elicited answers are self-assessments and generally appeared to over-state
competence, the questions were impressively discriminating and produced consistent patterns of variation.

The answers to the questions are set out in Tables 6.1 and 6.2, which
show the linguistic variable cross-tabulated with six hypothesised inde-

Table 6.1 Respondents' self-evaluation of their knowledge of the local language (%)

	Very fluent	Quite fluent	Some knowledge	A few words	None	n
By destination						
Tuscany	29.0	45.8	22.4	2.8	0.0	107
Malta	2.5	4.0	29.1	49.6	14.7	278
Costa del Sol	4.4	21.5	63.4	10.8	0.0	344
Algarve	2.3	24.5	54.1	17.7	1.4	220
Total	6.1	19.8	46.6	22.9	4.6	949
By year of arrival						
pre-1980	14.2	27.4	31.0	19.9	7.5	226
1980-4	6.7	19.5	53.0	17.4	3.4	149
1985-9	2.4	18.6	57.9	18.6	2.4	290
1990-6	3.3	14.1	44.9	32.6	5.1	276
Total	6.2	19.5	46.9	22.8	4.6	941
By age left education						
<17	2.3	14.2	49.4	29.0	5.1	435
17-18	4.4	21.2	47.6	23.2	3.6	250
19+	16.1	29.0	37.0	13.3	3.8	211
Total	6.1	19.9	46.0	23.7	4.3	896
By social class						
1 and 2	6.5	21.4	47.8	20.1	4.2	542
3, 4 and 5	5.6	15.6	47.2	27.2	4.4	250
Total	6.2	19.6	47.6	22.3	4.3	792
By gender						
Men	4.7	19.0	46.0	25.3	5.0	526
Women	7.8	20.8	47.3	19.8	4.3	423
Total	6.1	19.8	46.6	22.9	4.6	949
By civil status						
Married	5.4	19.2	48.2	23.6	3.6	645
Single/widowed/div.	7.6	21.1	43.2	21.1	6.9	303
Total	6.1	19.8	46.6	22.8	4.6	948

Source: Authors' survey.

Table 6.2 Respondents' reaction to the problem of dealing with the local language (%)

	Great problem	An irritant	No problem	An interesting challenge	n
By destination					
Tuscany	8.6	5.7	55.2	31.3	105
Malta	13.6	8.7	56.1	21.6	264
Costa del Sol	15.0	10.6	27.3	47.2	341
Algarve	27.4	15.1	25.1	32.4	219
Total	16.8	10.5	38.1	34.6	929
By year of arrival					
pre-1980	11.7	9.4	58.2	20.7	213
1980-4	15.4	13.4	37.6	33.6	149
1985-9	19.7	11.2	31.6	37.5	285
1990-6	18.9	9.5	29.1	42.5	275
Total	16.9	10.6	38.0	34.5	922
By age left education					
<17	19.6	10.0	35.8	34.6	428
17-18	15.6	12.8	39.1	32.5	243
19+	10.7	10.7	43.2	35.4	206
Total	16.4	10.9	38.4	34.2	877
By social class					
1 and 2	16.1	11.6	35.3	37.0	527
3, 4 and 5	20.1	9.2	39.0	31.7	249
Total	17.4	10.8	36.5	35.3	776
By gender					
Men	16.9	11.9	39.6	32.6	515
Women	16.7	8.9	37.4	37.0	414
Total	16.8	10.5	38.1	34.6	929
By civil status					
Married	15.9	11.8	37.1	35.2	634
Single/widowed/div.	18.7	7.8	40.1	33.3	294
Total	16.8	10.6	38.0	34.6	928

Source: Authors' survey.

pendent variables, namely destination region, year of arrival, social class, age left full-time education, sex and civil status. Some of these relationships show distinct patterns, others are less clear.

Starting with Table 6.1 we observe that, for the sample as a whole, just under half the respondents claimed 'some knowledge' of the local language, just over one quarter claimed to be very or quite fluent, and just over one quarter admitted to either no knowledge or just a few words. The clearest variation is by destination: three-quarters in Tuscany claimed fluency in the Italian language, whereas only about one quarter in the Costa del Sol and the Algarve were fluent in Spanish and Portuguese respectively, and only 6.5 per cent in Malta were fluent in Maltese. Putting the exceptional Maltese case to one side, the main contrast is between the British residents in Tuscany, most of whom have a good knowledge of the language, and the respondents in Spain and Portugal, most of whom had at best only 'some knowledge' of the language. There was less knowledge of Portuguese than of Spanish, possibly due to the greater difficulty of learning and understanding Portuguese, to the comparative recency of British settlement in the Algarve, or to a combination of these factors. The multi-generational residential history of the British in Tuscany and the high average duration of residence among our respondents will both have given more time for language skills to develop, but there are probably other influences: the positive images of Italian life and culture; the dispersed distribution which counteracts an 'enclave mentality'; the high level of education, making learning a foreign language a less daunting task; and the cosmopolitan backgrounds which mean that many are multilingual and used to adapting to new cultural and linguistic situations.

Table 6.1 also confirms that the duration of residence in the destination country correlates with linguistic ability. Thus 42 per cent of pre-1980 arrivals were fluent, compared to 26 per cent of 1980-4 arrivals, 21 per cent of the 1985-9 cohort, and only 17 per cent of the post-1990 group. Education is also an influence, for 45 per cent of those who finished full-time education at 19+ years had a fluent knowledge of the language, compared to 26 per cent of those leaving school at 17-18 and only 16.5 per cent of those who left at younger ages. The remaining three independent variables show less evidence of association with language competence although there is some indication that greater fluency is associated with high-status (partly reflecting educational differences), with women (consistent with the commonly-held view that they are better communicators and linguists than men), and with people who live alone (none of whom can rely on a spouse or partner to handle essential day-to-day exchanges).

Table 6.2 sets out respondents' assessments of the problems of using the local language. The responses are broadly consistent, with one or two exceptions, with those just discussed. Among the four regions, only 14 per cent in Tuscany found the local language a great problem or an irritant, compared to 22 per cent for Malta, 26 per cent for the Costa del Sol, and 43.5 per cent for the Algarve, showing some differences with the pattern of language knowledge. For instance, 56 per cent of the Maltese subsample maintained that the Maltese language was 'no problem' for them, yet only 6.5 per cent had any fluency in Maltese and two-thirds had only a few words or no knowledge of the language. Clearly the unproblematic nature of the Maltese language is related to the fact that nearly all Maltese speak English. As one informant said, 'I feel it is a waste of time to learn a language which only 300,000 people speak, and anyway most of them speak English.'

A similar interpretation can be applied to the Costa del Sol data. Here only a quarter of respondents declared that the local language was a great problem, and yet relatively few British retirees in Spain have a good knowledge of Spanish (as confirmed by other studies: O'Reilly 1995b: 35-6; Rodríguez *et al.* 1998: 194). A plausible explanation is that many local Spanish people who are heavily involved in the tourist industry speak English, which has become the *lingua franca* of the Costa del Sol. Another is that the density of British expatriate settlement on the Costa del Sol is such that most socialising occurs within the national group. In the Algarve, on the other hand, where British respondents' knowledge of Portuguese was only slightly worse than the case of Spain (Table 6.1), language was seen as more of a problem. Not only is Portuguese less commonly taught in Britain and inherently more difficult to learn than Spanish or Italian, but also fewer local Portuguese speak English, and there is little British enclavism in the Algarve, leading to a lesser degree of 'linguistic colonialism'.

The comparative frequency of reading local language newspapers reveals an even sharper division by destination. Tuscany is again the region where the respondents were most proficient, with 54 per cent regularly reading the press, while elsewhere most respondents did not read a newspaper in the local language; frequent readers were 17 per cent in the Costa del Sol, 9 per cent in the Algarve and 4 per cent in Malta (where some newspapers are in English).

Further insights into the role of language in retired migrants' lives come from participant observation and the in-depth interviews, and we consider this evidence regionally, leaving aside Malta.

Tuscany

Some elements of Tuscany's geographical diversity, as described in earlier chapters, are reflected in the historical patterning of British settlement (see also King and Patterson 1998). Knowledge of Italian and frequency of reading Italian newspapers are greatest in Florence where there is a long-standing community, many of whom lived and worked there before retirement; and least developed in Umbria, a region only relatively recently settled, and to where many retirees migrated directly from Britain (Table 6.3). Indeed there is a remarkably close correlation between the average duration of residence in each subregion and the respondents'

Table 6.3 Tuscany: knowledge of language and newspaper reading by subregion

Subregion	Knowledge of Italian language			Read Italian newspapers		Mean year of arrival in Tuscany or Umbria
	Very fluent	Quite fluent	Some; a few words	At least weekly	Occasionally; not at all	
Florence (n=17)	9	7	1	13	4	1974
Chianti (n=19)	4	12	3	11	8	1977
Lucca (n=22)	6	12	4	13	9	1978
Other Tuscany (n=26)	8	10	8	14	12	1981
Umbria (n=23)	4	8	11	7	16	1987
Total (n=107)	31	49	27	58	49	1980

Source: Authors' survey.

familiarity with Italian (although the subsample numbers are small).

Most retired British people in Florence had previously been involved in teaching, the arts or business in the city or elsewhere in Italy. While some retain an old-fashioned Britishness,[2] many have learnt good Italian through long years of residence. Indeed for many elderly British men and women in Florence, the language, art and culture are the main reason for being there. Several have local spouses and partners, which naturally enhances linguistic fluency. The reader is referred to the biography of Victoria, who had learnt French, Spanish and Italian in a global migration trajectory through India, Sussex, Egypt, South America and northern Italy before settling with her Florentine husband in his native city (Box 4.1).

A very different life was led by Albert, who now lives with his daughter and her Italian husband in a modest housing development on the out-skirts of Lucca. He moved to Lucca after his wife died, to live with his only daughter. Albert left school at 16 years of age and worked all his life in the police; he had no experience of foreign travel prior to coming to Lucca. Albert was engagingly honest about his lack of Italian, even after six years in Lucca:

> I don't manage with the language very well! I was never any good at languages at school. I did attend evening classes before I came out here but I didn't have the ability to learn... Now, I have a few words; I can just about make myself understood but can't understand the answers!

Albert exemplifies a retirement stream that is relatively small in our four study regions but, unlike the majority 'environmental preference' streams, will also be found throughout Western Europe and has been long established to Australia and North America: the migration to join married children abroad, often following bereavement. Despite the kin orientation, the problems of social and linguistic isolation among the participants in this migration may be much greater, even within the household. Albert's son-in-law spoke little English, and his main social contacts were with his daughter, now an invalid, and his bilingual granddaughter who lived nearby. Otherwise he spent his time walking in the countryside and visiting nearby historic towns, travelling by train, and the evenings were spent playing cards.

The language skills of most of our retirees in Tuscany were somewhere between the extremes of Victoria and Albert. Here is the example of Brian, a well-travelled retiree living in south-east Tuscany:

> We had both gone to evening classes in Australia so we had a basic grammar [but not] much conversation. I think that was a good thing because having had that grammar as a basis, all the other things fell into place – I knew how the words fitted in. I think we got on alright when we came, but we couldn't sit down and have an argument about politics and things like that. Now we can – we don't have any real problems now. We just need to build up our vocabulary. Also you run into this dialect problem... I still have a lot of problems with the *contadini* when they start talking.

Finally, let us enjoy the wit of Freddie, a semi-retired artist living in a secluded valley in northern Tuscany. Freddie had mentioned on his questionnaire that language was a major disadvantage for him, although during the follow-up interview it was observed that he coped more than adequately in Italian when workmen came in to fix his central heating. Nevertheless he insisted,

> My Italian is not good, but fortunately the Italian language is atrophying. If you read the newspaper, every second word is in English. Even in our own local paper, and all the advertisements. I say to people 'do you understand it?' But they think it's chic. It's all decoration, but gradually there are so many words being replaced by English all the time; there is no 'Académie Française Italiano' to look after the language. So Italian is dying – and I'm thrilled!

Costa del Sol

Recent ethnographic field research amongst the British population in and around Fuengirola found that 'many British migrants ... are not learning the Spanish language to a level that enables them to interact on any more than a superficial level' (O'Reilly 1995a: 35). Some who have lived in the area for thirty years speak fewer than twenty words of Spanish (O'Reilly 2000). Our research broadly confirms this disappointing picture, although we did find that many people had attained reasonable competence in Spanish, and many were still trying to learn. Like Brian in Tuscany, some residents appreciated having had a head start through work experience or by taking classes prior to their moves. It was also noticeable that those who spoke most Spanish, and who were continuing to improve it, lived in inland areas or in the city of Málaga which, despite being the capital of the region, has relatively few foreign residents. Aubrey is one of them, and he had made sensible preparations.

> When we decided to come to Spain, I bought *Teach Yourself Spanish* – they're excellent little books and you can learn a lot from them, and I also [had been] to an evening class in Leicester ... I tried to learn a bit before coming. I knew basically something on arrival ... very few people in Málaga spoke English.

The indefatigable Cyril, whose dancing, weight-lifting and marathon-running exploits were noted in Chapter 5, was no slouch when it came to learning Spanish. He was beginning to expand his social contacts with local people and also learning to avoid sensitive topics:

> I study Spanish at a class held at the university (in Málaga)... I have being going there for a year and a half. It started with 53 and now it's down to 28. Only seven Brits remain in the class. I'll carry on for another year or so. To speak fluent Spanish I need to go on a bit longer... All I want to do is to converse fluently with Spanish friends and neighbours ... if they know you're interested in their language ... most of them are only too ready to help out. I never speak about bull-fighting though, or any contentious issues... I now get invited to their parties. I don't speak fluently yet but I do get by... After [the class], I speak to a Spanish student who is learning English and we practice in a café or bar together.

Like many people who had taken lessons and learnt Castilian Spanish, Cyril had problems with the Andalusian accent: 'they chop the end off words'. Others agreed: 'the Spanish they speak here is doggerel... They swallow their words and speak so fast... I understand the people from Madrid much better.' There is another twist to the language situation: in areas 'saturated' with tourists and British residents, English is widely understood and the local Spanish people are accustomed to and tolerant towards British people trying to speak Spanish. In the words of Moira,

> Here in Fuengirola, the second language is English – they are used to hearing English spoken. When you speak Spanish with an English accent, they can understand you here. When you go to Málaga, it is all Spanish, and they don't understand when you speak Spanish to them.

On the whole, there is little incentive to learn Spanish in the main areas of British residential concentration, such as Fuengirola, Benalmadena and Torremolinos. Ninety-two-year-old Winston had been living in Spain for twenty-seven years, but 'I can't speak Spanish after all these years! The trouble is I was always with British people and we spoke English all the time.' This linguistic laziness has been reinforced by several local initiatives to serve tourists and foreign nationals. Interpreters are to be found in town halls, hospitals and medical centres (but rarely in police stations!). Some voluntary organisations offer interpreters/translators to cover emergency situations, whilst private intermediaries operate for profit.

The Algarve

The Algarve evinces a further variant on the linguistic relationship between the retired British population and the host society. Those who settle in Tuscany have the advantage of being in the region from which modern Italian originates, but for British people living in the Costa del Sol or the Algarve the situation is different: the language which some began to learn at a distance is very different from the earthy local dialects of Andalusian Spanish and Algarvean Portuguese. Moreover, Portuguese is widely regarded as a more difficult language (especially aurally) than Spanish or Italian, and, as noted, fewer Algarveans speak English than Andalusians in the Costa del Sol. Many of the British residents in the Algarve are frustrated by the difficulties of learning a tough language late in life, and lament having arrived at one of the 'plateaux' – well-known to language teachers – which define the limits of their competence no matter how hard they strive for improvement:

> I would get much more out of living here if I could learn the language. I find it very difficult. We have had lessons but we are too long in the tooth for classes now. You have to be dedicated ... it requires time and effort. We get by ... my wife understands more than I do (Henry, Portimão).

Henry noted that his wife was more fluent, and this gender comparison cropped up, unsolicited, in many interviews, confirming the survey finding indicated in Tables 6.1 and 6.2. According to an interviewee who had set up a self-help group for learning Portuguese, 'it is mostly the women who want to learn. The men just leave it to their wives. There is only one man in our group, all the rest are women.'

The Myth of Integration

Migration at a late age might be expected to mitigate against rapid integration, if only because of the absence of the 'integration channels' of work and schooling. Well-rooted integration is only likely to have occurred where the retiree had lived for some time in the country of retirement, especially before retirement age. Several such cases were encountered, especially in Tuscany and Malta. Integration usually involves a reciprocal exchange between the 'host' and the 'outsider' population, but for most people we interviewed it meant 'getting on well' with an indeterminate 'other', a much more restricted and partial conceptualisation than is commonly applied in the context of European labour migration (Favell 1998). The elderly British in southern Europe are not 'immigrants' in the commonly visualised sense, which implies powerlessness, marginality, minority status and a different cultural and racial background (Cashmore 1994: 188). Nor is their integration conditional on as many dimensions as apply to such immigrants: employment, schooling, civic rights, and over-coming of barriers of racial discrimination (Castles and Miller 1998: 212-52). Nor either are the 'philosophies of integration' promulgated by host countries – national essentialism, assimilation, multiculturalism and pluralism – yet strongly asserted in southern European countries which to date have less experience of mass labour immigration.[3]

It might be asked whether integration is a relevant concept at all for British residents and seasonal migrants along the Mediterranean coasts of southern Europe. Their own objectives are, perhaps, less integration with local Spaniards or Portuguese than access to local services and forging friendships within the local 'British' community. To put this starkly: if retired British people live on estates with other English-speaking neigh-bours and residents, if the local supermarket provides all their needs without a word needing to be spoken, if there are 'English' pubs and restaurants in the vicinity, and if the locals with whom they come into con-tact speak some English, why bother to learn the local language, and why bother to integrate? And in any case, integrate to what? Especially in the Costa del Sol, the local society is to a large extent a product of recent urbanisation driven by the needs of holiday-makers and foreign residents, and far removed from the Andalusian society that might have formed without mass tourism. On the other hand, British elderly residents in the Costa del Sol often make positive reference to enjoying and having adopt-ed the 'Spanish way of life' (O'Reilly 1995b: 30-5), which indicates a per-ception of having adopted some local ways.

The desire or need to integrate, and the social construction of integra-tion, clearly varies amongst British retired people living in southern Europe. For many, integration is largely irrelevant and their choice of location is based on individual preferences about climate, scenery, the res-idential environment, and the 'accident' of finding a suitable property. But we also found many people, especially 'early-retired' migrants, who were making determined efforts to integrate with the host community and to explore the culture of the Mediterranean. Integration may be a very personal matter and locally defined. While the questionnaire did not try to uncover the complex psychological dimensions of integration, two straightforward dimensions were approached: language, considered in the previous section; and involvement in social activities organised by var-ious types of club and association – exclusively British, primarily for the local indigenous population, and with mixed memberships.[4] Note that the question as posed was broader than membership: it asked about partici-pation in social activities arranged by various types of club. Hence it included attendance at concerts, nature rambles, coach trips, coffee mornings, as well as formal memberships of associations such as the British Legion, tennis clubs and volunteer groups.

Table 6.4 shows the key results from this question, categorised by desti-

Table 6.4 Participation in social activities arranged by various types of clubs and associations (%)

	Tuscany	Malta	Costa del Sol	Algarve	Total
British Clubs					
Yes	7.5	40.1	58.6	28.6	38.9
No	92.5	59.9	41.4	71.4	61.1
n =	106	279	266	220	871
Local (indigenous) clubs					
Yes	30.8	29.4	12.7	10.0	19.9
No	69.2	70.6	87.3	90.0	80.1
n =	104	279	229	219	831
Mixed (local/expat) clubs					
Yes	23.1	64.2	66.2	58.6	58.8
No	76.9	35.8	33.8	41.4	41.2
n =	104	279	302	220	905

Source. Authors' survey.

nation region. This proved to be the main discriminator in the pattern of responses; cross-tabulations by other variables such as age, social class and education were non-significant. Participation in British clubs' activities is much more common in the Costa del Sol (especially) and in Malta than in Tuscany and the Algarve. This partly reflects the divergent social meanings that British residents hold about 'their' clubs in the various destinations. In Tuscany, for example, where the British residents are scattered and might be broadly categorised as 'individualists', there are only two main 'British' clubs: the British Institute in Florence, and the 'Conservatives Abroad' in southern Tuscany and Umbria. In Spain, on the other hand, there are several British Legion branches plus a multiplicity of sports, social and volunteer associations which reflect not only the size and density of the British population in the Costa del Sol but also their keenness to engage in associative life. In Malta, the British Legion is as proudly Maltese as it is Anglo-Saxon.

With regard to taking part in the activities of local indigenous organisations, the four destinations divide in a different way. In Tuscany and Malta, about 30 per cent of the respondents participate in their activities, whereas in the Costa del Sol and the Algarve only 10-12 per cent do so. Finally, for 'mixed' clubs, Tuscany stood out as having a lower engagement than the other destinations where the participation was around 60 per cent.

Attempts to explain the differential pattern of responses in Table 6.4 should be grounded in the specific histories of the relationship between the British and each of the four destinations, following Anthias's (1992) argument that migrant identity and behaviour can only be understood with reference to the historical, social and geographical contexts. These contexts for British settlement and (non-)integration will now be explored in more detail, drawing from individual testimonies and taking each destination (and its various settings and places) in turn.

Tuscany

Historical accounts of the British in Tuscany tend to infer an innate unwillingness to integrate: 'So, an English colony took root, which like most expatriate communities remained thoroughly British. Its members absorbed the sunlight and did the things they liked best, adopting Italy in their minds as their own country, but not really mixing much with the Tuscans' (Raison 1983: viii). The allegation is that the British, while often capable of speaking Italian, were rarely interested in knowing how their Italian neighbours lived or in meaningful integration with Florentine society. A former member of the British Consular staff spoke posthumously of Harold Acton:

> It astounds me that Harold, as the old-type Englishman, the essence of courtesy, derived from the upper classes, was born, lived and died in this city at the age of 90 and was descended from people who came here in 1721... Harold, and his father and the earlier generations, were like metal seam in a rock; they didn't become part of Italy at all.

The size and coherence of the British community in Florence were greatly attenuated by the Second World War, and today retains only vestiges of its former character. A few elderly British congregate around the Anglican Church and the British Institute, including some who travel from the surrounding countryside. Apart from those (mainly women) who have Italian spouses and partners, there is little deep integration within Florentine society. Margaret, a retired teacher who has been living in Florence as a single woman since 1975, is fairly typical of others with a good knowledge of Italian and a profound admiration for Italian art and culture, but who remain quintessentially 'British'.

> I am an old-fashioned patriot, I would always stand up for the National Anthem... I always listen to the World Service. I'm always reading the English newspapers.

Key informants in the churches, the British Institute and the Consulate confirm that there are very many like Margaret in Florence. Nearly always highly educated, they tend to live individual, often frugal lives tucked away in the interstices of the city. By no means all are wealthy; indeed many are quite poor.

Out in the Tuscan and Umbrian countryside, integration is rather different. Here we find mainly professional and entrepreneurial retirees, most with high levels of education and aesthetic sensibilities. The integration of this mobile, cosmopolitan, often wealthy British population is largely a matter of individual choice, although it also reflects prior contacts with Italy. Those who live in the small towns and villages tend to have more intensive, everyday social contacts with their Italian neighbours than those who live in isolated farmhouses deep in the countryside. Larry, who lived in a converted farmhouse in the open, rolling countryside in the province of Grosseto, said that although the local people are friendly, 'I can go for days without speaking to anyone.' On the other hand, those who engage in farming, if only as a hobby, more frequently interact with other farmers and rural workers, most commonly in connection with the cultivation of vines and olives. For this group, integration involves not just contacts with the local people but also a deeper embedding within the local economy. Vernon was one such 'gentleman farmer':

> We bought this place in 1968 and we started the new olive grove in 1972... The actual planting of the new trees was done by a neighbouring farmer and we paid him for the work. Then there were people who helped with the harvest... We make oil and that requires a lot of preparation: it is not a simple process... About four years ago they asked me if I would join the extra-virgin olive oil cooperative ... it has been a fascinating experience. I have had a good insight into how the Italians go about organising their activities ... and produced a paper which set out the options for marketing in North America.

In a remote farming area of Le Marche a retired Scottish couple had been effectively 'adopted' by local farmers and shown the rudiments of subsistence agriculture:

> One of them has taken me under his wing, from an agricultural point of view. He has vacated a large corner of one of his fields and has brought everything down to us in seed form – peas and beans and so on – and told me what to do with them. He's told us all about the processes the vegetables have to go through. We have been invited to their home for a meal and we've had him and his wife up here. He's a wonderful old fellow! Basically our social life is with the local Italians. We can't, of course, have a proper conversation with them but we manage somehow.

As this quote makes clear, there are limitations to the extent to which people from very different backgrounds are able to communicate and integrate, but ultimately overtures towards the host community are rarely rebuffed, and the hospitality of Italian country people tends to be of an undemanding kind.

Finally, people who claim they *are* integrated often reinforce their claim by pointing to others who are not, as recognised by Buller and Hoggart (1994: 109-10) amongst the British in rural France. Jake and Pat were good examples. They had lived in Bologna and Perugia before retiring to a typical Umbrian farmhouse:

We have lived in Italy for 17 years and have lots of Italian friends. We are not in the category of those who retire to the sun-belt. We are much more integrated into Italian society as compared to those who came out on retirement in the UK... There is a sense that they act a bit superior, they don't really try to speak Italian properly and have a tendency to run down Italians... They go back to the UK regularly to recharge their batteries. They float around, do not stay here long enough to become integrated, [and] have a kind of colonial mentality.

Although some of the British in Tuscany – and in the Algarve and the Costa del Sol – are described as having a colonial attitude, in only one of our study regions is British retirement migration built upon a true colonial history. We move on to examine the extent to which this historical context has influenced the forms of integration.

Malta

A distinctive consequence of the long and complex history of British settlement on Malta and of contact between the two communities is the existence of a significant number of Anglo-Maltese retiree households. Intermarriage has occurred both between British service personnel stationed in Malta and the local people (mostly British husbands and Maltese wives), and between Maltese labour migrants in Britain (mostly males) and British women. Both types of cross-national households may retire to Malta. Two other retiree types may be found: those who have settled after a working life spent mainly in Britain (but who had probably made prior visits to Malta during the war or as a tourist); and British citizens who had spent most of their working lives abroad, for example in the Middle East or East Africa, and for whom the islands are a climatically attractive and tax-friendly destination (Warnes and Patterson 1998: 128-9).

There is another, more profound, aspect of integration in this specific case: the extent to which Maltese society has itself been retextured as a quasi-British society by a century and a half of British suzerainty and economic domination. A common view is that the British armed forces were generally on good terms with the Maltese, but real social contact between the two communities was rather limited. Moreover, it would be naive not to recognise that the Maltese, whilst often appearing pro-British and happy to emulate certain aspects of the British way of life, not least the language, have experienced an ambiguous identity and harboured some feelings of resentment (Boissevain 1977a).

In Malta language ability plays a minor role in defining the opportunity to communicate with the host population. At the same time, it is not clear how far the ability of the host population to communicate with the settler in English can be said to facilitate integration. The Maltese speak Maltese amongst themselves, thereby excluding the British residents, few of whom speak the language. And whilst the existence of a common language facilitates communication and the potential to integrate, the motivations for integration (on both sides) are not necessarily very strong.

141

Much depends on individual circumstance and the local setting. As in Tuscany, the local geography influences the amount of contact that different parts of Malta have with one another, and hence the degree of interaction between British residents and the local islanders. The British cluster in several areas, the main concentrations being situated on prominent headlands affording spectacular sea views, such as Mellieha Heights, St George's Hill in St Julian's, Juno Heights at Marsaxlokk, and the highrise blocks along the Sliema Strand. Inland from Sliema, the 'three villages' of Balzan, Lija and Attard are also popular with affluent retired British settlers, and there is a sprinkling in other inland settlements such as Mosta and Naxxar. For the British in these inland villages, what matters is not the view but the sense of living in the midst of a Maltese community, behind thick walls admittedly. The thickest walls on the islands belong to the fortified bastions which surround the Grand Harbour district known as the Three Cities, where some elderly British live in Senglea, marketed as the 'Maltese Chelsea' by developers in the 1960s. Finally, there is a small and rather tight-knit group of retired British on Gozo.

These places offer a variety of residential settings for integration. At one extreme is the Santa Maria estate on Mellieha Heights, a spacious and luxury development originally designed to exclude Maltese by means of a red, white and blue barrier gate. Subsequently, numerous well-off Maltese have moved into this cliff-top development, but it retains the atmosphere of an 'expatriate' enclave. At the other extreme are the Three Cities, the heartland of urban working-class Malta. The British living here are perceived to have crossed some sort of cultural divide. This is not to imply that they are speaking fluent Maltese or are necessarily fully integrated with the local population, but they live in close proximity to Maltese people in densely-packed but rather run-down neighbourhoods, compensated in some cases by stunning views of the Grand Harbour and its maritime traffic.

Although Malta has been an independent state since 1964, the underlying empathy between the two populations continues, at least amongst the older generations. The Maltese tend to have a greater knowledge of the British in Malta than the latter do of the hybrid Maltese culture which is simultaneously strongly Catholic and Mediterranean, and part Arab, part Italian and part British. Older Maltese have a curiously paternal attitude towards the local resident British, consistent with their intimate knowledge of the erstwhile colonial customs and institutions. A surprisingly large number of interviewees mentioned that they had been 'adopted' by neighbouring Maltese families. Eric and Dulcie were one couple who used this metaphor, as well as stressing the greater neighbourliness of the southern part of the island, which has fewer British settlers:

Here you are adopted by Maltese families. We 'clicked' with our housekeeper immediately and now we are part of her family. We are invited to their parties, weddings etc. and we are both close to all of her family. You would never find this in England... Down here in the south, which is industrial and commercial, you are on more easy terms with the locals ... this is the working part of the island.

For those who have married a Maltese spouse, very close to full assimilation is sometimes achieved. Michael, whose 'static displacement' in St Julians was described earlier, had married a Maltese woman. He was one of the few British retirees we met who had learnt to speak Maltese. Recently he had been widowed; nevertheless he was emphatic that

> I love this country... I have so many good friends and family here... I was welcomed and trusted [by my wife's family] from the time we got married... I became part of the family and was very close to them... The families all care for each other in Malta... I mix with Maltese by choice ... it helps by speaking Maltese, of course.

Some, however, found the 'integration' into the family of their spouse a little too suffocating. Tim, living near his wife's family, regretted being so close to his in-laws:

> Within three weeks I realised we should have retired to the other side of the island. I didn't appreciate *not* having in-laws before! They expect you to go out with them all the time, every weekend we spend with them. I'm rebelling.

Still relatively young and active (he had taken early retirement from the Army at 50), Tim had started work as a painter and decorator in order to 'escape' – being married to a Maltese enabled him to work legally. Some of the interviewees who were or who saw themselves as highly integrated were keen to point to others who were not – one stereotype was of upper-class 'ex-colonial' types who could not relate to the predominantly working-class Maltese population. According to Wilf, 'there are too many British people ... who have a colonial attitude. They think they are the bosses and the Maltese are skivvies! They don't try to integrate very much.'

Avenues to integration appear to be conditioned by professional background, type of associative activity engaged in, and the district of Malta chosen for retirement. Amongst professional-class retirees, contact with the Maltese might be channelled through common career background or perhaps the Yacht Club. Sandie had settled in Malta with her husband in 1968, both having taken early retirement, she from nursing, he from dentistry. Their social contacts in Malta had been mainly with local doctors, partly because of the professional link, and partly because her husband had had a long illness. Hilary's Maltese friends had been mostly down at the marina:

> We have met several Maltese boating types, and through them we have met other Maltese people... We find them very hospitable and they usually invite you to their homes when they know you. We meet most of our Maltese friends quite regularly.

One interviewee, Eric, managed to encapsulate many of the experiences and views that we encountered in Malta, and this interview clip makes a fine conclusion:

> In some ways the Maltese are more British than the British... The Maltese know the British, but the British are ignorant of the Maltese. The Maltese are strongly Arab, I feel. They can be deplorable at times with standards of honesty. They believe we British are naive... Everyone knows that the Maltese are, in fact, extremely astute in matters of trade, and in catering to the tastes of the British the Maltese have always known how to relieve the British of their money.

Costa del Sol and the Algarve

These two regions are taken together since they have more similarities than differences with regard to social integration. With climate and the ability to enjoy a relaxed outdoor life being the primary motives for British retirement to both regions, we found that the prospect of being able to integrate with 'the locals' was usually a secondary consideration. British retirees in Spain and Portugal were also more likely to be seasonal rather than permanent residents (see Table 5.6), further lessening the incentive for integration.[5] From the perspective of the host society, those who migrate upon retirement or who are seasonal residents may be indistinguishable from the floating population of tourists.

Tourism links places, but it also tends to separate the tourist from their surrounding environments. One can gain the impression that parts of the Costa del Sol have stronger functional links to Manchester and Gatwick than with Málaga or Granada. Some parts of the coast have an especially 'non-authentic' atmosphere, and the Costa del Sol has been described as a 'pseudo place' (Fussell 1980: 43). Neoteric and non-authentic qualities are also present in the Algarve, but are less marked. The distribution of retired British residents in southern Iberia is largely defined by the major resorts, the intervening extensive planned housing developments, and the adjacent inland villages and hills. Generalising, we may say that the further away from Málaga airport, and the further inland from the coast itself, the more contact people have with the local Spanish population. An equivalent rule for the Algarve is less easy to describe because, although nearness to Faro airport is not a relevant influence, some of the older-established and remoter inland residential developments accommodate elderly expatriates who have made little effort to integrate. Many retired British people live close to the airport but in dispersed rural settings near Loulé.

As with the other two destination regions, many interviewees commented on the ways by which the geography of British settlement influenced the forms of integration with local people. Taking some Algarve examples first, there was a distinct tendency to regard those who lived close to the airport at Faro as less integrated, whereas those who lived in the far west, beyond Portimão, or to the east and close to the Spanish border, were more in touch with the Portuguese. The 'colonial set' who had settled in the Monchique hills were also regarded as a group apart by other British retirees. In the words of Doreen, 'The people down here are more real. In Monchique it's rather the gin and tonic type – they are in the main retired colonial and service people.' The view from the other side was rather different, however. According to Murray:

> There is a different outlook between colonials like us and – with due respect – the Brits as such. We survived by getting out and taking an interest in the world around us... As colonials, we have a more outgoing character and that has allowed us to transplant here more easily... A lot of other people who retired in the Algarve bury their heads in the sand. They don't want to get involved in anything and they don't know what's going on... Some of them don't have a clue as to what to do when they have a problem.

In Spain, a retired policeman living in an inland village referred to various integration experiences:

> At one extreme, you get the type of English person who won't mix with anybody who isn't English. They are the worst type... There are also eccentrics here – one has literally 'gone native'. He dresses like a Spaniard and refuses to speak English! The locals think he is *loco*... We try to integrate as much as we can but we are limited by the language...

Others were equally disdainful, but it is also clear that some who say that they have adopted 'the Spanish way of life' have superficial views of what it means to be Spanish. A positive assertion of 'the Spanish way' is, for many, a way of expressing their disenchantment with Britain. O'Reilly (1995b: 30-1) develops this point further: the 'Spain' with which British residents identify is a construction in which Britain is 'bad' and Spain is 'good'. Britain signifies dullness, boredom, greyness, cold, old age, crime and lack of respect for the elderly. Spain signifies the opposite: warmth, sunshine, sociability, good health, leisure, safety and respect for older people. 'Bad news from Britain' fills the British newspapers and satellite television, but few British are watching Spanish television or reading Spanish newspapers, and therefore receive little bad news about Spain (O'Reilly 1995b: 31).

The weak integration between the British and the indigenous population in the Costa del Sol may be because a large proportion of the former live in the self-contained, self-administered environment of the *urbanización*. It would be a mistake, however, to regard these as wholly British residential settings. O'Reilly (1995a: 34-5) cautions against the use of the term ghettos for, as we also found, the British live side-by-side with other nationalities including Spaniards. Even so, 'interaction is usually superficial and transient' (O'Reilly 1995b: 35). More often than not, friendships develop only if the other nationalities can speak some English.

Our interviews with British retired residents living on purpose-built residential estates in both Spain and Portugal revealed a great deal about the extent and nature of interaction with the residents of other nationalities living on these estates, and also about the changing character of the estate populations over time. Many interviews were taken in the vast Calahonda complex, with its 4,500 properties. This development has grown incrementally over the past thirty to thirty-five years, so that different sectors have different ages and characters. Bertram bought into Calahonda in 1984, when it was about half its present size and, by his account, much quieter. He lives in a zone with twenty-one detached villas, owned by several nationalities:

> There are Germans, Spanish, Moroccans, some Indians from Glasgow and a Pakistani from Paris... There are five permanent residents, like me. The rest come and go ... one house is owned by a Moroccan minister and he only comes out in August. Most of the others come out three or four times a year... There are more Spanish people coming in now; once it was too expensive for them. The Spanish professional people here used to live in Málaga and come here just in the summer. Now there are more Spanish people living here permanently. There is one house up for sale and I have heard that it will probably go to a Spanish family.

A key change on several *urbanizaciones* is the in-movement of Spanish households. Properties are being bought as holiday homes by people from Madrid, Barcelona, other northern cities and also from Málaga, and as permanent residences by local people. The reaction of the retired British varies but is sometimes chauvinistic, as expressed by a British administrator of one of the estates:

> I would like to see more people integrate socially [here]. I don't think we have been too successful in that particular aspect of life here as regards foreign owners... Slowly we are educating the Spanish families into our way of life here.

Others expressed negative views of the rising presence of Spanish owners:

> I am, of course, pro-Spanish but we are a quiet community here and once the Spanish families come in, it will be full of noise – motor bikes, footballs, the lot. And the hours they keep are horrendous compared with the British sense of time. Two or three in the morning is usual for a Spanish party to be going on.

Even where more positive views are expressed, they are often etched with a tinge of national superiority, whilst the 'good things' about the Spanish way of life are often reduced to superficial differences. Here is Nora, a widow who lives with her mother on the El Faro *urbanización* in Mijas Costa.

> There are 12 houses in this little cul-de-sac. Our next door neighbours are British lawyers who come down regularly. There is a Spanish nurse on the other side. Across the road is a German man with his Italian wife. At the end of the cul-de-sac, there is a Spanish teacher with his Swiss wife and a Spaniard who owns an olive grove. The Spaniards come down here for the whole summer. We give their little children English lessons. We know everyone. We have a party

every summer... Our social life here is completely different. In England if you want to go and have a coffee or drink after an evening out, there is nothing open. In Spain, everything is open after 11 at night. That is the nice thing. There are so many different places to choose from here for simple things like having a coffee. There's so little choice in England.

In both the Costa del Sol and the Algarve, there is also a sense that some degree of contact with the local society can be achieved by collective action, and bridges are being built at the institutional level. Examples are fund-raising events held regularly by expatriate clubs to provide money or equipment for local Spanish or Portuguese charities. In Carvoeiro (Algarve), a theatrical group raises money for local charities. In the Costa del Sol, Betty and Cahill (1999) cite the case of the *Hogar del Jubilado* (day centre for elderly people) in Arroyo de Miel, Benalmádena, which has benefited from gifts of equipment from local British clubs. However they also report that when the centre asked for a Spanish-speaking Briton to join the committee, no volunteer was forthcoming. A more positive example, the well-known CUDECA organisation which provides palliative care, is described in Chapter 7. Other avenues for integration are provided by the multi-national memberships of clubs for sport, recreation and other interests. The Overtons are members of a gardening club on the Costa del Sol:

> Although it is basically an English club, there are other nationalities too including Spanish, French and Germans. We also belong to a Spanish bonsai class that has social activities. They are all Spanish there, except for three of us, and that is another way to learn the language and make friends. Trouble is, most of them want to improve their English!

Enda, who lives in the Algarve resort town of Carvoeiro, enjoys the multinational social round at the local tennis club:

> The tennis club is quite a part of my social life now ... I play four times a week and in fact I am playing in a competition soon... I play through the winter... I have made a lot of friends there, all sorts of people, a real mixture. Not only British but Dutch, Belgians, Germans, Scandinavians and South Africans too.

Whilst there are similarities between the social geographies of the retired British in the Costa del Sol and the Algarve, we also found differences in their contacts with indigenous people. There was much less organised social life in the Algarve, probably because of the smaller number; as a result, relationships (and conflicts!) with the local people tended to be more individual. Glen, an artist who lives in Lagos towards the quieter, western end of the Algarve, commented: 'Social life is quite limited in this part, and there is no social pressure ... it's just plain country living ... everyday living here is perfection for me.' For others the 'plain country living' of the Algarve hinterland was more problematic, and some found the local people diffident. According to William:

The Portuguese were initially quite welcoming but it is not easy to make real friends with them. It is rare that you get invited into a Portuguese home... There is also a different attitude toward women in Portugal. It's a different culture, although things are changing slowly.

Social Life with Other British People

Many British seek their own wherever they go, but perhaps with more enthusiasm than other nationalities. This provides a counterpoint to the occasionally negative reactions to local people which we have noted above. Social life with other British residents also involves other processes of social integration, but the retirees resident in southern Europe are far from socially homogenous. We have already presented much evidence on the ways in which they perceive themselves to be fragmented, often into geographically defined social groups. There are other divisions too, from those who pursue intensely social lives within the British community, to the individuals who deliberately shun the company of their compatriots and, as often as not, act in a social vacuum when it comes to the host country.

One important influence on the nature of 'in-group' social life is time – both the years that the retiree has been living in the region, and the months each year spent in this destination. In the early stages of relocation, the support received from other expatriates is often important in cementing friendships and forming social networks. The newcomer is typically ascribed a subordinate or dependent role, seniority among expatriates being mainly determined by their length of residence. This is one context in which social relationships and hierarchies may be constructed anew. Another is the need to adjust to a complete change of environment, a 'total displacement', which makes people uncertain of where they stand in an unfamiliar setting where the conventional props of their lives are missing. Individuals may find themselves living in what J. G. Ballard (1996) calls an 'affectless zone', without conventionally defining activities and structures (work, family, neighbourhood etc.). This allows them to invent new roles for themselves. One role which is adopted by older people, some soon after their arrival, is that of a volunteer.

The second conditioning influence of time is with respect to the degree of permanence versus seasonality of residence. Long-term and permanent residents tend to look down on tourists, even (and sometimes especially) those of their own nationality. James, who had settled in a remote Italian valley, had scathing views about holiday visitors to the area:

We avoid the people who have holiday homes here. We have nothing in common with them. It may sound snobby but British people who have holiday homes out here come to Italy and think they are really 'somebody'. They think they have made it. This comes over all the time – they are so self-centred – they believe they have achieved something.

The seasonal retired migrant has an ambivalent standing within the resident/tourist dichotomy, and several authors have used the term 'residential tourists' to denote this group (O'Reilly 1995b). As we have seen, the 'snowbirds' who flee the winter cold of the north are a substantial part of the expatriate population. Their social networks tend to be dichotomised geographically according to season but are not necessarily any less intense as a result, as other research has shown (Buller and Hoggart 1994; Myklebost 1989).

Given the sharp contrast in British in-group social interaction as between in the Costa del Sol and Tuscany, these processes in the two regions are now examined in more detail. What follows is a contrast between 'Eldorado' and 'Chiantishire'. Later some data from the other two settings will be introduced.

The myth of Eldorado: living in a 'soap bubble'

In 1992 the BBC set an ill-fated soap drama near Mijas, creating a mind-closing cliché that the British expatriate community in the Costa del Sol lives in an artificial world akin to a TV soap. British readers may remember the wooden acting, feeble story-lines and stereotypical scenes that led to *Eldorado* being soon abandoned. As Karen O'Reilly (2000) has pointed out, the programme built on a stereotype of the 'Brits in Spain' which had been constructed by newspaper and television journalism. This stereotype presented them as living lazy lives in the sun, drinking too much alcohol, behaving like old colonials, and certainly not integrating. Sometimes the 'expats' were portrayed as having a wonderful time, on other occasions as being poor and isolated, whilst the presence of a few exiled criminals of tabloid notoriety was extrapolated into all manner of salacious stories. These imaginations have flourished in the absence of academic research, and we hope that the field evidence collected by Betty and Cahill (1999), by O'Reilly (1995b; 2000) and by ourselves will both construct and disseminate more accurate accounts of the lives of expatriate older people in the region. Betty and Cahill (1999) claim that whilst elderly British residents rarely integrate effectively with local Spaniards, they enjoy a well-structured lifestyle which on the whole keeps them busy, happy and healthy. They also stress the role of expatriate clubs in the 'rich and varied lifestyle' of the elderly British.[6] A wide range of activities and interests is catered for by these associations. In addition, there are local coach trips to places of interest, some longer-distance holiday trips (to discover the 'real Spain'), small British lending libraries, talks by 'experts' on Spanish life and customs, and, always popular, information sessions on Spanish health, legal and financial matters. Many retired British felt it was necessary to join these clubs to meet people of similar backgrounds and interests, to widen their social circles, and to receive practical information about living in Spain.

Another sign of the high level of in-group British activity is the proliferation of English-language media. English, Scottish and Irish newspapers are available on the morning of publication, and there are several locally-produced papers and magazines such as the *Sur in English* (a weekly subsidiary of the regional daily *Sur*), *The Entertainer, Lookout,* and *The Reporter,* as well as local English-language radio stations, the most important of which is *Onda Cer,* broadcast from Marbella. Betty and Cahill (1999) consider the significance of this large output, firstly confirming that very few elderly Britons read Spanish newspapers or watch Spanish television (apart from the weather forecast!), and secondly suggesting that the arrival of American and British satellite TV has made the community even more linguistically self-contained.

Returning to the social geography of British residential settlement, it is clear that the expatriate-dominated villages such as Mijas Pueblo and *urbanizaciones* such as Calahonda provide spatial frameworks for within-group social contacts which do not exist for the more dispersed rural settlements of Tuscany or interior Algarve. The *urbanización,* with its inward-facing cul-de-sacs and residents' committees, is in effect a miniature village, within which virtually every permanent resident is known. One of the characteristics of such small communities is that new arrivals tend to find themselves quickly incorporated into the local social networks. O'Reilly (1995b: 33) describes how already-settled expatriates in Fuengirola make newcomers welcome, 'drawing them into the symbolic community via informal networks'. For some, the presence of close friends in the area was one of the main factors leading to retirement abroad. Murdo, who had lived in Scotland and Canada before retiring to Mijas Pueblo, remarked 'we already had friends here. This was very important.... When you first come, you need to know people to lessen the culture shock.'

Although O'Reilly (1995a: 34-5) firmly rejects the use of the term 'ghetto' to portray the concentrations of foreign settlers in the Costa del Sol on ethical and philological grounds, the word was often used by our interviewees, both retirees and others. For instance Moira and Paul, whose social life centred around the Anglican Church and a theatre group, said that they lived in 'an English ghetto'. The term ghetto has long historical associations with Spain (as in Toledo) but its present-day racial, genocidal and socially dysfunctional connotations make it highly unsuitable for this application, and O'Reilly is right to question its use. But there are clear single-nationality residential concentrations along the Spanish coast; she herself points to the 'gilded ghetto' of the Avenida Finlandia, a 'clearly demarcated residential area' populated by Finns (O'Reilly 1995a: 36), and other examples of national residential concentrations are given by Rodríguez *et al.* (1998: 195).

We now turn to the types of social interaction engaged in. Some play bingo and spend evenings in British pubs and restaurants; others head for the golf course or join in bridge parties or amateur dramatics. Here are some accounts of social life which enable us to appreciate the extent to which it is conducted in the company of other British people. Frank, in

Estepona, described his social life in the following terms:

> We never consciously wanted to escape from the other Brits here... We belong
> to a club which is for English-speaking people. This is an active group and holds
> many activities. My wife has taken on bowls but I don't like sport much. She also
> does Scottish dancing... There are also good theatrical facilities here – a small
> theatre company which puts on plays. They tour all along the coast... We also
> belong to the Anglican Church – there is a little community there with good
> friends of ours... The Labour Party group is now getting going ... I have been to
> all their meetings so far.

Others were more oriented to the Royal British Legion, which has five
branches and over a thousand members in the Costa del Sol. The British
Legion is the most wide-ranging British organisation in Spain. Although
confined to ex-Service personnel and their dependants, its members assist
with welfare work and are actively engaged in promoting the needs of the
elderly British expatriate community as a whole. In this extract from
Hilary's interview, she describes her involvement as a welfare officer.

> A few of us used to go to the Torremolinos Social Club but we weren't very
> pleased with it, so we joined the British Legion... The local branch has about
> twenty members ... we have a social secretary and I am the welfare officer...
> Fortunately we are healthy but if anyone became ill or had an accident, we
> would arrange to go and visit them... We have wheelchairs and crutches ... zim-
> mer frames as well.

We conclude with some comments drawn from British clergy of different Christian denominations. With their pastoral roles and accumulated
experience of British congregations, in one case going back to the 1950s,
ministers can be very useful key informants. One should appreciate, however, that, like consular staff and doctors, they tend to be involved disproportionately in cases of illness, bereavement, isolation and disturbance.

> As a chaplain, I find there is a lot of narrow-mindedness here. Some of the
> British retirees find their life centres around medical associations and doctors.
> They need to learn Spanish and get on with their lives! They have *Sky TV* but
> what is happening in the rest of the world doesn't seem to interest them.

All of the ministers that we interviewed acknowledged a problem of exces-
sive alcohol consumption amongst some retired Britons:

> There is a drink problem here ... even within my congregation there are peo-
> ple who have succumbed. Sometimes it happens because of boredom – some
> people find their existence here rather superficial... Some people go into bars
> for hours, for them it is a way of life... I am surprised at the level of the alcohol
> problem, and it's my guess that the problem exists more outside the church
> than within!

A former chaplain of St George's Church in Málaga (also responsible for

Nerja) describes the community at the eastern extremity of the Costa del Sol, outside the area where we concentrated our field research.

> There is a staunch British community in Nerja... We have a good congregation there... Most of them came out early on in their retirement and they are mostly middle-class, not particularly wealthy. I don't think many of them have much contact with the Spanish population. They live in the big urbanisations up the hill, and some in the town itself... They are a bit parochial and insular... It's not a happy place ... well, I don't want to talk too much about it!... They are perfectly normal people but a bit blinkered. They don't want to integrate.

All the clergy confirmed the elderly character of their congregations:

> The youngest would be in their late 40s; most are retired, several are in their 70s or older. We don't have any children at all in our congregation ... no baptisms for a long time.

While the church congregations are swollen during the tourist season, it is the permanent and long-stay retired residents who are their backbone.

The church also provides a wider social function, strengthening British communal identity beyond the immediate congregation. Several denominations bring expatriates of different nationalities together, while the Roman Catholic Church fosters associations with Spanish individuals and welfare organisations. An ecumenical centre in Fuengirola, *Lux Mundi*, hosts and organises a wide range of cultural, social and community activities, from quizzes to Alcoholics Anonymous and hospital visitors. It has a branch centre in Torre del Mar and affiliates Belgian, Danish, Dutch, English, Finnish, German, Norwegian, Scottish and Swedish churches.

Chiantishire: in a class of their own

It would be difficult to imagine a setting for British retirement more different from the high-density holiday complexes of Torremolinos or Fuengirola than the sparsely-settled hills and valleys of Chianti. But geography is only part of the social context. Shared backgrounds, tastes and values are the social glue which holds the majority of older expatriates in Tuscany together. They are, to a large extent, in a class of their own. As we have demonstrated abundantly in Chapter 4, this predominantly upper- and upper-middle-class group has a fine sensitivity to the region's artistic and environmental endowment. Their language skills and their previous contacts with Italy mean that they are usually able to communicate with local people, but while this does not necessarily mean that they are highly integrated, nor did our fieldwork reveal the kind of intense in-group social interaction observed in the Costa del Sol. The British in Tuscany are too spatially dispersed, and their social background does not, on the whole, predispose them to bingo or bowls, or sinking a pint in the John Bull Tavern. Nevertheless for many, probably the majority, of the older British in rural Tuscany, most of their meaningful social contacts are with their peers. We found that they tended to choose their friends carefully, relying on what one interviewee described as 'small webs' of close friends for support and entertainment. The various small webs correspond to subtle divisions in social background, wealth, education, political allegiance and other factors. Some indication of their boundaries and of the nature of intra-group social life are gained from a selection of interview quotes. First, Peter, who lives in Greve in the Chianti heartland:

> We entertain quite a lot, we invite our friends over for dinner, and in the summer go to concerts with them, maybe to Florence once a week. We used to go to the opera but it has become too expensive; now we have CDs instead! Some of the British who live out here still go to the opera, but we have become lazy... We also play bridge among friends ... mostly British friends but some Dutch and Americans, people we've met at dinners mainly.

Lloyd and Erica drew a contrast between themselves as gregarious ex-Army retirees and others who wanted a more solitary life:

> In the last few years we have got to know a lot of English people here... It is inevitable that you gravitate to people speaking your own language... We have quite a good social life here and hold parties. It probably comes from the Army background ... where entertaining is normal. Some people come and live tucked up in the hills and don't wish to see other people. This is not the way we live.

The third extract is from Douglas, whose interview in 1995 we have already quoted at length (Box 5.1):

> We have made a lot of English friends here. The way we entertain ... is generally that we have four or six people to dinner, certainly once a week, and we go to someone else's house once a week. We had a play reading some months ago and had twelve sitting down to dinner... The English we know out here could be divided into three distinct categories. Generally speaking these categories don't mix... First, there are the retired army and navy officers, ex-diplomats, people of that ilk ... the upper middle class. All of them are retired, all middle-aged or elderly people ... including some Americans... Anyway, our social life revolves around that category. The next category are mature English people – professional or semi-professional people – working here, like the estate agent ... there is also an English dentist... That group is not so free for lunch or dinner. Then there are the refugees from Mrs Thatcher's Britain; building workers whose homes have been repossessed by the building society and who ... hope to get a job here ... working-class English people.

There is a sense in which 'Chiantishire' has (or had) a social cachet as an area of British 'colonisation' which was unparalleled: an extension of the most well-heeled parts of the Home Counties. Today this image is kept alive by newspaper articles about prominent politicians and media stars visiting the area (recently the family holidays of Tony Blair in Tuscany have been widely reported), by the 1996 Bertolucci film *Stealing Beauty*, and by the popular books of the British writer John Mortimer, notably *Summer's Lease* (Mortimer 1988). To understand fully the social construction of the term Chiantishire, the origins of which are disputed,[7] one needs to go back to the pioneer British settlers in Chianti in the early 1960s. We interviewed nearly all of the early settlers who are still alive and still resident in the area. The fullest account comes from Raymond Flower, the first British person to buy a Chianti farm and the author of a book on the region. Box 6.2 is an extended extract from two interviews in October 1995: a comparable account appears in Flower's book (1988: 211-20, 229-30). Flower was brought up in Egypt. He had enjoyed a polymath career as a businessman, racing-driver and writer, and had been in central Italy as a soldier during the war. At the time of the interview he was 74 years of age and still active as a writer and in buying and selling property around Castellina-in-Chianti and in the Marche.

Box 6.2 The social construction of Chiantishire: a first-hand account

I came because I was doing a lot of motor racing ... we were living in Egypt and I was running the family business but I spent a lot of time in Europe because of the racing... Then came the Suez Affair, and we were all suddenly chucked out, hopeless... It became obvious that I would have to have a place in Europe ... and my mother said she wanted to find a place in Tuscany [so] I came and I was the first of the British, in 1962, and then my friends came, and the friends of my friends, and then it got completely out of control... There were 60,000 houses available in those days in the whole of Tuscany, and around here practically every other house was abandoned... And then we got the smart lot who came in: Teddy Goldsmith; Alistair Londonderry, who bought a farmhouse of mine when there was trouble at Lloyds in '68 and I needed to raise some cash ... [a lengthy list follows] ... That's how it grew up... So we really did get the heavy cream of society, you know, coming along and buying. And – this is where the Chiantishire thing came in – you had this extraordinary situation of going into a Tuscan farmhouse ... and finding all the Central Bank heads of Europe sitting under an olive tree by a swimming pool debating... And then you'd go to the little bar in Castellina – there were no telephones in the houses in those days – and you'd find Oliver Poole, who was Chairman of Lazard's, as I did one day, and he was trying to get through to London, having a coffee while he was waiting, to arrange the merger between Leyland and the British Motor Corporation! So yes, I suppose there was a sort of Chiantishire feel about the place in those days ... *all* the big names were here, and they brought other names, and it was actually very jolly, but only in the summer ... that is what we mean by Chiantishire ... but it only lasted a very short time ... a ten-year period when it was a jet-set... So, how have things changed? Well, they have changed. This has become the smart money area; it's lost its virginity, if one can put it that way.

Flower's account gives unique insights into the way in which Chiantishire, although a geographical term deriving from the Chianti region, is (or was) for some a social construction which refers to the periodic coming together, mainly in the summer, and for a period of around ten to fifteen years during the 1960s and 1970s, of a powerful group of people – politicians, industrialists, financiers, aristocrats – who symbolised the ruling classes of Britain (and to some extent also, of the European and international economy) at the time. The term lingers on, perhaps justifiably so, as the Chianti region continues to be a playground of the rich and famous and summer tourism has replaced wine and olive oil as the main income earner of the district.

Other settings

'Eldorado' and Chiantishire have been employed here as highly polarised variants of British residential settlement and expatriate life. There are many other settings too. Up in the Serra de Monchique in the inland Algarve there is a mainly ex-colonial group of people with similar social origins and composition to the British in Tuscany; while along the Algarve coast are *urbanizações* which mirror closely their Costa del Sol counterparts. Parts of the Costa del Sol and the Algarve especially attract the golfing fraternity, while there is a small concentration of sailing buffs in Malta. Torremolinos has a betting shop patronised by the close-knit working-class retired British community, while Gibraltar attracts those who deal in stocks and shares. Yet most of the communities we encountered had fewer idiosyncratic traits.

In the Algarve, one of the bulwarks of the British community is the Association of Foreign Property Owners in Portugal, AFPOP. Founded in the late 1980s, AFPOP's 2,700 members are mainly British living in the Algarve. Social life in the Algarve is less organised than in the Costa del Sol but more organised than in Tuscany and Umbria. Apart from purely informal interaction, the main activities amongst the British include golf, bridge, walking and a few speciality groups such as theatre and bird-watching. There are also a couple of English-language newspapers – the *Algarve News* and *The Resident* – and an English-language radio station based in Albufeira. Nevertheless, for many, a low-profile retirement life is the main priority, and the main social contact is with other British retirees.

> We came here for seclusion and so we don't go to the local bars. That's where the Brits and other Europeans sit every weekend and drink. There are places in the vicinity where the Brits play bingo – but it's not our scene ... we aren't really interested in joining clubs as such. We are quite comfortable with the friends we have made ... we have a little Sunday lunch club, when we all go to a restaurant – all English people.

The next interviewee was keener on socialising, and acknowledged the role of AFPOP:

> If you want a social life, you have to work hard at it in the initial stages. When we came, we decided to join everything we could to meet people... What really opened up our social life was AFPOP and the archaeological society. AFPOP

have regular lunches, and everyone comes from all over the place... (Duncan, near Lagos).

Others, like Ivor, were less impressed with AFPOP and its perceived association with the more wealthy and snobbish elements of the retired British population:

I am a member of AFPOP but that doesn't provide me with anything! Most of the people there are the moneyed ones, very well-heeled and a bit out of touch with people like me. You get invited to a luncheon with a lecturer, it's expensive and you can't guarantee it will be very good. It's not my scene to be perfectly honest. I like music and nature, I don't belong to clubs.

In Malta the British Residents' Association (BRA) has some similarities with AFPOP. The BRA was founded in 1970, one of its purposes being 'to foster friendly and harmonious relations between members of the Association and the people of Malta'. It is also a social focus for many British residents who, in practice, have little contact with the Maltese. The Association had considerable success initially as an unofficial pressure group which sorted out the inequities of a tax system which, according to one of its officials, made Malta 'a very good place to live, but not to die'. The BRA has around 1,000 members in five branches. In recent years it has opened its doors to all foreign residents of Malta, but it remains a predominantly British association, and does not appeal to most of the British nationals married to Maltese. The Association is required by law not to engage in electoral politics, but it does act vigorously as a special interest group (it was influential in negotiating the terms of the reciprocal health care agreement) and as a welfare adviser.

Large numbers of the British retirees we interviewed in Malta were BRA members. Many had appreciated both the social activities and the practical advice on tax and legal matters. Here are two characteristic plaudits:

You meet many people [at BRA meetings] but the main thing is their wonderful welfare system. This year I had pneumonia and they visited and helped me... They were also a good back-up when my husband died ... they assisted with the burial arrangements.

There are many benefits to being a member... Cheap food! There are various places you can get a discount. In the BRA, we have very good connections with the British High Commission and if you have any problems, [they] will sort it out with the government... The BRA has some clout here.

As with AFPOP, there were others who held a more detached and even negative view of the BRA and the social character of its membership:

My wife did get me enrolled once. I went along as they had some interesting quizzes ... but after one or two years I never went again. Most of the British there said that they were highly-placed ex-service members and I didn't like their attitude ... they were acting as being something they weren't.

For a large group of British retirees today, social life is mainly with other British retirees through membership of several clubs and networks: the BRA, the Union Club, and the various Anglian churches – St Paul's Pro-Cathedral, Holy Trinity in Sliema and St Andrew's Church of Scotland. The Union Club is regarded as something of an institution in Malta. Some of our interviewees described it as a 'geriatric club', or as 'God's Waiting Room'. According to another informant, the Union Club is a 'home from home ... a little bit of old England in a way, which is probably what attracts us'. Another social circuit revolves around the International Wives' Association, set up in 1983 by the British wife of a Maltese dentist. This association is for foreign women married to Maltese.[8] These women, traditionally shunned by the wealthier settler population, have a strong sense of community, and seek to put people who arrive in touch with others from the same area of the United Kingdom. Alongside these voluntaristic associations, it should be remembered that many British retired citizens are either natives of Malta or have a Maltese spouse; they live dominantly family-centred lives that are structured around the vital events and celebrations of all ages and generations rather than the preoccupations of retirement. Links with the UK are another dimension of retaining a British identity, and these links are analysed in more detail in the next section.

Links to Britain: Return Visits and Visits from Family and Friends

This section brings together the evidence on links with Britain (see especially pp.109-12 and Table 5.6) with the material on social life and integration. We have found that contact and integration with local people is greatest in Tuscany, whereas in the Costa del Sol and the Algarve retirees on average spend greater amounts of the year back in Britain, integration with local Spaniards and Portuguese is minimal, and nearly all social life revolves around the British expatriate communities.

Many return visits to the UK (and for a few, elsewhere) are made to keep in touch with friends and relatives, above all children and grandchildren. Being distant from family was one of the most frequently reported disadvantages and the third cited problem of living abroad (Table 5.9). Another factor found to prompt return visits is the wish to escape the heat and tourist influx of high summer. Less instrumental motivations associated with a person's identity and self-image may also play a part, such as the need to reclaim a few of those immovable aspects of Britain and British culture which are 'missed' in exile. Having said this, relatively few people pointed to things that they missed in Britain (apart from family members), although real ale, good public libraries, value-for-money clothing stores, sausages and Radio 3 were mentioned.

Instead, there is an unspoken consensus not to complain about life abroad – except about the bureaucracy! O'Reilly (1995b) found that among her informants there was a determined approval of all things Spanish coupled with a rejection of all things British. She also noted how little ceremony attended anyone's leaving the Costa. A comparable attitude was identified by the Australian husband of a British retiree in Tuscany, who referred to the often-voiced determination to go on living in Italy rather than return home as the 'burnt bridges syndrome'. According to this perceptive informant, 'those who suffer from it have the wherewithal to return from whence they came, or to venture to pastures new, but the great decision to come to Italy has been made and, come what may, true Brits ... will see it out to the bitter end'. Many others, in all regions, saw things in a different light: 'most of our elderly friends in this area find that as time goes by, and they haven't integrated into the local community, they need to go home'. O'Reilly (1995b: 32-3) cites examples of the discrepancy between retirees' public and private statements as regards feelings towards Britain. Publicly, the impression is given that they are happy and settled in Spain and have no wish to return to Britain; privately and in confidence, some of O'Reilly's closest informants, especially the women, expressed feelings of isolation and of sadness over the remoteness of close friends and family (O'Reilly 2000).

On return visits to the UK, the questionnaire returns suggest that respondents had made, on average, 1.4 visits to Britain during the previous twelve months. Those living in the Algarve (1.6) and the Costa del Sol (1.5) tended to visit the UK more often than retirees in Tuscany (1.2) and Malta (1.0). Possible reasons for the differentials are that flights are cheaper and more frequent from Faro and Málaga; retirees in Portugal and Spain are younger (hence perhaps fitter and more mobile) than their counterparts in Tuscany and Malta; retirees in Tuscany and Malta have more family, and former work and friendship links in the destination region; whilst retirees in Spain and Portugal are more likely to have made a 'clean break' retirement migration, leaving their family and lifelong friends in Britain.

Most return visits were timed to take place during the summer or at Christmas. Whilst necessary to retain contacts with family and friends, some were seen as duty visits and quite stressful, reinforcing the self-assessed wisdom of the decision to retire abroad:

> We go back to the UK once a year to see our parents. We usually go at Christmas. We don't spend a lot of time there. We don't like the weather and it all seems so stressful... We run from one point to another trying to see everyone. The life in England doesn't appeal any more... We didn't notice it so much when we lived there. Being in Spain has made a difference. Now we couldn't live in England (Percy and Sue, early retired from a family business, Calahonda, Spain).

> If I go on holiday, I go back to England and visit friends. I do a round trip in England to see everyone. It's not a real holiday, though, tramping round everywhere... If I go over to the UK now, I stay with one son or the other, but they

don't trust me to drive their cars so I get a bit housebound! Travelling around by train is so expensive (Harriet, Vilamoura, Algarve).

Several key informants and retirees, both male and female, drew attention to a gender contrast in attitudes to family relationships. The message that was conveyed time and again was that women miss their relatives (and friends) more than men, corroborating an established tenet of family sociology that 'women develop skills that facilitate intimate relationships ... and not only have more friends but they are often close confidantes' (Arber 1996: 562). Some saw the complement, that men are more active and settled in the retirement destination than women:

> The men are happier here than the women. My husband paints and rides and is totally absorbed with what he is doing. Also, he doesn't feel the need to be with his grandchildren as they grow up, as I do. There are some men here who are quite happy to sit and read their English newspapers all day, while they have a drink... The men are more contented because they've led active lives, and most women here have not – well, the majority of them (Cherie, Vilamoura, Algarve).

Visits to the UK are reciprocated by visits from friends and relatives, the majority pleased enough to stay for a while in a pleasant environment and having what is, in effect, a cut-price holiday. Table 6.5 sets out some detailed statistics on the numbers and types of visitors drawn from the questionnaire. The table shows the total and the main categories of visitor in the previous year for each destination region. Averages are calculated on the basis of both the total sample of respondents and those who actually received visitors of each category. Interpolating between these two totals, it is clear that a significant minority (17 per cent of the total sample) received no visitors during the previous twelve months. This percentage was particularly high in Malta (24) and Tuscany (22) and lowest (7) in the Algarve.

On average, the 957 respondents included in the total valid sample received seven visitors during the year, increasing to eight if those who received no visitors are discounted. Retired migrants in Tuscany and the Algarve received, on average, twice as many visitors as those in Malta. The most common visitor was a non-kin adult, followed by the respondents' own children and grandchildren, and non-kin children. Amongst the more noteworthy inter-destination contrasts, the number of child visitors is unusually low in Spain, there are a high number of grandchildren visiting Malta, and a high number of non-kin adult visitors to Tuscany. Tentative suggestions can be offered to explain such differences:

- a propensity in Tuscany to host friends accumulated through high-status, professional and cosmopolitan careers;
- close-knit family structures in Malta account for a high frequency of grandchildren visits;
- in the Costa del Sol especially, a significant segment of retirees are to

Table 6.5 Visitors hosted over the past year

	Total visitors	Own adult children	Own grand-children	Other (non-kin) adults	Other (non-kin) children
Average number of visitors for total sample (n = 957)	6.92	1.47	1.46	3.21	0.41
Tuscany (n = 109)	9.72	1.99	1.65	5.65	0.72
Malta (n = 281)	4.54	1.48	1.70	1.89	0.44
Costa del Sol (n = 346)	6.18	1.01	1.01	2.74	0.15
Algarve (n = 221)	9.73	1.93	1.75	4.41	0.63
Average number of visitors for those who received visitors (n in brackets under each average)	8.33 (795)	2.94 (479)	3.97 (352)	5.23 (587)	3.85 (102)
Tuscany	11.90 (89)	3.88 (56)	4.86 (37)	8.21 (75)	3.25 (24)
Malta	5.96 (214)	3.59 (116)	6.06 (79)	3.83 (139)	6.25 (20)
Costa del Sol	7.45 (287)	2.11 (166)	2.61 (134)	4.50 (211)	2.22 (23)
Algarve	10.50 (205)	3.02 (141)	3.79 (102)	6.01 (162)	3.97 (35)

Source: Authors' survey.
Note: Total visitors includes other visitor subcategories such as other kin adults and some possible double-counting of visitor types.

some extent 'living an escape' (O'Reilly 1995b: 29), and detached from family and friends in Britain.[9]

Whilst visits from friends and relatives are at least as important as return visits to Britain in maintaining social and family networks, not all are regarded with undiluted pleasure. In the questionnaire, respondents were invited to evaluate such visits as 'a great pleasure', 'good and bad' or 'disruptive'. Overall, 77 per cent who answered this question found the visits highly pleasurable, 21 per cent had mixed reactions, and 2 per cent found them disruptive; these proportions varied little across the destinations. For some, it seemed, their relaxing routines are interrupted by boisterous family guests or by visitors who overstay their welcome, expect too much and become expensive. Gilbert, living in Gozo, explains that, after a couple of trying visitors, he and his wife bought a small apartment around the corner to keep their guests at bay:

> A friend of my in-laws came here for a visit. When we met her at the airport, we asked her how long she was staying. She said certainly not less than a month. She was a middle-aged single lady who drank a lot. We had to take her to the beach every day, and on tours of the island. Cooked breakfasts every day and a midday meal – it was a bit too much, and expensive. I am only living on an RAF pension and she never spent a penny on us! Then friends from the RAF came. We began to think about a little flat around that time ... we decided to dig into [our capital] to buy the other apartment.

Leonard and Millie both have children from previous marriages, whose visits to their Algarve home they found both demanding and expensive:

> I haven't lived with my children since they were 15 but they come here twice a year. Millie and I don't have children ourselves – we haven't been together that long... When you have little children coming, they need to eat at specified hours and they are wandering around all the time, they don't respect your property. You notice these things... My eldest son is 40 [and] they brought their children out. When they came here, we had to fit in with them, not the other way round... Next time when they come, we'll give them a set of house rules – and a charge! It cost us over £300 to provide everything for them: wine, cake, biscuits, plus all the electricity and water, as we saw from the bills which came after. They used the pool every day too.

Many interviewees said that they saw at least as much of their family, especially their children and grandchildren, as they would have done had they stayed in Britain. In some cases this bonus was unexpected, but in others the opportunity for relations, especially children and grandchildren, to make frequent visits in a holiday atmosphere had been part of the rationale of retiring in a sunny destination:

> I have two sons, a daughter and three grandchildren. They all visit me here and I go over there – I'm visiting them next week in fact... In my job, my family were used to me travelling around. I see more of them now than I would have done back home! (Michael, widower, St Julians, Malta).

Conclusion: Where is Home?

In the last quote Michael is clearly referring to Britain as 'home'. Others, however, had very different ideas of where home was. Douglas, in Italy as a retiree for ten years, was clear he was staying for good and derided those who were still oriented towards Britain: 'we have a list of our friends who we call "wimps" who keep talking of home in terms of England. This is our home and we have no intention of going back.' A similar view was expressed by Shirley in the Algarve: 'Some people who have been here for years still keep talking about going home when they visit the UK [but] as

I fly back into Faro I always think to myself, "I am home!"'

Many retirees in Malta were adamant that the island was now their home, indicating a stronger attachment than found in the other regions. But others are ambivalent about where their roots and identities lie. As O'Reilly (1995b) has deftly shown, people do not conceive a simple dichotomy or even a continuum between Britain and Spain (or wherever) and then place their 'identity' along this uni-dimensional scale. Many retired British migrants seem to be creating new identities which comprise a mixture of elements of 'here', 'there' and other ingredients which they share only with other British retirees who live in the same place in similar circumstances. Deirdre's complex identity derives from her British birth, forty-four years in Kenya, and ten retirement years in Malta:

> Well, I miss Africa all the time! I was brought up there. Until you have visited there, you couldn't understand what Kenya is like. The scenery is absolutely marvellous. Malta is the second compromise... When I go to England, I am always looking forward to coming back to Malta. But, then, I was born in England! I remember wartime Britain, I am very fond of the Royal Family – well, the Queen, not the other lot! I will never give up my British passport.

We have shown that southern Europe attracts many people like Deirdre who do not have deep roots in one place, people who are (or have been) extremely mobile and who maintain multiple place affiliations. One might say that their identity is not 'place-specific' but that they have a more abstract sense of themselves. Some are perhaps reluctant (or even unable) to say where they 'come from', whatever their passport states. To appreciate the full flavour of their mobility, and its centrality to their lives, one has only to compare their life histories with those of their parents or grandparents, on whose graves is sometimes found the name of a house or farm in which a whole life was spent. With the majority of the retired British population in southern Europe comprising professional people, it is easy to agree with the postmodern notion of their being located more in fields of expertise than in places.

Our evidence, and the findings of others whom we have cited (notably Betty and Cahill 1999; O'Reilly 1995b, 2000), demonstrate that many British retirees in the study regions have rich and multifaceted lifestyles which are more varied and pleasurable, and involve more intense social contacts and physical activity, than they would have experienced in the UK. The majority of these contacts and activities take place however in the company of other British people, and the level of integration with the indigenous society is generally low.

Language is undoubtedly the main stumbling-block, but 'incompatible traditions' also repel, such as bullfighting (in Spain), trapping birds (Malta) and hunting (Italy). Given the realities of language and cultural barriers and the predominance of climate and lifestyle as the key motives for retirement abroad, 'integration' with local people, to the extent that it has occurred, may be regarded as a bonus rather than a necessity. What was more important was neighbourliness and the friendly smile from 'the locals' – features of the standard experience of the tourist and traveller.

Ultimately what both the migrant and the tourist want is to feel at home. Hence the effort made by many retirees to create a home from home, the attempt to fashion their own cultural environment within their new home – the fully carpeted Essex bungalow on the Costa del Sol or the Staffordshire manor house in Tuscany. But popular accounts of the British in Spain which describe maverick individuals remaking a 'little England in the sun' are gross distortions. What one can say is that the tourist resort, or even the cosmopolitan countryside of Tuscany, with its confusion of cultures and manners, allows everyone the illusion of being 'at home' and the freedom to 'be themselves'.

Notes

1. Taken from *French Property Buyer*, October 1991, p. 22, quoted in Buller and Hoggart (1994a: 100).
2. See the case of 'Margaret', described in King and Patterson (1998: 173).
3. Although it has begun to change since the mid-1980s: see King and Black (1997); King and Rybaczuk (1993).
4. We need to acknowledge here the diversity of types of club and association in the retirement destination regions. Clubs generally have premises, associations often do not. Hence we can differentiate sports or recreational clubs with fixed premises (tennis, bowls, golf) from those which do not and are more associated with pastimes such as rambling, bird-watching and gardening. We can also identify associative activities based around churches, charities and cultural activities – volunteer work, coffee mornings, amateur dramatics. Political associations are another subgroup, either linked to political parties in the UK ('Conservatives Abroad') or to promoting the interests of British residents in the destination region.
5. Buller and Hoggart (1994: 112-14) also found that British permanent residents in France were more likely to have achieved some integration with the local French society than those who were second-home owners and who visited their French property for certain phases of the year.
6. Although the British are the largest tourist and residential group in the Costa del Sol and therefore have given rise to the largest number of nationality-specific clubs, other nationality groups have an equally lively organised and informal social life. Betty and Cahill (1999) specifically mention the Nordic Club in Estepona, with 500 members, as well as Irish, North American and South American clubs and organisations. They believe that there are nearly a hundred such organisations in the region.
7. The first coining of the term is variously credited to the German mag-

azine *Der Spiegel*, the Italian weekly *L'Espresso*, and spurious claims that John Mortimer 'invented' the term.

8. Its main objective is 'to promote understanding and friendship between members and the local community, to help members deal with differences in culture and temperament, thereby helping them adjust more easily to their new life'. There are some 250 members, a large proportion of new members (and about one quarter of total current membership) being Associate Members, i.e. British or foreign wives married to non-Maltese men.

9. Although we did not collect systematic data on marital histories, anecdotal evidence and the in-depth interviews indicated that a high proportion of retirees in southern Spain were in second and subsequent marriages or partnerships. Such arrangements may well lead to a partial rupture of kinship and friendship links and to a lower intensity of visiting from the UK.

Seven

Retirement Abroad and Health and Welfare

Introduction: Paradoxes of Retirement Abroad

This chapter examines several aspects of health and well-being associated with retirement residence abroad. The issues are wide-ranging, complex and in some respects contradictory. It is frequently said, for example, that a move to a warmer and drier winter climate improves one's physical health or mental state, although the objective evidence for this is elusive. On the other hand, some warn that moving abroad can produce serious or even critical difficulties when an expatriate retiree becomes seriously ill. The chapter identifies the major welfare and health benefits and problems that are consequences of retirement abroad, which groups of people are most affected, in which circumstances and when. It will also examine the differences in the health and welfare services of the destination countries and Britain, and how the migrants adjust to these.

We begin by clarifying the definition and meaning of health and well-being both in general and, for there are important differences, with particular reference to older people. We then examine the health and welfare entitlements of expatriate retirees in the Mediterranean countries. These have been changing rapidly in EU member states through the social provisions of recent European treaties and bilateral agreements between the UK and other countries. The chapter next turns to health and social services in the destination areas, with both a description of current provision and a review of the British expatriates' experience of their use, drawing on interview and questionnaire responses. Several problems are identified, and a number of interesting communal responses by expatriate communities are examined. Finally the chapter synthesises the health and welfare consequences of retiring abroad.

Health, welfare and well-being in retirement

What is meant by health and well-being? The social sciences abound with the difficulties of giving stable and precise meanings to everyday speech terms, but these two have few rivals for ambivalence. A homely metaphor may be allowed. Health and well-being are like onions; the outer appearance is readily described but when you begin a close examination, the surface flakes and drifts away. Underneath one finds layer upon layer of potent contents. When you divide the flesh, the pieces become difficult to handle, indistinguishable, and less and less resemble the organic whole. The longer your examination, the more you may wish to cry.

Definitions of health and well-being

The understanding and definition of health involve many conceptual and technical problems, as the following quotations quickly show. 'There is no simple definition of health ... [it] may be conceptualised in a variety of ways including the absence of specific disease states or as a state of mind. ... [it] often defies the best efforts of researchers either to define or measure [and] is a much broader and socially defined concept than the simple absence of disease.' [There are] 'three distinct dimensions: the absence of disease, a functional concept, *i.e.* the ability to cope with daily activities, and ... ideas about general fitness and general well-being' (Victor 1991: 2, 94-5). Definitions of health moreover are culturally specific and change through time. 'For the past 150 years, rising expectations have changed the definition of health in the United States from "survival" to "freedom from disease", to an ability to perform "daily activities", to a sense of happiness and "well-being"' (McDowell and Newell 1987: 14). All investigators agree that health is multi-dimensional, but although they share a foundation in 'disease and disorder', there is no agreement upon where the boundaries (if any) lie between health and other states, such as well-being and quality of life. Many now argue that the 'disease model', with its focus on the presence or absence of pathologies and disorders, inadequately conceptualises health and is a poor basis for a practical definition. The current consensus is rather that an holistic view of health is more appropriate, because affluent Western populations have expectations beyond the absence of disease, disorder and pain (Wilkin, Hallam and Doggett 1992: 15).

The holistic rendering of health is rarely expanded to cover all aspects of well-being as conceived by social scientists, politicians and the general public. Physicians, for example, ordinarily do not see civil rights or the state of law and order as a dimension of health. The wider interest in *well-being* has had several roots and lines of development, including: utilitarianism and other philosophical theories of ethics which explore the actions and states that lead to the greatest happiness of the greatest number in society (Bond 1996; Griffin 1986); medicine's interest in the quality of life outcomes of interventions, including specific indicators for elderly patients with chronic conditions (Fillenbaum 1985; Maddox 1992); development studies, in which comparisons of the transformations of rich and poor countries have expanded from material indicators to welfare and quality of life measures (OECD 1976); the 'social indicators' schools of applied sociology and economics, which focus on short-term 'performance measures' for government, industry and commerce (Andrews and Withey 1976); and, finally, sociologists' and social psychologists' interests in subjective measures of satisfaction, contentment and happiness (George 1992; Ryff 1996). By any standard, this is an eclectic collection.

Health and well-being in old age

Health in old age has distinctive features. They arise partly from the diseases and disorders which are most prevalent in the age group, and partly from older people's own health expectations and the comparative standards that they apply when assessing their own condition and prospects. These in turn are conditioned by societal and professional attitudes and behaviour towards older people (Bytheway 1995). Describing health in old age poses difficulties at many levels, from its conceptual definition to identifying valid indicators. Minor complaints and chronic disorders have a high prevalence among older people. When people are asked to describe their own state of health or to describe a healthy person, they generally think of someone of about their own age. Younger people stress being physically active or the absence of symptoms, while 'older people [are] more likely to represent health as ... social functioning' or being active: 'health is described by phrases such as being happy, being unstressed and being able to cope' (Victor 1991: 97).

Health and Social Welfare in the Destination Countries

A frequent assertion by expatriates who move from Britain and northern Europe to the Mediterranean is that they feel healthier: some say they will live longer. These benefits are most often ascribed to the climate, the more active lifestyle, reduced stress, and the diet. It may be true that increased physical activity, more excursions, and new social activities characterise early retirement, but the resulting benefits could be enjoyed in Britain as well as southern Europe. Several factors can raise or lower survival in one region compared to another. The variations in the local complement of pathogens and toxins are commonly understood, as is the proficiency of the local medical services, from the diagnostic and prescriptive skills of primary care, through the ambulance and emergency services, to the quality of community nursing. If a region has poor stroke management services, then both the mortality and the disability rates from the condition will be relatively high. Two questions arise: firstly, do the environmental, lifestyle and medical service attributes of the Mediterranean countries produce a healthier setting than Britain and other northern European countries? Partial answers are provided by the comparative levels of life expectancy and mortality, although to examine 'healthiness' by studying deaths is never satisfactory. The second and far more difficult question is whether migrants from northern to southern Europe, particularly at the end of their working life, are affected by local epidemiological and health service conditions. Are the health advantages and disadvantages of a new area of residence overridden by the health and mortality risks that people have acquired earlier in their lives?

The epidemiological evidence does not show that Italy, Malta, Spain and Portugal have a uniform old-age mortality advantage over the United Kingdom (or indeed other northern European countries). Every one of the five countries has the highest and also the lowest death rate in at least one older age group for one major cause of death (Warnes 1999). Two contrasts warrant emphasis. Cardiovascular death rates among men are very much higher in Malta and the UK than in Italy, Portugal and Spain; and stroke death rates among men and the oldest women are exceptionally high in Portugal. In all the countries, old-age death rates have been changing rapidly, and we do not know the relative contributions of: childhood and adult lifestyles (notably tobacco consumption, nutrition and exercise); current lifestyles; and the effectiveness of a country's medical services. There is therefore no basis on which to argue that the mortality risks in any one of the five countries will be distinctly high or low over the next decade and beyond.

Turning to social welfare, by world standards, all western European countries have well-developed social security systems and health and social services, and the differences between north and south have narrowed during the last half-century. The reasons include the progressively closer economic and social interdependence of the western European nations, their membership of the European Union, and the consequential, and spontaneous, processes of convergence. Most EU countries, including Italy, Portugal and Spain, now have a national health service. Even countries outside the EU have elaborated recognisably similar systems. In Malta, for example, the new Republic of 1974 rapidly instituted a much more generous system of social security, and from 1987 it invested heavily in public health care.

The national 'welfare states' and systems of health services have developed in contrasting ways, some reflecting deep-seated cultural and political variations. Three models are frequently described (Esping-Andersen 1990; 1996). The *Nordic* model stresses 'social inclusion' and income support for all households, producing exceptional benefits for female-headed households and young adults. The model depends upon high labour-force participation among women and low private-sector supplementation of state income benefits and health care. The *Continental European* model organises state support largely through the full-time, long-term employed male householder, and has been generous neither to the unemployed nor to young independent or maternal females. Pensions are managed through employment-based social insurance schemes, with private-sector supplementation, and therefore produce greater income inequalities among older people than the Nordic schemes. A subdivision between the *Bismarckian* or Germanic and the *southern European* forms is sometimes made. In the former, a wide range of high-value social welfare benefits have been developed but there are fewer social services than in the Nordic group; in the latter, both services and benefits are relatively few but family support through co-residence and church-organised provision is comparatively high. The difference may be one of stage of development rather than principle. Italy is a special case, closer to the German model than its neighbours. The *Anglo-Saxon* model of Britain (and Canada, the United States and New Zealand) is distinguished by fewer (and reducing) entitlements during sickness, pregnancy, early retirement and disablement, and an increasing role for private sector insurance, particularly for pensions and health-care costs, with the state progressively targeting benefits and consolidating a 'safety net' rather than elaborating universal insurance schemes by which to raise the living standards of all.

The structure and comparative provision of the national systems of social security, health services and personal social services are of great significance to a retirement migrant. Young adult labour migrants may be most concerned with salaries, wage rates and housing costs but, as shown in Chapter 1, the quality of life of retired people, even the more affluent, is strongly influenced by government social expenditures (and related policies on the taxation of older people's and expatriate residents' income). Advanced age also brings relatively high rates of sickness and disorder, creating above average dependency on informal care and the formal health and social services (which in every country are substantially underwritten by public expenditure). Numerous factors therefore come into play in assessing the suitability of a nation for retirement residence, from personal taxation to the availability and quality of primary, hospital, community health and domiciliary social services.

There are additional complications across Europe today. Countries vary in the extent to which they allow the 'export' of the social security benefits to which a resident citizen is eligible. Characteristically, income benefits which are related to past earnings (and contributions) are payable to expatriate retirees, but not means-tested or special-needs income benefits (as for disability or to meet care costs), or those which meet housing or residential-care charges. As to health service entitlements, there are bilateral agreements which give the citizens of one country reciprocal rights of access in the other (although usually they are only partial). We now turn to the ways in which social security, health services and social care systems vary among the four IRM study countries and in comparison to the United Kingdom, and review the 'exportability' of social security and health-care entitlements from the UK to the southern countries and the regulations that those countries currently apply to foreign citizens of different residence status.

Italy

'Italy has a system of social protection which is a combination of employment-based insurance and universal provision, but where corporatism and patronage continue to play a large role' (Hantrais 1995: 222). These arrangements do not lead to well-developed income protection or health services for immigrant retirees of modest or average income. Even though Italian social expenditure during the 1960s was high by OECD standards, it was not until the late 1970s that the country adopted a universalist approach to the delivery of health care and extended its social security system to most groups in society (Niero 1996: 117). Partly to tackle a considerable problem of resources not being directed towards those most in need, in 1995 new legislation separated the state pension fund from all other social security payments (Brugiavini 1999; Europa Directories 1998: 1824).

The National Health Service, the *Sistema Sanitario Nazionale* (SSN), was implemented in 1980 to provide free health care as a 'constitutional right', although charges are made for essential medicines, medical examinations and hospital treatment. Initially local authorities were made responsible for providing hospital, primary care, psychiatric and public health services through an agency lacking budgetary constraints and directed by a political appointee. This did little either to control costs or to reduce the profound inequalities in provision and utilisation by region, by the rural-urban divide, and by educational and occupational groups. In 1986, Italy had 1,752 hospital establishments with 450,400 beds, one for every 79 people (Europa Directories 1998: 1824). Expenditure generally diminishes from north to south, while physicians and ancillary staff are insufficient in most Italian regions, one consequence being a strong 'sanitary migration' of patients from the south to northern hospitals (Palagiano 1994: 295), and another that Italy is by far the major importer of health-care services in the EC, the patients affected normally having to travel abroad (France 1997: 18). For those who can afford to pay or are well insured, the quality of medicine in the best northern Italian private hospitals is second to none. By the 1990s, Tuscany (5.1) and Umbria (5.2) had above the national average (4.7) number of doctors per 1,000 population, but contrasting ratios of hospital beds (8.1 and 6.0 respectively compared to 7.5 nationally).

Since its inception, the SSN has been stigmatised for its lack of quality: a *Eurobarometer Survey* of 1993 showed that among European citizens, the Italians were the least satisfied with their health services. It is for this reason that the controversial reform of the SSN in 1992 took place with 'total public indifference' (Niero 1996: 126-7). This reform will remove health service delivery from the local authorities, pass the responsibility to independent organisations similar to British NHS Trusts and, another obvious borrowing, reorganise the family doctor services into fund-holding practices. The reforms were accompanied by 'advice and recommendations' to promote reform of the 'geriatric care system', by establishing community-based geriatric evaluation units that, in collaboration with general practitioners, will allocate frail older people to integrated home-care, skilled nursing facilities, or long-stay geriatric wards. Among European countries, Italy has the lowest provision of nursing-home beds (24 per 1,000 people aged 65 years or more). Moreover, most 'provide a level of care closer to a board-and-care home than a skilled nursing facility' (Carbonin, Bernabei, Zuccalà and Gambassi 1997: 1520-1). The availability of home-care services is even lower than that of nursing-home beds, for long-term care is provided primarily by families or long-stay hospital beds.

Malta

The social security system of Malta is the responsibility of the Ministry of Labour and Social Services; there are flat-rate and earnings-related pensions, and the statutory retirement age is 61 years for men, 60 for women (Barnard 1993: 398). The Maltese health-care system has well-developed private and public sectors. The latter, the responsibility of the Ministry for Health, Care of the Elderly and Family Affairs, provides free hospital and community health services, and during hospitalisation medicines are also free. A person who suffers from one or more specified chronic diseases, e.g. rheumatoid arthritis, is entitled to receive free treatment irrespective of means (Clews 1998: 270). For most patients, however, drugs are highly priced because of the small total demand, agents' fees, and weak competition. At the end of 1995, there were 889 practising physicians, 603 in the government's employment.

As in Britain but unlike most countries, the primary health-care centres provide the normal point of first contact with medical services. There is however no binding registration system: patients move (and are allocated) from one doctor to another; and there are charges although in the public sector they are modest. In 1995, there were 7 health centres in Malta and one in Gozo, 41 satellite clinics in Malta and 12 in Gozo, and numerous pharmacies. Collectively they provide 24-hour general practitioner services, emergency and accident services, chiropody, diabetic and ophthalmic clinics, an emergency dental service, and physiotherapy. Malta's hospitals and particularly their specialist services have developed rapidly in recent years, but policies for the care and treatment of seriously dependent older people are in flux. In 1997 there were five public hospitals with 1,944 beds, and three private hospitals with 168 beds (Europa Directories 1998: 2256). There is a palliative care organisation but no hospice for terminally ill people. Nurse training has recently been upgraded but the status of the profession remains low. The St Vincent de Paule 'Residence' was established over a century ago as a workhouse and now has 1,100 places including some medical beds and staff for the long-term care of older people: it caters for both independent and chronically sick and bed-ridden residents. The islands' single consultant geriatrician operates from this complex and from Zammit Clapp Hospital, a modern geriatric assessment and medical rehabilitation unit with fifty beds, physiotherapists, occupational therapists, and social workers.

In 1987 the Secretariat for the Elderly introduced policies to support more older people in their own homes. All community nursing has been contracted to a long-established private organisation, the Malta Memorial District Nursing Association, and there are several other domiciliary services for older people. The home help and care service, with 2,066 clients in 1992, provides help with shopping, errands, bed making, laundry, ironing, house cleaning and personal care such as dressing and the preparation of meals (Garrett and Scerri 1994). A *Handyman* service carries out odd jobs for needy older people and there are meals-on-wheels. *Telecare*, a telephonic alarm system, provides emergency help and by 1993 was linked to 2,400 homes. Most of the domiciliary services are priced according to means but are subsidised. The first private sector sheltered homes were being built in 1996.

Portugal

Reflecting the recency of the country's modernisation, Portugal has the least well developed social welfare and health service systems of the IRM countries (a similar assessment would apply to Greece). Social security in Portugal is a relatively new concept originating in the constitution of 1976 and covering both contributory and non-contributory schemes, while health care is provided on a universal basis free of charge and administered by a national health service (Hantrais 1995: 226). A 1992 Eurobarometer attitude survey found that the Portuguese sample returned the highest percentage (73.7) who believed that 'pensions are too low and should be raised even if this means raising taxes' and the lowest percentage (2.4) who said that 'pensions are about right' (Walker and Maltby 1997: 62). Spending on public pensions was 6.1 per cent of GDP in 1994, well below the European average, although overall social security spending has recently increased more rapidly in Portugal than in the rest of the OECD (Terribile 1996: 38).

A national health service was created in 1979 but there are separate systems of health care for some occupational groups, provision is markedly poorer in rural areas, and patients have to pay, on average, 30 per cent of health-care costs (Williams 1993: 467). In 1990, the government approved new measures and increased spending on health care. By the end of 1995, Portugal had 40,548 hospital beds and there were over 29,000 physicians working in the country (Europa Directories 1998: 2773). Around 1990, 17 per cent of hospital beds were in the private sector. The number of physicians per 100,000 inhabitants increased from 228 in 1983 to 261 in 1988. In 1988 there were 147 general hospitals and 82 specialised hospitals, 371 health centres, and 2,450 pharmacies. The general standard of health facilities is significantly lower than in other western European countries and 'more on a par with some in eastern Europe' (Palagiano 1994: 293-4).

A comparison of general practitioner services in Portugal, six northern European countries and Israel found that exceptionally few Portuguese GPs participated in out-of-hours services or home visits (Wensing *et al.* 1998). As many GPs practise independently and few at multi-disciplinary health centres, visiting hours are commonly restricted, appointments systems crude, and waiting times long.

Spain

The Church and the family remained virtually the sole providers of social services in Spain until well into the 1970s, since when the role of state-organised social provision has rapidly grown. As recently as 1988, only 6 per cent of men aged 60 years or more lived alone, the lowest in western Europe (the comparable percentages for Italy, Germany and Denmark being 13, 15 and 20) (Dooghe 1991: Table 4.3). Several reasons for the perpetuation of multi-generational households can be advanced, including the persistence until recently of low incomes, Roman Catholic family values, and a large farm population. Until the demise of the Franco dictatorship, other important structural factors were the paucity of community health and social services and the weakness of pensions.

The changes in both social forms and social policy since the restoration of democracy have been substantial. The social welfare system that Spain is building follows the 'Continental European' model in that it is 'service-lean' but 'transfer-heavy' and benefits are most generous for those who have had full-time employment records. The pace of adjustment to new social and economic forms over the last thirty years has been impressive, particularly given the country's persistent economic difficulties. As their pensions have been largely unaffected by the cuts since 1985, older people have been the major beneficiaries of the expansion of social provision (Boldrin, Jimenez-Martin and Peracchi 1999). The 'grey vote' is, as in other Western countries, an increasingly important factor, as manifest in the 'Toledo Pact' of 1995 by which all the major political parties agreed not to make pensions a general election issue. Once elected Prime Minister in 1996, José María Aznar explicitly excluded pensioners' benefits from the proposals to reduce public spending (Ross 1997: 207).

Despite democratic Spain's economic weaknesses, a leading social policy achievement has been to raise the material standard of life of its older population. The next challenge will be to raise their quality of life, particularly for those with low incomes and without family carers. To date it has elaborated ambitious social service and community development policies but not achieved widespread implementation. The post-Franco local authorities quickly established domiciliary provision and, to support and co-ordinate these efforts, in 1978 the central government set up the National Social Services Agency. There are impressive programmes to develop residential homes, day centres and even supported vacations. Shortages of funds have retarded their growth and some programmes, such as 'vacations for third agers', are provided on a relatively small scale.

At the end of the Franco regime, while Spain had a system of compulsory health insurance that covered most families, medical facilities had fallen far behind western European standards. Only around a fifth of hospitals and clinics were in public hands, most being run by private organisations more or less directly linked to the Church. There was no established system of primary care (Ross 1997: 201, 204). While a Ministry of Health was created in 1977, fundamental reforms of the inherited system did not come until the 1986 General Health-Care Act, which created a National Health Service very much on the British model, decentralised the compulsory health insurance system (INSALUD) to the seventeen autonomous regions, and guaranteed the right to health care for all Spaniards and all foreign citizens resident in Spain. By the 1990s universality of provision 'free at the point of delivery' had effectively been achieved, although patients bear 40 per cent of the cost of prescriptions and there are charges for dental and psychiatric services. A massive hospital building programme has greatly reduced the importance of privately-run facilities, yet the latter still account for over 30 per cent of all hospitals and about 20 per cent of available beds (Ross 1997: 202). In 1995, there were 787 hospitals (of which 441 were private) with 168,000 beds, and 163,000 physicians worked in the country (Europa Directories 1998: 3016).

Despite these major achievements, the Spanish health service has substantial problems, such as long waiting lists for many types of treatment. There is a shortage of trained nurses and nursing auxiliaries, also insufficient hospital beds. The provision of acute beds is close to the EU average (3.5 per 1,000 population) but long-stay beds, especially for medical geriatric care, are in short supply. In addition, the available beds are unevenly distributed, being scarcer in rural areas and the south. Physicians are exceptionally concentrated in the large cities; 28 per cent of Andalusia's doctors work in Seville (Palagiano 1994: 294). There is a strong emphasis on hospital-based specialist care at the expense of primary and community care services. A significant reform of primary care services was, however, initiated in 1984, to introduce multi-disciplinary team practices at health centres (*centros de salud*), 'to increase accessibility, comprehensiveness, co-ordination of care and patients' satisfaction', and replace the 'solo practice and episodic care' previously provided from independent physicians' surgeries (Larizgoitia and Starfield 1997). The reform has advanced most in Spain's northern regions but, as we shall see, has also taken great strides in Andalusia. The local health centres remain underfunded by comparison with the hospitals, and suffer more from shortages of nursing staff; and too few newly-trained doctors wish to become GPs. The development of community health services during the 1980s was uneven, 'being the responsibility of the Autonomous Regions each of which produced their own legislation at different times' (Almeda and Sarasa 1996: 158). Home-care services are practically non-existent.

The European Union's Social and Welfare Policies

A recent influence upon the quality of life of a retired citizen of one EU member state who lives in another has been changes in their social security, social service and health service entitlements as a result of the European Union's developing social policies. At present most northern Europeans who contemplate moving to a southern European country or to another continent for retirement are not entirely reliant on social security pensions or benefits for their income. Nor will eligibility to such benefits, or their value, play much part in an individual's assessment of the advantages and disadvantages. Yet the quality of a country's (or region's) health services, the regulations governing eligibility and access to various services, and the charges that are levied, are very important. This generalised contrast requires two qualifications. A country's social security benefits for citizens and long-term or 'permanent' residents in the retirement age groups will affect many expatriate retirees after extended residence. This is because the real value of occupational pensions and dividends usually declines over time, savings are depleted, and commonly (in the present cohorts) a husband's death leaves his widow with a severely reduced income. The second qualification is for the future. The Commission of the European Union is keen to elaborate its 'social dimension' and to promote the convergence of social entitlements and health care. The agenda is long, and still focusses mainly on the labour force and people of working age, but some are already arguing that the principles should be extended to the 'economically unproductive' population. Why shouldn't a Dutch older person, the proponents argue, be supported in a nursing home in Spain rather than the Netherlands, especially if their quality of life is significantly raised and the costs of providing the care are lower? If such measures are introduced, there will be profound changes in the influences upon international migration by older people within Europe.

In 1989, the member states (apart from the UK) adopted the *Community Charter on the Fundamental Social Rights of Workers*, which included the following provisions on the protection of elderly people: 'every worker of the EU must, at the time of retirement, be able to enjoy resources affording him or her a decent standard of living', and 'any person who has reached retirement age but who is not entitled to a pension or who does not have other means of subsistence, must be entitled to sufficient resources and to medical and social assistance specifically suited to their needs' (Fontaine 1994: 43). Then, in 1990, the member states adopted directives which extended the right of abode (freedom of movement for residence) to students, unemployed people and retired workers 'who have a pension and health insurance or sufficient resources to prevent their becoming a charge on the host country during their stay' (Fontaine 1994: 39). Residence permits granted under these conditions are valid for five years and renewable. Under a European Economic Area (EEA) agreement, the EU regulations on social security apply to all EEA countries.

The signatories in Maastricht to the *Treaty on European Union* (excluding the UK) agreed a social policy based on the *Social Charter* and specified ways of its implementation, including the refined deference to national sovereignty in the social field through 'subsidiarity'. A key innovation of the Maastricht Treaty is that 'European Union citizenship' is conferred on everyone holding the nationality of a member state. The rights accorded are, firstly, to move and reside freely within the territory of the member states. Secondly, a citizen residing in a member state of which he or she is not a national has the right to vote and to stand as a candidate in local and European Parliamentary elections. Thirdly, every citizen is entitled to the diplomatic or consular protection of any member state in the territory of a non-member country if his or her country is not represented there (Fontaine 1994: 17). Alongside these fine words are deep reservations about the creation of a unified European 'social welfare space' (Van Kersbergen 1997: 6-7). Specific references to expatriate older people's rights are few but contain important provisions. Retired people may remain permanently in the member state in which they have worked, as long as they lived in the state for three years and worked there for twelve months. Another important general provision is that EU law guarantees equality of treatment for EU nationals as regards the ownership and use of property in member states other than their own (although there are restrictions in Italy, Greece and Spain regarding land in border areas).

Social security entitlements

Currently there are marked discrepancies among the EU nations in the formal provision of social security payments, public-sector medicine, and specific measures for older and disabled people (Hantrais 1995: 133-4). EU Regulations intend that people from every member state are treated equally and have their benefits rights protected so long as they are or have been (self) employed and are receiving benefit (Benefits Agency 1998: 2). They apply to nationals of any member country and to those who at some time have lived or worked in an EU country, to a stateless person or refugee who lives in an EU country, and to a dependant or widow(er) of anyone covered by the regulations. There are reciprocal arrangements between the UK and the other member states, except Greece on social security entitlements.

The explanations of social security entitlements, as set out in widely available leaflets from the UK Benefits Agency, convey the key points but characteristically become opaque on detail. Benefit entitlements depend upon an individual's contributions and, for a widow, her husband's contributions (or for a dependant, their supporter's). Each individual's entitlement has to be assessed, an inevitably intricate procedure which often takes many months. For those who have worked in more than one country, a separate assessment is made in each country. When these assessments are determined, then the international divisions of each country's

Table 7.1 Entitlement of UK citizens to health care in the four IRM countries, 1998

Service	Italy	Malta	Portugal	Spain
Information point	Local health unit or centre: *Unità Sanitaria Locale* (USL)	Area health centre (polyclinic)	Regional offices of National Health Service: *Administração Regional de Saúde*	District offices of the Social Security Institute: *Instituto Nacional de la Seguridad Social*
Procedure to access primary and emergency care	E111 to be exchanged for a USL certificate of entitlement	E111 does not apply. Bilateral agreement entitles visitors holding UK passport to urgent treatment at a polyclinic	E111 not required for UK visitors. Treatment available on production of passport at health centre: *Centro de Saúde*	Treatment under E111 only by NHS practitioners at a surgery (*consultoria*), health centre (*centro sanitaro*) or hospital clinic (*ambulatorio*)
Primary care and prescription charges	USL certificate reduces consultation and prescription fees	Visitors of up to 30 days are entitled to immediately necessary free treatment from a polyclinic or district dispensary	Consultation and prescription charges. Under EU agreements, basic hospital care is free but charges for secondary procedures	Prescriptions from any pharmacy, on payment of up to 40% of the cost except for EEA pensioners, for whom they are free
Hospital treatment	USL *proposta di recovero* certificate generally entitles holder to reduced cost treatment in certain hospitals	Visitors of up to 30 days are entitled to immediately necessary free medical treatment from a government hospital	E111 not required for UK visitors. Basic treatment free on production of passport but fees for secondary examinations and tests	Free treatment only in a public ward of a public hospital on admission as an NHS patient (photocopy of E111 required)
Notes	Some regions have few NHS facilities	Covered by bilateral, not EU/EEA, agreements	Few public sector facilities in Madeira or the Azores	Fewer public facilities in Balearic and Canary Islands

Source: Department of Health (1997).

social security agencies negotiate the aggregate entitlement and which countries will pay. In the UK, most of the additional benefits for low-income, retired, dependent and disabled people[1] have a residential quali-fication and are not payable to a citizen who has retired abroad – even a visit abroad can compromise a person's eligibility. In short, at present this group is strongly disadvantaged if they move from their home country to another EU state.

Health-care entitlements

Under EU reciprocal health-care arrangements, travellers from the UK are eligible to free or reduced-cost emergency medical treatment in all EEA countries, in most cases on production of a completed E111 form which is available from all UK post offices (Department of Health 1997). Within Europe but outside the EEA/EU, there are bilateral agreements with several countries including Malta. The specific arrangements with our four case-study countries are summarised on Table 7.1. Within Europe, there are no reciprocal agreements with Cyprus or Switzerland; and there are none with any African, continental American or Asian coun-try.

EU retirees are faced with a dilemma when they move to another mem-ber country, namely whether or not to declare themselves as permanently resident. The advantages and disadvantages of so doing are particularly difficult to estimate when the individual has properties in, or income from, more than one country, and when they spend substantial time in two or more countries. Whatever the optimal solution today, it can quickly be overturned by changes in national and international regulations or in the individual's circumstances. The principal factors to be considered are per-sonal and property taxation rates, health-care costs and social security entitlements.

The health-care element is complicated by country variations in a visi-tor's entitlements to urgent care, the relative availability and quality of public and private sector health care, the coverage that an individual holds through private insurance, and their health-care needs. Some coun-tries have more impelling rules and can apply them more effectively than others, e.g. among the four study countries, a long-term resident of Malta is least able to dissemble as a visitor because the islands have few entry points and vigilant immigration surveillance. The improving quality of the health services in Italy, Malta and Spain encourages northern European retirees to declare their permanent residence in the country. The stronger the perception of improvement, the greater the incentive to opt for the host country's NHS (as the expatriates become assessable for tax). Registration with the local NHS does however create a disadvantage when the individual either visits the UK (or another EU member state), or returns at short notice, for although he or she is entitled to NHS emer-gency treatment, they are disbarred from other UK NHS services. The EU territory is not yet a seamless health-care entitlement domain.

The most common resolutions of the health-care decision by UK retired people in southern Europe are presently that many young and healthy retired people do not declare as permanent residents. They retain their registration for UK NHS services, and rely on their private health insurance and entitlement to urgent treatment on the NHS. This stratagem is consistent with the age group's relatively numerous trips to and sojourns in the UK (and elsewhere). On the other hand, according to a British health-care expert whom we interviewed in Spain, the older age groups and those 'with a major health problem ... [tend to] go with the [local] NHS'. This decision is most common in Malta and Spain, while British retirees in Italy and Portugal make less use of those countries' public sector medicine, although in Italy at least a change is beginning.

The Well-Being of British Expatriate Retirees

The rest of this chapter focuses on the well-being of British retirees in the four study regions. It examines both the experience of overseas retirement and the participants' assessments of their chosen places and ways of life. Three kinds of information are compiled. First the responses to the self-completion questionnaire with explicit health content are examined, then selected evidence from in-depth follow-up and key informant interviews is presented by destination region, and finally a synthesis is constructed.

Although the self-completion questionnaire did not have targeted questions about the respondent's health or their use of health services, it gave many opportunities to refer to the health-related advantages, problems and disappointments of expatriate retirement, and these subjects were frequently mentioned. There is comparative information on the extent to which 'my or my partner's health' featured in the decision to live in Tuscany, Malta, Andalusia and the Algarve, and on the relative frequency of spontaneous reports of the health advantages that had been experienced. The antithesis of health is a health problem, to which people's reactions are much influenced by the advice and treatment they receive, so the spontaneous and structured assessments of the quality of the health services are of great interest.

As was explained in Chapter 5, pp.93-6, among the *first* reasons given for moving to the retirement area, 'for my (or another's) health' ranked in second place, being volunteered by 9.9 per cent of the 925 respondents who gave any reason. Several surveys have found that the predominant response to this question is 'the climate': it was given by 38.2 per cent of our respondents (and other environmental reasons by 2.2 per cent): see Table 5.1. The questionnaire provided eight opportunities to give *other* reasons for retiring to the area. Across these, nearly a fifth (19.0 per cent) of the respondents mentioned that they 'felt or were healthier'.

What is meant, and what lies behind, the dominating prevalence of references to the favourable climate? The most appreciated elements are the mildness, sunshine and relative dryness of the winters, including the absence of frosts – the general effect is liberating and cheering. The Mediterranean winter climate not only allows but encourages people to be active out-of-doors; which for a few means golf, tennis or adventurous rambles, and for many more means meals on the patio, leisurely sight-seeing or shopping, and meeting friends by the harbour or at a club. The heat of summer is appreciated by some but not others, but is a minor qualification for the hundreds of our informants who were clear that the climate raised their morale. The Costa del Sol produced the highest relative frequency of 'for my health' main reasons for the move and Tuscany the lowest, and there were even stronger differentials in the shares who made favourable references to the climate (Table 5.2). The relative frequency of such main reasons in the two Iberian regions was five times higher than in Tuscany. Although the percentage giving accolades for Malta's climate was closer to the Iberian than the Tuscan level, the share of its respondents citing the climate as a reason for moving was significantly below the figures for the Algarve and the Costa del Sol.

The questionnaire produced two other frequently mentioned reasons for the move that have lifestyle and well-being connotations. The 'pace-of-life' was rarely mentioned as a main reason for moving but was spontaneously offered as a subsidiary reason by a quarter of the respondents. The share giving this answer in Tuscany was significantly lower than in the two Iberian areas, and the Maltese share was closer to the Tuscan than the Iberian score. Finally, the ability to pursue outdoor activities was mentioned as a reason for moving by 7.6 per cent of the respondents, but by many fewer in Tuscany than in all other areas. Elsewhere on the questionnaire, the respondents were asked to mention up to four advantages that they had experienced since their retirement move. Nearly half (47.4 per cent) volunteered a health-related reason, ranging from 57 per cent in the Algarve, to 39 per cent in Malta.

It will be remembered that the respondents were also invited to nominate particular problems that they had experienced while in the country (pp. 122-3). Table 5.9 set out the first-ranked disadvantages; Table 7.2 includes all mentions of health problems. Just over 15 per cent mentioned health services, with considerable variation among the four countries. The share mentioning such problems in the Algarve (31.9 per cent) was significantly higher than in any other, while the share in Tuscany was nearly double that in Malta and Spain. Fuller assessments come from two questions which asked the respondents to compare the quality of health services in the UK with where they lived, one with reference to primary and community services, the other to hospital services. Remarkable differences among the four retirement areas were produced (Table 7.2). More than half (51 per cent) of the respondents on the Costa del Sol rated Spanish hospital services as superior to the British, but only 1.1 per cent in the Algarve gave the equivalent opinion. Five in six of the Algarve respondents indicated that Portuguese hospitals were worse than the

Table 7.2 Assessments of local health services (%)

Characteristic	Tuscany	Malta	Costa del Sol	Algarve	All
States health services as problem	16.5	9.3	9.0	31.9	15.3
n =	104	271	337	217	929
Hospital services are better than UK	14.6	16.4	51.0	1.1	25.4
Hospital services are worse than UK	50.0	43.4	13.0	83.7	42.3
n =	82	230	300	190	802
Primary/community care are better	16.5	22.7	31.7	1.6	20.3
Primary/community care are worse	46.8	34.1	32.7	87.4	48.0
n =	79	220	290	191	780

Source: Authors' survey.

British, but only 13 per cent on the Costa del Sol saw Spanish hospitals that way. Maltese and Italian hospital services were rated between these extremes (the scores being significantly different from both). In Tuscany, one half of those who made the comparison rated Italian hospitals as worse. The comparative assessments are consistent with the strengths and weaknesses of hospital services among the four countries described earlier in the chapter. Opinions about the quality of local primary and community care services had a similar pattern and were only slightly less polarised. The Spanish services came out very well and the Portuguese very badly. The main changes were that the rating of Malta's services rose from near the Italian towards the Spanish level. Over all four areas rather more thought these services 'worse' and a smaller share gave 'better' ratings. The principal influence on all these comparisons is the very high positive ratings of hospital services in Spain.

Many of the in-depth interviews included accounts of episodes of ill-health that required treatment from local doctors and hospitals, and several key informant interviews were arranged with managers and practitioners in medicine, nursing, and residential and palliative care. Interviews with ministers of religion and officials of British residents' clubs, among others, added to the information on the expatriate retirees' health and well-being. Here we highlight the repeated and strongest expressions of their experiences. Reactions of course varied. There was much praise for the skills of medical professionals and for the time and consideration they gave, the latter often being compared favourably with actual contacts or assumed practice in the UK. More generalised plaudits were relatively common for the Costa del Sol's hospitals, and in Malta for the primary care centres and community nursing. There were also many complaints, but as often astonishment, frustration and a lack of understanding of the different organisation and customs of medical services in the interviewee's adopted country. Not knowing what is and is not provided leads to surprise and disappointments, which then circulate and produce generalised anxieties. These most commonly concerned hospital nursing and follow-up care. The respondents' comments are presented sequentially for each country, beginning with those from southern Spain.

The Costa del Sol

Positive experiences of hospital treatment in Spain and the visible investments in modern (and luxurious) facilities are creating a favourable impression among the expatriate community:

> The Spanish hospitals are very good. They have first class equipment.

> The health system is so much better here [and] the hospital in Marbella is excellent. The doctors arrive very promptly if you call them and health insurance is cheap.

The improvements in the Spanish NHS services and the opening of the Costa del Sol hospital in 1993 have encouraged many older British residents to declare as permanent residents and to cede their UK health service entitlements (Elliott 1995: 28). The trend is likely to continue, especially if the planned improvements in the primary care service are realised. The Autonomous Region of Andalusia aims to establish a *centro de salud* in every main settlement (one for every 10,000 inhabitants). They will offer general practice services, a 24-hour emergency service and advanced diagnostic facilities. When British-origin residents register with the Spanish NHS, they hold a red card, the *tarjeta sanitaria*, which declares their entitlement to the national health services administered by the *Servicio Andaluz de Salud*. Some direct experiences were related to us:

> I got *pensionista* status in 1989 when I arrived here permanently, not on age grounds but because I was on invalidity in England. I went to the Social Security Office and handed in our E121s and while we waited the papers were filled in and we became *pensionistas*. We are better off here – we don't pay for prescriptions.

> I am a resident here and automatically entitled to free treatment. I now go to a rheumatologist here who deals with my arthritis. The results of the X-rays come through quickly and you get a thorough examination. They never get irate even though everything needs to be translated to you. They are so patient with you.

One quotation refers to the common difficulties that British residents have in their medical contacts and consultations because they do not understand Spanish:

It is not so good being here when you fall ill. One point is the problem of language. One woman had to make an appointment back in the UK as she couldn't find any interpreters when she went to the doctors.

This issue prompted a doctor at a Benalmádena health centre to carry out a 'satisfaction survey' of the expatriate patients which demonstrated a high level of concern about the translation issue. This led Charles Betty, a British retired local resident, to establish a volunteer interpreter service. 'He has real dynamism and his activities stretch from Fuengirola to Estepona and Torremolinos' (Elliott 1995). In 1997, there were 'twelve unpaid interpreters who between them speak Spanish, English, Dutch, French, Italian and German [and to date] 80 per cent of the foreigners seeking assistance from the service have been British people aged at least 60 years' (Betty 1997). There are also an increasing number of translators working in the Costa del Sol's hospitals.

We heard many complaints about hospital nursing and the lack of follow-up or 'after-care'. The problems are both the virtual absence of community health services and poor communication between hospital consultants and the health centre or private 'family doctors' (for primary care has not been the customary gateway for specialist care). A procedure nominally exists for a patient who requires home support and treatment to be placed by a hospital social worker into a nursing home or the care of local authority social services. In most cases, however, an expatriate patient is discharged into the care of their family or, in serious cases, their general practitioner.

Many people here are worried about after-care and nursing. Traditional Spanish attitudes are that the family and friends will look after them [in hospital]. There has not been good training for nurses because of that attitude but it is now improving. For instance, at one time there were no visiting hours because families could come in at any time of the day or night... Now they are starting visiting hours.

I was [in] a little ward with four others, and there was no real nursing back-up. In the rooms here there are fold-up beds which your relations can use and stay overnight. The relations do most of the work of looking after you.

Several of the issues feature in the 'case study' presented in Box 7.1. This shows the interactions between three ingredients that make for satisfactory or unsatisfactory care: (a) the British resident's expectations of the local health services and of their insurance coverage; (b) the absence of a standard (and known) procedure for determining the respective roles of the primary and hospital services and the public and private sectors; and (c) hospital policies and practice with respect to admissions, the supply of nursing and non-medical services, and the provision of information to the patients and their relatives. The account features a woman in her late eighties who was living with her daughter and son-in-law. They were willing to pay for private health insurance but as their mother was registered with the Spanish NHS, believed that its services would meet her medical needs. In a strict sense, it did, but a great deal of discontent was produced by the small attention that the system gives to nursing care and to the forms of patient-centred attention that are taken for granted in the United Kingdom.

Box 7.1 Two confused hospital episodes on the Costa del Sol

This 1996 interview was with a lady aged 64 years and her mother (89 years) who moved to the Costa del Sol from London in 1988 with the daughter's husband. The mother was registered as a permanent resident and was therefore entitled to all Spanish NHS services, but they also had a range of private health insurances. The mother fell over in the town and broke her hip. She was taken by ambulance to three hospitals. The daughter explained, 'at the first hospital she was asked to show evidence of insurance, and they sent someone to the house to collect my papers. Because she didn't have insurance for the clinic, she was taken to another hospital where she stayed six hours, and then to the third where they deal with fractures.' The mother said, 'they couldn't do the operation for 10 days because of the trauma. I had a private room for two, and a Spanish lady was in the next bed: her daughters looked after me at night – this was very kind.' The daughter continued, 'she then had the operation and you couldn't fault them on the medical side. But they left her lying in bed too long ... [and] started physiotherapy far too late. They left her sitting on the side of the bed – these things are not right here. In the end, two porters literally dropped her into the bed (they are the equivalent of male nurses). The Spanish daughters just looked after her for things like bedpans. They are under-staffed here and the nurses are not the same as they are in the UK. When she came home, she was very dehydrated and there was no follow-up.'

Much later the mother broke her other hip. The daughter explained: 'We rang the helicopters and they took her to the hospital she had been in before. They said they didn't have a casualty department. Then she was told she didn't have a fractured hip – they had X-rayed her knee. I spoke in Spanish, but of course it wasn't fluent. They ended up by sending her to another hospital ... where she spent two weeks and they said she had a bad chest. Then they said they would send her to another clinic. When she moved I stayed to look after her. The nurses bring the meal in on a tray and leave it on the table: you bring it to the patient. Eventually the operation was done but after one delay after another ... the medical care was fine, it was just that the nursing side was bad.'

It may seem unusual for the married couple to have health insurance but not the mother in her eighties. The explanation was given later: the mother had permanent residency and therefore was entitled to Spanish NHS services 'as a *pensionista*'. But the household also had miscellaneous insurance, and this complicated the care.

Malta

The concerns of the Malta respondents were similar to those in Spain except that language was hardly an issue. The accounts reflect the country's more comprehensive network of health centres than are yet established on the Costa del Sol, and contain much appreciation of the islands' well-developed community nursing service. The following are *verbatim* extracts from the in-depth interviews with retired British residents in Malta and Gozo:

> I find my doctor quite wonderful – he has absorbed me into his family. Hospital services are excellent here.

> The Cancer Department here was superb and I find Maltese doctors first class.

As on the Costa del Sol, the praise was qualified by complaints about nursing, the cost of medicines, and the quality of hospital 'hotel services'. There were more references to the absence, until the last few years, of specific specialties and procedures in the hospitals:

> There is a lack of equipment and nursing here but they are now forging ahead. The treatment is good but medication is very expensive.

> People seem to think the doctors here are as good as in the UK. But the standard of nursing training is very low.

There were many appreciative comments about the Malta Memorial District Nursing Association's care:

> The nurses visit or do whatever is needed, such as bathing, insertion of eye-drops, even help get people out of bed. Whether this is done daily depends on availability. All that is needed is that the doctor will leave a note to the nurse as to what is needed by the patient.

One respondent had made good use of the *Telecare* service described earlier, but a second was less than clear about what it offered:

> My son insisted that I should get *Telecare* as I am 70 and live alone. It's a phone. If I bang the red button, a doctor, the police and the ambulance would arrive. There are two specialist buttons as well for certain services. I don't even need to lift the handset to operate those buttons. They also give you a device which you wear around your neck and you press it for help. It is absolutely fabulous. I have already used the emergency button... I've told other people about it but they are not too interested – there are not many single people who I know.

> There is another system where elderly people wear something around their neck and help always arrives.

A case study from a couple who are both qualified nurses and who moved to Malta in 1990 when in their early sixties is presented in Box 7.2. After their move, the husband worked as a surgical theatre nurse in St Luke's Hospital, a shortage of specialist nurses enabling the required work

Box 7.2 A couple's assessments of Maltese health services

The opening quotations are from the wife who explained that while shopping in Valletta she had a fall. 'Everyone rushed to help me. We went to St Luke's and they put an ice pack on my ankle and X-rayed... Ten days later I had to return for more treatment, and I called the community nursing service [MMDNA] the night before. I found them very good. We pay only £1 annual subscription because we belong to the British Residents' Association.' At the hospital, 'the doctor put on a full plaster ... he was a consultant surgeon: excellent treatment.'

On his 18 months' experience in the hospital operating theatre, the husband said, 'the standard of care was equal to anything in the UK, but after-care is a problem... In the hospitals here we have rest rooms and the surgeons would have a coffee with the nurses and discuss the operations beforehand ... it does improve working relationships. There is however limited choice [of hospitals and specialists] unless you are prepared to pay.' The couple believed that 'the primary health-care and community services are in some ways better [than in England]. My mother-in-law came over and was badly bitten by mosquitoes. We took her to the doctor and she was seen immediately, and when later I called him late one Sunday night he came to our home within 15 minutes. When I apologised for calling him late he said, "I am a doctor and it's my job to come and see you. Send for me at any time." ... The doctors have time to talk to you in Malta.' Overall, the couple believed that if the Maltese nursing services and the facilities were 'brought up to scratch', the health services would be absolutely first class.

The couple do not have private health insurance, and when asked if the UK-Malta reciprocal arrangements helped them, said, 'it doesn't work, well, only one way. People from England get hospital treatment free of charge, but when my wife's plaster was to be removed, it was the day after we flew to England.' Their Maltese doctor gave them a copy of the note he had sent to the hospital in England. We were told that 'as we had been living abroad for more than 6 months, we would be charged £50, with extra for any X-rays... They said the reciprocal agreement didn't apply unless I was receiving a disability pension, was on social security or serving in the Forces. That's the reciprocal agreement for you!'

permit. Added to these insights, the wife experienced the hospital and community nursing services as a patient, and both had made use of the local primary care centre. Their assessments of the Maltese health services are unusually well informed by a 'system view'.

Tuscany

Our respondents in Tuscany and Umbria on the whole made similar comments to their counterparts in Spain and Malta. Their assessments of the physician and hospital services were more variable however, expressing both high praise for the 'centre of excellence' hospitals and deep disgust with the quality of nursing care. Many more were exercised to find the best tactics for utilising the Italian public and private sectors, and rather more made use of services in the UK and other countries (Switzerland and

Germany were mentioned). Several, for example, continued to have all their dental treatment in England. There was a kaleidoscope of opinions:

> We have good doctors here and yet ... if I became ill, I would want to go back to England.

> I'm happy with the health services here; they are certainly more prompt. It is different here, as I saw the specialist privately. There was no delay in getting into [the private] hospital.

> We really are worried about the health situation in Italy as I have been in hospital in Italy and it really is very frightening in many ways. That is the only area of worry which I have here.

> The doctors are good in town hospitals but not in country areas. In Venice, Ancona or Padua, the expertise and apparatus is as good as any in London ... but that's a long way to go.

Several respondents were making use of the Italian NHS for both primary care and hospital treatment. One respondent with a nursing background found the services straightforward to use, but some were confused about their entitlements and how the system operated:

> Yes, I have been very happy [to have] had everything done on the National Health. They took me to hospital immediately in Viareggio and I was put in intensive care. They took immensely good care of me and I was very impressed ... I think the much-maligned Italian health service is quite good.

> I have found it quite clear. You go to your local doctor and if you need to see a specialist, you make an appointment as you would do at home. If you need emergency treatment, you are taken to hospital and you do not need to pay... Essentially, you can take advantage of what there is locally.

> I'm a bit unsure of what one should pay for here. We don't really understand. There are some things we find difficult after the UK. We assumed the service was totally free as in the UK. It is not. Some things you pay for and some things you don't.

There were no comments about community health services (there are none). The strongest echoes of Spain and Malta were the amazement and concern about hospital nursing:

> Here the families are expected to sleep in the hospital ... because there is no one else. The Italians like being present, of course. But as a foreigner without an extended family, it is very alarming.

> When my husband went to hospital, it was as if Italy was 30 years behind England in hospital care. The nursing was bad – I was a British nurse who didn't want to threaten them – but I had battles in every way possible to get my husband better care in the hospital.

The Algarve

The comments from the interviewees in the Algarve had several distinctive themes: heightened awareness of the limitations of the local hospitals and the need to travel to Lisbon (or the UK) for specialised treatment; awareness of inconsistency in the type and quality of general practitioner (family doctor) services; and recognition of the importance, compared to the other study areas, of private consultations for both primary care and hospital treatment. There were also many more references to the services provided locally by British, German and other foreign physicians. The in-depth interviews amply confirmed the concerns with the local health-care system that were revealed by Table 7.2.

As indicated by the comparative audit of services, the Algarve's health-care services do not yet provide a well-integrated service, partly because the Portuguese NHS reforms are in their early stages, and partly because the region is both peripheral and neglected by the medical profession. The situation is however changing, and multi-disciplinary primary health-care centres are opening, so some positive comments were heard among a litany of complaints:

> We belong to the *Caixa*, the state system – national health. The general practitioners are awful. They are never there when you want them; you can't get prescriptions.

> The doctor in this country is a demi-God and you do what he says, without asking questions. The system is less well funded and more old-fashioned than at home... The local health centres ... can't afford to pay doctors and nurses.

> A lot of people choose to use the Portuguese public health system [and attend] the health centres. There is a lot of waiting time ... especially in the larger centres. The national health service is good and I was twice in the Portimão Hospital. I found the service was very good.

The interviewees' understanding of the limitations of the health-care system in the Algarve and the need for more serious conditions to be treated in Lisbon and the United Kingdom is redolent more of the colonial era than of harmonised European provision. Such expressions are leavened by the observation of a medical 'key informant' that attitudes in the Algarve are slow to recognise the widening range of specialties in local hospitals:

> He diagnosed cancer and sent me to Lisbon which was the only place [in 1992] where you could get radiotherapy.

> If I had to have cardiac surgery, I would go home for it. But for less than that, I would stay.

> We now have a new hospital but ... there is no blood bank in the Algarve [and] no intensive care. The quality of nursing in the Lisbon hospitals ... isn't too bad.

The [national health] hospital at Faro has improved beyond recognition: experienced surgeons and good equipment ... [and] the nursing has changed completely.

Limited trust in the local health-care system appears to be a foundation for the relatively widespread opinion that residence in the Algarve becomes problematic in advanced old age and for those with a chronic or serious condition.

Health services and well-being

The evaluations about health and social services across the destination regions have four main elements: praise for some hospital and primary care physicians, frequent references to language difficulties, common amazement about the relative scarcity of in-hospital nursing care, community health services and 'after care', and the universal concern about the cost and quality of life in residential and nursing homes. The distaste and anxieties about hospital nursing have three elements. Firstly, the language differences in Italy, Spain and Portugal make rare both friendly and professional conversations with the nurses. Secondly, 'holistic care' simply is not practised; and thirdly, the expectation is that relatives will provide the non-medical care of patients while in hospital. This not only presents practical and quite often insoluble problems for an elderly single person or couple who have no relatives in the country, it also means that some behaviour on the hospital ward is viewed by many older British people as more appropriate to a private bedroom than a public institution. Many expatriate retirees are poorly prepared and quite simply shocked by the lack of privacy and the intrusions during their most private acts at times of vulnerability. It is well documented in Britain that a large proportion of frail older people find help with toileting and bathing more acceptable from a professional and qualified carer than from a close relative: to receive such help from an unqualified stranger, with whom they cannot converse, is for some people no less than repulsive.

To allay their sometimes misplaced but usually prudent concerns, the British (and other) expatriate retiree communities adopt several stratagems. At a general level they are well informed about the need for, and coverage provided by, health insurance, through both the informal dissemination of experience and the more systematic advice of the Residents' Associations, as most clearly seen in Malta and the Algarve. In detail, however, not only does the nature of risk-avoidance actions make 'optimal coverage' a chimera, but an individual's decisions are confounded by two forms of rapid change: the rapidity of public health reforms and their unpredictable rate of implementation; and the complexity and volatility of the private insurance market. International, UK and local companies vie for trade, offer a bewildering range of policies, indulge in abrupt price changes, and are taken over. Several of our respondents had been insured with companies that had gone into receivership.

Table 7.3 Possession and coverage of private health insurance by country (%)

	Tuscany	Malta	Spain	Portugal	All
Possesses health insurance	45.0	61.2	56.1	69.7	59.5
Coverage:					
Hospital care costs locally	36.7	34.5	56.4	60.6	48.7
Hospital care costs in UK	32.1	26.7	34.4	56.6	37.0
Cost of travel to UK for treatment	12.8	8.5	15.0	24.9	15.2
Nursing home fees locally	25.7	24.9	27.2	31.2	27.3
Nursing home fees in UK	23.9	13.9	15.3	30.8	19.4
No health insurance	55.0	38.8	43.9	30.3	40.5

Source: Authors' survey.

Given the rapid improvement of Spain's hospital services, the growth of national health provision in Italy, Spain and Portugal, and the development of reciprocal agreements with the United Kingdom, one problem for the expatriate retiree is what private health insurance coverage to take out. The Costa del Sol representative of BUPA International, Ronald Elliott, who has written an informative guide to health-care services on the coast (Elliott 1995), believes that out-dated attitudes 'go back to the days when many Brits lived in Africa and were offered policies that covered flights back home for treatment. Obviously in parts of Africa, there is no treatment ... [but] in Spain, you can receive high standard treatment for just about any medical complaint. It's a personal decision, but you can over-insure' (personal interview, 1996).

Around 60 per cent of the respondents to the questionnaire survey reported that they had private health insurance (Table 7.3). The commonest form, held by nearly half of the respondents, was coverage for hospital treatment in the country of residence (the range of treatment was not specified). More than a third (37 per cent) had coverage for UK hospital treatment, but only 15 per cent had policies that covered the travel costs. Coverage of nursing home fees was less common (and neither the circumstances nor duration were specified). Just over a quarter (27 per cent) had coverage of the fees in local nursing homes. The variations among the four countries were not great. The Algarve respondents were the most likely to have private health insurance and coverage for all five of the itemised services. Respondents in Tuscany had the lowest share with health insurance, but their policies must be relatively comprehensive compared to those held by the Maltese respondents, for a greater proportion had coverage in each of the five fields. A significantly lower share of the Costa del Sol than the Algarve sample had private health insurance, and the strongest differential among the specific forms of coverage was for hospital charges in the United·Kingdom. The least variation was in the coverage of local nursing home fees, while in the Algarve the share with coverage of UK nursing home fees was significantly higher than in either Malta or Spain.

Another interesting response is various voluntary association initiatives to fill the gaps in local health and care systems and to introduce new forms of provision. Most of the residents' and church-based associations have primarily social and religious objectives but some had taken on a welfare role, which was usually restricted to information exchange, advocacy and discrete surveillance. In exceptional circumstances they would summon and orchestrate help for others but normally, and rationally, the members drew back from the direct provision of care. The elaboration of help with language interpretation has moved beyond random neighbourly help to various levels of systematic organisation in many expatriate retirement communities besides the example described in Benalmádena (O'Reilly, 2000). In a few places, the scope of active community concern is wider. The British Residents' Association in Malta established a 'welfare section' in 1971. Its activities have divided between advocacy and representation to the Maltese authorities, and 'playing an active role in making sure that everyone is cared for'. They have a bank of wheelchairs and prosthetics for people with impaired functions, and visit members and non-members who are ill or housebound.

The custom and expectation of family care in southern Europe under-lies not only the marked differences in hospital and community nursing practice but also makes palliative care and hospices an alien tradition. The lack is keenly appreciated in the expatriate community. It has led some nursing homes to develop expertise in this form of care, but the most interesting developments have been on the Costa del Sol. In 1990 an enterprising clinical group opened a palliative care unit of twelve beds at the NHS Red Cross Hospital in Málaga, since when it has provided great-ly appreciated care for terminally ill expatriates (and Spanish people) who were unable or unwilling to return to their country or place of origin. The initiative has indirectly stimulated a hospice movement around Fuengirola. The *Asociación para Cuidados del Cáncer* (Association for Cancer Care, or CUDECA) was founded in 1991 by a British woman, Joan Hunt, following the Red Cross Hospital's terminal care of her husband (Hunt and Martin 1997). Its activities have burgeoned: during 1992-3, a volunteer home-care team cared for 29 patients; from 1994 a professional team looked after 49, 74 and 118 patients in successive years; and in 1997 and 1998 two full professional teams cared for more than 150 patients. CUDECA has more than 450 volunteers, many of whom work in the charity's shops (nine in 1999). For those who assist in home care, careful selection and nine months' training and probation are applied. By 1998, CUDECA claimed that through collaboration with the hospital oncological services, health centres, emergency services, and the Palliative Care Unit, 'we hope [soon to] take care of the needs of almost all the population of Málaga [province]'.

An interesting feature of this initiative, British in origin but developed by retired people from many northern European countries, the Americas and the Antipodes, is that it has attracted the active support of local Spanish doctors, priests, political organisations and agencies. Remarkably, the charity received exceptional help from not only local lawyers in drafting its articles of association, but also managed to register as a charity – approval of the Statutes was gained from Madrid 'in record time'. In 1995 the Benalmádena municipality donated the land for a hospice, construction began in April 1998, and some administrative rooms are now functioning. There will be twelve beds, a day hospital, a home-care centre, consultation rooms, a training centre, and administration, fund-raising and service departments. CUDECA is thriving through a productive collaboration between a dedicated group of British expatriates and Spanish physicians, with support from the wider expatriate and Spanish communities.[2] The fund-raising activity, so much a part of its success, is supported by charity shops, dinners and fêtes. Its success is undoubtedly associated with the awesome need that it seeks to meet and with which all expatriates and many Spanish citizens can identify. The fact that several of the elderly volunteers have themselves become patients illustrates how appropriate the association's goals are to the community's needs.

Variations in well-being

This section focuses on the net advantages and disadvantages and overall well-being that are associated with overseas residence in later life. Its aim is to synthesise, by some complex data-processing presented in a relatively simple table and an equally simple diagram, some of the dimensions of well-being differentiated by destination region and by other respondent characteristics.

To build an understanding of the personal implications of retiring abroad, we return to the several linked decisions involved in moving to another country: when to retire, which country and region to move to, what kind of property to secure, the selection of a particular dwelling, who forms the household, whether or not to retain one or more properties elsewhere, and if so, how to divide time among them. Chapter 5 has analysed the evidence collected on the self-completion questionnaire about these decisions. As we have seen, 'the climate' dominated the replies, followed by two facets of a better lifestyle, 'the slower pace of life', and 'feel or am healthier here'. The expressed reasons for moving or living abroad for later life include factors of all the principal dimensions of well-being described in the theoretical and 'indicators' literature. Material, family and social advantages predominate, while references to civic issues, including political rights, discrimination, personal security and business ethics (or corruption) are not rare. Status and power considerations were occasionally expressed, as in references to the opportunities to hold executive positions in British retiree organisations. Several of the most prevalent reasons span two or more of the material, social,

Table 7.4 Expressed advantages, problems and disappointments in the study areas

Area	Percentage expressing at least one factor in the category				
	Financial	Civic & Legal	Lifestyle	Social	Services
A. Advantages					
Tuscany	34	2	78^m	10	1
Malta	47	4^c	65^{tca}	11	2
Costa del Sol	41	1^m	82^m	6	1
Algarve	39	2	90^m	8	0
All	42	2	78	8	1
B. Better than expected					
Tuscany	4	8^m	42	9^a	12
Malta	1	0ta	29^c	16	13
Costa del Sol	2	2	43^m	19	13
Algarve	2	6^m	38	24^t	14
All	2	3	38	18	13
C. Problems					
Tuscany	24^m	4	12^m	47^m	60^{mca}
Malta	43^{tca}	7	25^{tc}	21^{tca}	28ta
Costa del Sol	18^m	7	8ma	61^m	36ta
Algarve	21^m	7	23^c	57^m	76^{tmc}
All	27	6	17	46	46
D. Disappointments					
Tuscany	5^m	5^a	7ma	19	18
Malta	18^t	4^a	18^{tc}	9^{ca}	16
Costa del Sol	10	3^a	6ma	23^m	13^a
Algarve	10	12^{tmc}	19^{mc}	28^m	25^c
All	12	6	13	20	17

Source: Based on data from Authors' survey.
Notes: Sample sizes are Tuscany 109, Malta 281, Costa del Sol 346 and Algarve 221.
The lifestyle dimension includes references to climate and physical environment.
Superscripts t, m, c and a indicate that the percentage is significantly different
(p<0.05) from the value for, respectively, Tuscany, Malta, the Costa del Sol and the
Algarve.

health, psychological, and civic dimensions of life, with 'admiration of country', 'for a better life', and 'the climate' being unusually equivocal. But a majority of the answers fall clearly into one of the dimensions, and this taxonomy is employed in the comparative analysis which follows.

The four sets of evaluative responses (on reasons, advantages, problems and disappointments) have been coded into the material, social, instrumental, civic and lifestyle dimensions of well-being. The percentages of respondents in the four study areas who stated at least one reason in each category are compared in Table 7.4. Malta produced the most distinctive replies, with relatively frequent mentions of financial problems, disappointments and advantages. This may well be because in Malta there is a relatively large proportion of retirees in the oldest age groups and with relatively low incomes. They also made the fewest references to environmental and lifestyle advantages and unanticipated benefits, complemented by significantly frequent references to problems and disappointments in this category. On their social life, they made frequent references to advantages and few to problems and disappointments. Given the above-average complement of family-orientated retirement migrations to the Maltese islands, a high proportion knew what kind of social life they would join.

The Tuscan respondents reported significantly low frequencies of financial benefits, problems and, most of all, disappointments, but consistently positive civic and lifestyle evaluations. Their only significant negative evaluation concerned instrumental services. Respondents from the Costa del Sol gave distinctive evaluations in the civic, lifestyle, social and services domains. Most exceptional were the scarcity of reported problems and disappointments with the lifestyle and the environment, and few complaints about domestic, retail and transport services. They mentioned more unanticipated lifestyle benefits than respondents elsewhere. The Algarve produced a distinctive array of complaints, with high frequencies in the civic, lifestyle, social and instrumental-services domains.

The evaluative questions described and analysed above were complemented by the following items in the self-completion questionnaire:

- specific questions on the number and agreeableness of overnight visitors to the home, and on the use of social clubs (analysed in Chapter 6);
- seven questions which requested of respondents a rating of housing costs, various medical services, and their social life in their adopted residential area as compared to the United Kingdom; and
- questions about whether the subject would stay, move locally, return to the UK or move elsewhere in response to nine adverse and positive events, e.g. a health change, bereavement, or winning £100,000.

An aggregate well-being measure has been developed by summing: (a) the number of cited advantages and benefits (positive) and problems and disappointments (negative), (b) the 'better' or 'worse' ratings of social life, hospital services and community health services, and (c) the responses to the hypothesised events, to stay or move locally (positive), or to return to the UK (negative). The range of the aggregate scores was from -19 to +20 and the mean was +5.4.[3] Few systematic variations in well-being by personal or household characteristics were found, and none by age, sex, marital status, education, former occupation and employment status, or current household size or tenure were significant. Nor did language competence, prior residence abroad, or prior connections to the area produce significant differences. It was found however that well-being associated strongly with destination-specific problems, as with the local language and health services, but these variables are components of the regional well-being indicator (Figure 7.1) and the relationship is tautological.

Several lifestyle variables produced significant associations. Those currently living in a house had relatively low well-being (5.8), while those in apartments, hotels and boats scored 7.0, the most likely explanation being that the latter were not experiencing the legal, fiscal and maintenance inconveniences of property acquisition and ownership. There was also significant variation by residential mobility in the study area, for those who had moved just once had a significantly lower score (5.3) than those who had moved three or more times (8.0). The most unusual contrast was between the low score (5.3) of those who, before retirement, had lived exclusively abroad *for work*, and the 7.4 among those who also had lived exclusively abroad but *not for work*. The latter group included many relatively affluent, high-status and widowed women in their seventies or older.

Three measures of social life and integration produced distinctive subgroup means. While the use of expatriate, exclusively British, mixed or any social clubs was not significantly related to well-being, the 165 respondents who used clubs for the indigenous population scored 7.4 while those who did not scored only 5.7. The strongest difference was between those who patronised just one type of club (5.1) and those who used three or four (7.7). It seems that the socially most active did have high well-being scores. On the association between visitors and well-being, while the frequency during the previous year of most categories was unrelated, children's visits were an exception. Those receiving six or more had a low score (5.4) compared to those hosting 0-2 (6.5). There was a similar inverse relationship with the total number of visitors, the 6.7 score of those entertaining 0-5 being significantly higher than the 5.4 among those who received ten or more.

The strongest comparisons came from three residential 'choice and use' variables (Figure 7.1). There was a strong positive relationship between well-being and the number of weeks spent in the retirement area during the previous year, with those present for less than six months scoring 3.1, and those staying 45-49 weeks scoring 7.6. Corroboration comes from a similarly strong inverse association with the number of trips made to the UK during the past year, from a well-being score of 7.2 for those who made none, to 0.6 for the eleven people who made five or more (the maximum was eight trips). It is recognised that people who find the sum-

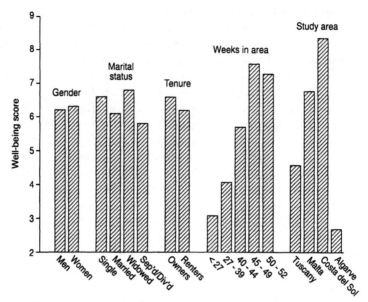

Figure 7.1 Average well-being scores by selected characteristics

mer heat most oppressive, have the strongest emotional or social ties in another country, or have family or business problems back home, will spend less time in the adopted country than those who are more settled or committed.

There were also age and duration-of-residence effects. It is clear, for example, that those who had only recently moved – and therefore many in their late fifties and early sixties – travelled a great deal and spent relatively few weeks in their adopted areas. This group were also closest in time to the legal, financial and practical necessities of establishing a new home, of arranging their UK affairs, and of adjustment to retirement. The higher well-being scores of the older respondents result partly from being 'more settled' and adjusted, and partly from selection effects: those who are most dissatisfied are least likely to stay. Nonetheless the evidence is clear that even if income, health and mobility problems do multiply with increasing age, satisfaction with living in southern Europe, far from declining, improves with time. It is striking, however, that among retired migrants systematic variations in well-being by personal characteristics are relatively few, weak and minor compared to the variations by the region of residence.[4]

Remarkably, all four country well-being mean scores were significantly different from each other (Figure 7.1). The scores in Malta (6.8) and Tuscany (4.6) were closest to the overall mean, while the Costa del Sol's was exceptionally high (8.4), and the Algarve's very low (2.7). It is clear that the high well-being in southern Spain is associated with the climate, active lifestyles, high ratings of hospital services, recreational and social facilities, good travel connections to the UK, and few complaints about local services. The low Algarve score reflects most the high frequency of problems and disappointments: 11.8 per cent complained about the roads and driving standards, and 13.6 per cent about the difficulty of getting jobs done in their homes. Other disappointments which were at least 2½ times more common in the Algarve included: dirt, litter or pollution; the gas, water and electricity utilities; the rising cost of living; and the high cost of air travel. Of the four areas, the Algarve is most rapidly developing as a tourist and retirement area and the resulting disruption and environmental changes actively irritate.

Conclusions

There are two widespread concerns about later-life residence abroad: the welfare of the participants, and the impacts on the destinations (Mullan 1992). Advances in the mass long-distance travel market and telecommunications underpin the accelerating globalisation of work experience, vacations and, potentially, retirement residence. As the proliferating 'retirement guides' show, people seek guidance about where it would be agreeable to live and how to settle successfully. This study has demonstrated that among those who have already moved and stayed, the great majority have found many advantages in residence abroad. In response to an open question to name personal advantages of living abroad in retirement, one third of questionnaire respondents reported that the pace of life was healthier or more appropriate than in Britain, while 11 per cent explicitly wrote that they were or felt healthier. A quarter mentioned financial advantages, while nearly half found the cost of living lower than in the UK. One fifth informed us that the locals were friendlier than they had expected, and 15 per cent mentioned advantages of the social life. This is an impressively positive audit of the decision to live abroad.

Every expatriate retiree is aware of ill-advised moves. Those who made the wrong decisions tend to move away or return with short delay. Journalists readily find instances of impoverishment, social isolation, neglect, and constricted activity, but these are rare and many the consequence of life events that would have occurred elsewhere. We neither advocate overseas residence in later life nor argue that it invariably raises wellbeing. Our interpretation is rather that the hurdles to be overcome, particularly in moving to countries of different language, legal systems and social customs, are so great that most who proceed have strong motivations for doing so and sufficient material, cultural and mental resources to achieve success. The practical conclusion from the findings of our analysis is that careful surveillance of the intended destination area is most important. Even when a decision to move has been made, the common practice of initially renting a second home and retaining one's base in the

197

home country should be followed. The commitment to the area should be staged. Successful ageing abroad depends as much on learnt adjustments as on prior fitness and resources.

Notes

1. Including in 1999, the Severe Disablement Allowance, Attendance Allowance, Invalid Care Allowance, Disability Working Allowance, Disability Living Allowance, Social Fund payments (funeral expenses), Community Care grants, Crisis loans, and Cold Weather payments.
2. The multi-national need and the increasing utilisation by the Spanish are demonstrated by changing nationalities of the patients. In 1996 the British made up 47 per cent and the Spanish 48 per cent; in 1998 the respective figures were 23 per cent and 64 per cent, with 11 per cent from other EU countries.
3. For the comparative ratings, not all the scenarios (for example, bereavement of spouse) applied to all respondents so these scores were weighted according to the number of applicable questions. The distribution of scores was negatively skewed, the mode being 11.0-11.9, and only ten respondents scored below minus 11, but readily transforms to a quasi-normal form.
4. The observed associations are consistent with meta-analyses of subjective well-being. For variations in individual well-being, 'ascribed social status variables (age, sex and race) and role-related variables (worker, spouse and grandparent) are only weakly related ... [and] achieved social status variables, particularly income, are modestly correlated. Life-style variables (social activity, housing, transport) also appear to be modestly related ... [while] health emerges as the most potent predictor' (Okun 1987: 400).

Eight

Impacts and Prospects

Introduction

The final chapter reflects upon our study's contribution to the understanding of international retirement migration and looks to the future of this previously neglected form of population mobility. It briefly summarises the principal results, and points to the most obvious gaps in knowledge and the insistent questions for further study. The chapter is organised around a sequence of syntheses, which begin with an examination of the underlying influences upon or 'drivers' of IRM. The second synthesis recaps the diversity of types and pathways of IRM, bearing in mind that the stereotypical British construction of retired migrants – that they are people who have lived their working lives in the UK and who, on retirement, make a 'total displacement' move to a Mediterranean resort which they know only through summer holidays – describes no more than half of the cases. Both the prior connections with the destinations, and earlier residential histories are much more complex. It is also argued strongly that a shift in the motivations and aspirations of retirement moves has occurred during the last two decades, with 'environmental' and 'lifestyle' preferences coming more strongly to the fore.

The third synthesis is about the immense differences in the regional geographies of the four study areas, particularly as regards the influence of the settlement patterns, landscapes, societies and economies on the tourist and retirement-residence developments. The following complementary synthesis examines the impacts of retirement settlement on the landscape, economy and society of a destination region. Its pervasive themes are the tensions between tourism and retirement functions, and the difficulty of isolating the independent effect of retirement in-migration from the other sources of demand for residence and for change in the built environment. Then follows a synthesis about the personal outcomes of retirement migration. The evidence is drawn from our survey respondents and the in-depth interviewees. Although many problems and disappointments were experienced (as detailed in Chapter 6), these were outweighed by the respondents' positive reports. In all four areas, the migrants were on average satisfied with their move and current situation, although with marked differences among the destination areas. The book concludes with a short and largely speculative statement on the likely futures for IRM in Europe. Contradictory influences and trends are identified, but overall it is concluded that there is much potential for growth in the retirement flows. The fortunes of individual favoured destination areas are, however, very difficult to predict, and some likely variations are described.

Underlying Influences on Retirement Abroad

It was argued in the opening chapter that the fundamental causes of the growth of retirement migration during the twentieth century were rising affluence and housing wealth, increased longevity, earlier retirement, and changes in lifestyle preferences that are difficult to specify but which may be indicated by rising educational standards. While our detailed study of British retirees in four southern European areas prompts no revision of that assessment, it has altered and deepened our understanding of the factors behind the *increase* of retirement migration from northern to southern Europe. In this context it is paradoxical that the dominant reason given by expatriate retirees for their move to the south is 'for the climate', when among the few certainties is that latitudinal differentials in temperature and sunshine are (for this purpose) a constant and cannot explain the change. Climate and residential environments have a large role in moulding the selection of destinations, but we must look to social and economic and political transformations for the main influences upon the growth of the flow.

The many socio-political transformations that are conditioning the development of international retirement migration may be generalised in both structural and life-course terms. On the one hand, we have shown that multiple macro-societal changes have had a bearing: from the revolutions in transport and communications technology, through countless expressions of entrepreneurial capitalism, to the democratisation of southern Europe. Indeed there are so many plausible influences that it is impossible to assess their relative contributions in general terms let alone to quantify them. On the other hand, it is still the case that only a small minority of those who reach retirement decide to migrate to another country. The 'behaviour' is highly selective of individuals, and our best chance of identifying who migrates is to identify the personal and life-course traits that are 'risk factors' or antecedents.

The associations between the development of mass tourism, the creation of new residential opportunities, and the subsequent growth of a large retirement flow were apparent long ago, especially for parts of the Iberian coast, for the sequence replicated the early twentieth-century experience of British and French coastal resorts. Much clearer now is the important influence of 'Europeanisation' in two special senses: of British

working lives and leisure patterns, and of commerce and consumer services. While both the legacy of the British Empire and the success of British
multi-national corporations have sustained strong commercial, professional and diplomatic links with many countries in the Middle East, South
and South-East Asia and North America (but less so Latin America), since
the 1950s the *relative* growth of Britons' international employment and settlement links has been in Europe. Skilled and manual labour migration,
UK membership of the European Union, the lengthy postings in Germany
of hundreds of thousands of British armed service personnel, and the
innumerable 'twinnings' and exchanges of schools and civic and cultural
associations have all encouraged study, residence and work abroad, as well
as dual-nationality friendships, marriages and identities. Among our
respondents in their seventies who had lived abroad in the five years
before retiring to southern Europe, 40 per cent had lived in Europe, but
among those twenty years younger, the majority (55 per cent) had done
so. For more and more people, retirement in southern Europe has been
preceded by lengthy periods of residence in the destination countries or
elsewhere on the continent. While this well-established trend will exert an
increasing influence, it will not necessarily produce a matching growth of
retirement flows to southern Europe, for there are many attractive alternative European destinations, in rural areas and in well-serviced,
'unspoilt' small towns.

The influence of 'economic harmonisation' can be illuminated by reference to everyday analogies and marketing jargon. Today, if a person
knows how to make an international telephone call from a public booth
in Britain, to do their weekly shopping in a supermarket, or to draw
money from their bank account through a 'cash machine', they rarely
have trouble doing the same things in any part of western Europe – which
was not the case twenty years ago. These activities reflect a general process
of 'cultural and economic convergence' which has involved the standard-
isation of product ranges, and simplification of the 'customer-interface' in
many convenience, telecommunications and financial services. While
western Europe is far short of the homogenised 'capitalist cultural realm'
of North America, moving from one of its countries to another implies
ever fewer inconveniences or reasons for anxiety with both mundane and
momentous personal transactions.

It will be apparent that it is impossible to separate the deep-seated structural or socio-political changes that have been affecting European lives
from the characteristics of the people that experience them. If we couch
our explanations of changed residential and migration decisions in terms
of the characteristics of successive birth-cohorts, we cite social, economic
and political transformations (and to some extent the reverse applies).
The best behavioural explanations for the increase of international retirement migration rest on two characteristics of people: their resources and
their preferences or aspirations. Change in the latter, people's lifestyle
preferences, are not entirely explained by either economic or political

change, and their roots are elusive modifications in people's self-concepts, identity and egocentric motivations. These defy comprehensive under- standing but may be well indexed by behavioural change, as in marital pat- terns, the use of time, and the decreasing part that extended family members play in people's social networks and lives.

One clear trend that we have described is the rise of amenity and lifestyle influences on the selection of retirement locations and, corre- spondingly, that family-related locational decisions are now quite rare: they were found mainly among Anglo-Maltese and Anglo-Italian families and to a small extent on the Costa del Sol, where some moves have been influenced by a child's success in setting up a small business. The shift from 'family-related' to 'lifestyle' retirement migration has several dimen- sions, and a full assessment requires study of other contemporary flows (as from Britain to Australia and northern Europe). It can be demonstrated however that the importance attached to a location that enables frequent contacts with children and grandchildren is much less among our respon- dents than among a sample of long-distance retirement migrants in England and Wales twenty years ago. In that group, some moves were pur- posefully to destinations that were attractive for children's and grandchil- dren's holidays, while others, as from London suburbs to the extra-metropolitan fringe, leap-frogged earlier suburbanisation moves by a retiree's child and either improved or had a neutral effect on the jour- ney time to their homes.

A second change, particularly during the 1990s, has been the decline of emigrations from the UK by widows, many well into their seventies and older, to the 'Old Commonwealth' nations and the United States. Family- related migrations continue, of course, and we have much evidence of fre- quent children's visits, but the insistent impression is that this aspect of the retirement migration decision has receded. The following quotations from the in-depth interviews give some indication of currently widespread attitudes:

Interviewer: Were you thinking of [your grandchildren] when you bought [this house], perhaps as a place they could come on holiday?
Respondent: No. I wanted a place of my own and not a rented one. I knew they could come when they wanted.

Officer of a residents' association: [Their] average age is 60 and they are nearly all permanent residents. There is a tremendous lack of children here – generally just grandchildren visiting.

Interviewer: Do you have many visitors?
Respondent: No. My only daughter is in New Zealand. [My wife's] son and grandchildren have only come out here twice.

Minister of religion: Many of the older ladies out here who find them- selves bereaved, are very close to their grandchildren and want to go home because they then feel isolated. The children often want to bring them back and keep an eye on them – and their inheritance! But I don't see a lot of the people here going back. Many think about it as they get older but most of them don't really want to give up the life out here.

The change may be associated with a general decrease in the importance attached to kin ties and the spread of individualistic attitudes. Giddens (1992) believes that 'the "baby boom" generation [also the latest cohort of retirees] ... has distinguished itself through rejection of moral restraint in favour of the values of emotional intimacy, hedonism and "self-actualisation"'. One manifestation has been the spread of divorce and the increasing frequency of second (or later) marriages or partnerships. The proportion of women in England and Wales who had ever divorced by the age of 45 years doubled from 14 per cent among those born in 1931, to 29 per cent among those born just sixteen years later (Falkingham 1997: Table 1.9).[1] Among our respondents, the most frequent situation was for wives to be 0-4 years younger than husbands, but only 44 per cent were in this category compared to 62 per cent of a sample of migrants for retirement within England and Wales in 1976 (Law and Warnes 1977: Table 4.10). While the share of couples in which the wives are much younger than their husbands has increased, as lay observers assert, pairings in which the woman is older than the man have grown much more strongly (from around 12 to 17 per cent, and to 20 per cent in the younger cohort of our respondents). The migration decision of some respondents was explicitly or manifestly linked to a new intimate relationship, but without data from previous cohorts we cannot judge whether this is an incidental change or a rapidly growing stimulus to international migration.

Types of International Retirement Residence

Within the four study areas, we have found great variety among the expatriate retirees, not only in the expected dimensions of income, educational level and occupational background, but also in less predictable biographical attributes, such as the influence, in childhood and youth, of contacts with extended family and parents' generation friends on the countries which people get to know. Most of all, we have demonstrated much more diversity in the pathways by which British expatriates arrive at their retirement home than most commentators have previously acknowledged. Both the Costa del Sol and Tuscany were included as study areas because we were aware that among 'environmental preference and amenity' migrations there are strong contrasts among those seeking similitudes of imagined 'rural idylls', those drawn by indigenous cultural veracity, and those wanting transposed British services and customs. Less appreciated was that in all four areas there are British retirees whose connections with the retirement areas (and indeed foreign countries) range from 'holidays only', through extended employment, to lifetime residence. Nor did we understand as well as we do now that there is no clear break between 'amenity' and 'family connections and support' retirement migration. In Malta and Tuscany particularly, many permutations of bi-national identities and of levels of integration into local economic life and family networks are found. In some cases the connections stem from several generations of a family's work and residence in both Britain and the overseas country; more frequently they are the product of recent cross-national marriages – made in Britain, in the destination European country, and in other parts of the world.

Our respondents in Malta and Tuscany displayed the most comprehensive range of biographies, pathways, motivations and social profiles that we encountered. On a wider canvas, international retirement migration ranges from the highly organised 'extraction' of elderly Jewish citizens from the pre-1990 Soviet Union to Israel (including many who were frail or seriously ill), through a spectrum of family-orientated moves, to the various forms of amenity moves. At one extreme, a small number of family-orientated international moves are virtually imposed by both responsible and over-protective children upon, say, a bereaved mother of declining health. Dysfunctional examples remove widowed people from a socially rich and well-supported setting (about which they may have been largely silent or unconscious), and take them to a residential arrangement in another country where most of their interests and habitual activities are frustrated and their dependency is heightened and confirmed. At the other extreme, some international retirement moves might be described as 'unconsciously' undertaken, as by the many Irish citizens who return from working lives in the UK to their home country. As with similar flows of retirement migrants between relatively proximate countries, 'returns' are a common realisation.

The diversity of environmentally motivated retirement migrations should also be emphasised. Among our respondents can be counted a dedicated field student of Carthaginian archaeology, an avid researcher of local church liturgy, several keen yachtswomen, and others who were selflessly dedicated to community service; all very different people from the also relatively rare relentless party-goers, ex-colonial chauvinists and 'alternative' commune dwellers. Around the world, 'amenity' retirement migrations will have an even greater spread and might be classified on several scales, including hedonism to cultural inquisitiveness, and psychological self-sufficiency to crowd-dependency. Not all types of people and expatriate retirement communities are found in the four study areas. We have not been able to detail, for example, instances of retirement into a 'world city' for its metropolitan amenities, or into humble third-world settings for financial, intellectual or spiritual motivations. And while international retirement moves in Europe are becoming ever easier to arrange and undertake, few moves across a European border involve slighter financial difficulties or less of a cultural transition than a Canadian's purchase of a retirement home in a southern US state. Nor should it be forgotten that work-related migrations continue into the last years of working life, particularly among 'skilled labour', and that for the growing number of self-employed international consultants and advisers, no fixed retirement age applies.

Notwithstanding the great heterogeneity of international migrations by older people, we have presented strong indications of a changing pattern of motivations and 'place-time usage'. The main trend of recent decades has been the rise of environmental preference (or amenity) migrations, and among these the most evident are the net movements from urbanised and high-income regions (in the northern latitudes of America, Europe and the eastern Pacific), to less developed, often rural and lower-income regions (in lower latitudes of the northern hemisphere). International retirement migration is both distinctive, because it takes generally affluent people into relatively poor and ill-serviced regions, and problematic for those regions and potentially for the participants. The influx makes heavy demands on the service infrastructure, raises the prices of housing and stimulates consumer services – from bars and banks to building services – and creates population clusters that have the potential to make large demands on health and social services.

The Destination Areas and Degrees of Change

Before large-scale retirement settlement began, the four study areas had different spatial and social structures, most clearly of climate, landscape, level of economic development, and external relationships with the UK and the rest of the world. Furthermore the regions were not homogeneous economic and social spaces; rather, there were considerable differences between, for example, the interior and the coast of Málaga province, and between Florence and southern Tuscany. Through their contrasting locations, accessibility to different parts of Europe, and prior associations, each retirement region has attracted different combinations of retirees from northern European countries. The British predominate in the Costa del Sol and in Malta, while in parts of the Canary and Balearic Islands and in northern Italy, the Germans are more numerous. The regions of Italy and Spain contiguous to France accommodate many of that country's retirees, while East European retirees are most evident in Malta (where there are also exceptional numbers who have worked in Australia), and Americans on the Costa del Sol. There are also marked differences in the combination of 'permanent' and 'circulating' retiree residents, and in their occupational and educational backgrounds.

One of the clearest influences on change in the destination areas' economies, social formations and settlement has been the nature of tourism development and particularly a region's involvement in mass-market or package holidays. Tourism and retirement residence increasingly contest the appropriation of land in the four areas, the general result being the displacement of the more recent retiree settlers from the tourist nodes to their hinterlands – even though significant retirement communities cling on in even the most intense centres of mass tourism. The following paragraphs summarise the distinctive features of each region, its recent history of tourist development and retirement settlement, and the scale of the associated transformations.

Tuscany

Tuscany has the longest associations with the UK for both tourism and settlement. The Grand Tour, the numerous literary associations and commercial contacts have given it a special affinity and laid the foundations for one of the earliest large flows of 'environmental preference' retirement migrants from the UK. This was encouraged during the 1960s, when agrarian reforms released numerous attractive rural properties on to the market. Our respondents in Tuscany were the longest-established British retirement community of the four we studied. Tuscany has also been particularly attractive to the upper middle-classes, especially to those who have lived abroad or worked in the arts and media. Not surprisingly, family and work ties were relatively important in the decision to move to Tuscany. There was also a notably positive affirmation and attraction to *Italian* history and the region's harmonious landscape and culture. For these reasons, and perhaps also because of respondents' greater experience of living abroad and ability to speak foreign languages (three quarters considered themselves quite or very fluent in Italian), they sought rural properties and were not keen to affiliate with the small established clusters of British residents as in Florence.

Linguistic skills and geographical dispersal did not, however, mean that they became well integrated with the host community, except when engaged in farming. Nonetheless, the migrants expressed a generally high level of contentment with their new homes, and they had especially positive lifestyle and civic evaluations. The British are not the largest foreign population living in Tuscany (the Germans are), but their numbers are swelled by tourists and second-home owners in the summer. Although Harold Acton (1986: 55) observed the English 'home counties' atmosphere of Chiantishire, it should be remembered that many of the British retirees have spent much of their working lives far from England, and a prevalent 'lifestyle preference' is less to re-create English country life than to draw selectively from British, Italian and expatriate customs and conveniences.

Malta

British tourism and retirement migration to Malta over the last thirty years has consolidated rather than been the foundation of the northern European impact on the local society and economy. The long British colonial association is responsible for English being widely spoken, and the substantial emigration from the 1950s of the Maltese to the UK has added many more friendships and dual-nationality marriages to those begun in Malta through the armed services and their shore establishments. One consequence has been that British retirees on the islands are the most integrated with the indigenous society of the four studied populations. The Maltese respondents were the second longest established and the second oldest. With on average the lowest social status, not surprisingly they were the most likely to cite financial advantages in their decisions to migrate to Malta and to refer to financial problems, but they were the least likely to experience problems with their social life or to expect to return to the UK. We have argued that the relatively strong family connections and social integration of the retirees and the well-serviced settlements probably produce a more supportive environment for those who become widowed or frail and dependent upon informal (non-spouse) and formal help. There are indications that the growth of the retired British community in Malta is not keeping pace with that in the other areas (although the settlement of Germans and Scandinavians is increasing). The reasons include the fading ties with Britain and the reduction of 'return' migration by Anglo-Maltese couples from the UK.

The Costa del Sol

The Costa del Sol has been radically transformed through tourism and related recreational provision since the early 1960s. It has been successively a fashionable tourist magnet, one of the earliest and most popular zones for mass-market holidays, and the region of Europe which has attracted the largest number and highest density of expatriate retired residents. Its latitude, absence of winter frosts and extensive areas of undeveloped land have been vital, and its phenomenal air transport connectivity to northern Europe has been both cause and effect of the rapid evolution. The absence of earlier strong ties with northern Europe means that the coast's retired respondents were the second youngest of the four areas and had the second most recent average year of arrival. The retirees have been attracted overwhelmingly by the climate and the 'way of life': the latter refers more to the adopted lifestyle than to the few assimilated Spanish customs and attitudes. This adopted lifestyle might be described as relaxed while less sedentary than that enforced by northern winters. Outdoor activities are a feature. Compared to Tuscany and Malta, the expatriate retirees are relatively segregated (or at least suburbanised), although most of the national enclaves that have formed have been spontaneous and ephemeral. Poor language skills further deter integration, especially as the size of the foreign communities supports many retail and personal services run and staffed by their compatriots. The large numbers also support numerous Dutch, English, Finnish, German and Swedish newspaper and radio and television stations, several northern European churches, and both national and cross-national voluntary associations.

The relatively low level of social integration should not however be exaggerated. On the *urbanizaciones*, many Spanish occupiers are from the middle class of Madrid and other northern cities and no more Andalusian than the foreigners. Property owners in particular have shared interests, and we encountered residents' associations with both Spanish and expatriate officers. There is also institutionalised bridge building through other special-interest associations, and in the rural hinterland informal ties with Spanish neighbours are quite strong. Moreover, no other area displayed stronger signs of a recognition of common instrumental interests among the various expatriate retired communities. Maybe the newness of the settlements and the diversity of the people who have come explain the relatively common references to disappointments with the social life – a rare case of difficulties being more prevalent in this area than elsewhere. Nonetheless, the British retiree respondents were generally satisfied with their moves, stated relatively few problems, and scored high on overall well-being. They particularly valued the quality of the health services, and reported many unanticipated benefits from their moves. On this coast, Spanish entrepreneurs, international holiday companies and northern European residents have totally transformed large tracts of what was until recently a dominantly rural area and, in the process, created an unprecedented and distinctively European 'rainbow' society. It has two elements, with the young Andalusian families suburbanising from Málaga oriented towards work and a still-novel comparative prosperity, alongside multinational foreigners oriented towards recreation in its many different forms. It is precisely these qualities which have attracted many Britons to retire to the area, while repelling many others.

The Algarve

The mass tourism functions of the Algarve have been the most recently developed among the study areas and the speed of the region's transformations has been the fastest. Our survey respondents were the youngest and most recently arrived of the four groups. But many of our informants complained about the ubiquitous building work and the loss of many of the 'unspoilt' features which first attracted them to the area – a factor, it seems clear, in the strong displacement to the rural interior of the most recent cohort of British retirees (Williams and Patterson 1998). Apart from its chronology, the evolution of the tourism and retirement impacts has brought about several similarities with the Costa del Sol and two major differences: a lower volume of visitors and settlers, and a physical environment that has less constrained the settlement to a narrow coastal strip.

As the Algarve was a relatively isolated rural region before the arrival of mass tourism, the retired migrants had few prior connections aside from holidays. Without the working-age and marital connections of Malta, or the intensity of mass-market tourism found on the Costa del Sol, retirement migration to the Algarve has been more socially selective, and the occupational status of the respondents is relatively high. They were more likely than those in either Malta or the Costa del Sol to have lived abroad in the five years before they moved, but less likely to be socially integrated with the local and foreign residents. Only about a quarter considered themselves fluent in Portuguese, they had the most complaints about the health service, and the lowest level of well-being. This was associated with relatively frequent visits to the UK and above average intentions to return. Their dissatisfaction should not be exaggerated, however, because both the index of their overall well-being and the balance of expressed advantages and disadvantages were strongly positive. Their *relative* dissatisfaction could be transitory, another expression of the newness of the settlements and the communities, or simply of the 'adjustment' problems of newly arrived migrants, or alternatively may persist if the tensions between tourism and retirement residence are not reduced.

The Impacts of Retirement Settlement

A simple way to indicate the impact of the growing retired foreign population is to monitor this changing share of the total population (although under-registration may disguise the true extent). In only a few municipalities of the Costa del Sol would *all* the foreign residents approach one half of the population. Nevertheless in many more districts the impacts have been substantial. A broader assessment can be made using four themes: settlement and housing; the economy; health and welfare; and government.

The variable impact of expatriate retirement on settlement patterns reflects the environmental and social contrasts described above as well as the specific forms of the regions' tourist developments. In simple terms, alterations to the settlement patterns and landscape have been least in Tuscany and greatest on the Costa del Sol. In Tuscany, although tourist visits have a major impact on the cities of Florence and Siena, there are relatively few foreign European residents. In its rural areas, retirement migration has had little effect on the overall settlement pattern, although – along with tourism – it has brought considerable investment in the buildings. Much of Tuscany is protected by strong planning and conservation regulations which prevent new building and control renovation. One result has been that house prices have soared, tending to exclude young local people. On the Costa del Sol, by contrast, the population has increased many times over, the workaday port of Málaga has grown into a vibrant, multi-functional city with ever-expanding land demands, and the coast to the west, which formerly was largely undeveloped outside the fishing villages, has become a near-continuous tourist and residential urban strip. No other part of Europe has changed so much through recreational and retirement residential developments over the last thirty years; the nearest global parallels are parts of the Californian, Floridia and Queensland coasts.

In Malta and the Algarve, the impacts on the settlement pattern and landscape have been less radical than on the Costa del Sol. The principal landscape change in Malta since independence has been a substantial expansion of the built-up area, mainly through the construction of new housing for the Maltese, but with contributions from light-industry estates and tourist facilities. The new developments are widespread on both Malta and Gozo, but concentrate in the 'outer fringes' of the Harbours Conurbation focused on Valletta. It is impossible to isolate the independent role of retirement settlement, not least because most expatriate retirees are spatially well integrated with the local population. It has however been argued that during the 1970s the pressure to relax building controls came from both tourism and retirement settlement (Boissevain 1977b).

In the Algarve there have been contrasting impacts on the settlement pattern. Tourist infrastructure and housing for foreign retirees have filled the interstices between the original settlements and early tourist nodes and produced a linear city. As on the Costa del Sol, the developments have been accompanied by substantial labour in-migration and second-home purchases, making it difficult to isolate the effect of foreign retiree immigration. In the rural hinterland, the impacts of retirement settlement have been similar to those in Tuscany despite less stringent planning controls – there have been few new housing developments but much renovation, so the main effect has been the consolidation of the pre-existing settlement pattern.

The landscape and settlement impacts in the four areas have therefore been first and foremost place-specific, although the Iberian coastal areas show many similarities. All four destinations have, however, shared two strong effects: steep increases in house and apartment rents and prices, and irresistible pressures for change in the functions and social character, if not the built appearance, of their villages, towns and harbours. Otherwise the common elements have been few: some are obvious, such as new retail services, and some are visible but less widely recognised, one example being the damage to the landscapes of all four areas by the expansion of quarrying for building and road materials, especially evident in Malta.

The economic impacts of the retirement influx have also been diverse, although one general benefit when compared to tourism is the generation of year-round and more diverse expenditure. The most obvious stimulus has been on building and construction supplies. Most new-build has been by indigenous entrepreneurs, although British development and construction companies have operated in the Costa del Sol and parts of the Algarve. Similarly, most renovation has been by local sellers or commissioned from local builders by the purchasers (although, as in France, self-employed roofers, electricians, and plumbers are an early form of expatriate economic activity in areas of foreign settlement). There is a complementary impact on agriculture, both through the loss of land to new-build and because, when farmhouses are converted for retirement residence, some of the attached farm land is often acquired. Retirement migration has directly stimulated tourism, for visits by friends and relatives bring substantial spending even without payments for accommodation. Retirees tend however to oppose further tourism development, in places through residents' or special interest associations.

The impacts of retirement migration on health and welfare services in the destination areas were discussed in Chapter 7. A marked increase of the older population inevitably makes demands on health and welfare services, and brings into sharp focus the differences between provision in northern and southern Europe. In all four study countries, the support and care of widowed and frail older people in the host society still relies heavily on family care. As a result, there is comparatively little residential and nursing-home care and even fewer domiciliary services, as are customary in northern Europe. The quality and the coverage of health-care services are improving rapidly – especially in Spain – through national modernisation and reform programmes. The under-registration of residents adds to the difficulties of the responsible agencies in the destination countries, as health and welfare resources are usually allocated through capitation formulae. The prevalence of ill-health among young retirees is however frequently exaggerated, and it should be remembered that retirement migration is socially selective. The migrants have above-average incomes, 60 per cent have private insurance cover, and their expenditure not only supports increased health and welfare employment but also stimulates capital investments and innovations which benefit all sections of the population.

Finally, there are important effects on political and associational activity and local government. Our interviews revealed a high level of concern with both the quality of the local administrations and the returns from local taxes, but much indifference to national politics. This apparent contradiction is consistent with the exclusion of foreigners from national elections. Even now, when the Treaty on European Union has extended local government electoral rights to citizens living in other member states, the engagement with local politics is slim. In most areas retired residents still have slight electoral weight, and language differences and non-registration are also barriers to participation. The emergence of new forms of cross-national engagement in local politics is, however, evident in the Balearic Islands and the Costa del Sol. Perhaps of greater importance than participation in the formal structures of local government will be the involvement of foreign nationals in special-interest associations and campaigns, as with charitable initiatives to establish new services, and challenges locally and through European institutions to discriminatory regulations.

Effects on the Migrants

This study of British retirees' experience and opinions about their residence in a southern European country has produced two dominant findings – that the balance of assessment is strongly positive, and that variation in individual well-being is primarily associated with the area of choice. On the former, the advantages and surpassed expectations clearly exceeded the problems and disappointments, so that 80 per cent of the respondents had positive well-being scores. The reason most commonly given for moving to southern Europe and the most frequently acknowledged advantage was the climate. The in-depth interviews yielded hundreds of such references, but apart from the occasional cross-reference to a health or longevity benefit, as with 'my husband wasn't well and he didn't want to go through more English winters' and 'the dampness is terrible in England and that makes you old', the accumulated explanation of why the climate is so advantageous has been slight. As much is revealed by the references to the cold, dampness, greyness and long winter nights of the British climate (and latitude) as by the connections that the respondents occasionally made between the climate and their new lives, as with 'we were sun-bathing in January – it was wonderful' and '[it] keeps the older people more active – no long, dark, cold evenings'. The climate's advantages are truly taken for granted; as one informant said, 'the climate is obviously attractive'. For more expressive remarks, if not more penetrating understanding, one exemplary environmental observer's remarks can be quoted: the Mediterranean climate 'feels quite delicious – the atmosphere so dry, and the heavens so clear and blue with the sun shining brightly, that all nature seems sparkling with life.... I [never] ceased from wonder at finding each succeeding day as fine as the foregoing. What a difference does climate make in the enjoyment of life!' (Darwin 1997: 241-2).[2]

Other evidence of the generally high degree of satisfaction with their moves was revealed in the low frequency of wishes to return to the British Isles even if personal or financial circumstances deteriorated. The ratio of the predictions between staying and moving away was 4.6 to stay; less than one fifth of the sample (18.7 per cent) produced a net 'would move away' response.[3] The Costa del Sol and Malta informants produced the highest 'stay' scores (5.0-5.2), the Algarve the lowest (3.3), and the Tuscan were in between (4.2). The overwhelming evidence is that our respondents are highly satisfied with their chosen area of residence and only a minority are likely to leave.

Uncertain Destinies: Probable Futures for the Destination Areas

There will be further radical changes in the already favoured areas, and many of the effects that we have observed are likely to spread. One control will be the extent to which IRM from the UK and northern Europe continues to increase, and the ways in which a rising demand for 'sun-belt retirement' is met. A key issue for any favoured region must be its relative attractiveness in an internationally competitive market. As tourism is the most important initial affiliation with retirement destinations, its development may be a guide to future trends. On this basis, Turkey and Greece are likely to become more important, while the proportion selecting Malta and Spain will probably decline (Williams 1997). More speculatively, how long will it be before entrepreneurs succeed in attracting European retirees to sections of the North African, Persian Gulf and Brazilian coasts? Another dynamic feature is the relative size of the retirement flows from different northern European countries. While by design the British have dominated the flows to our study areas, Germans predominate in Majorca, while in parts of northern Spain and northern Italy the French are the most numerous foreign residents. In the future there are likely to be stronger flows from elsewhere in northern Europe. It is possible that the international provenance of retirees is of little significance for the host communities, although Rodríguez *et al.* (1998) have identified some social and behavioural differences among those from the UK, Germany, and the Benelux and the Nordic countries on the Costa del Sol. At the neighbourhood level, as on the *urbanizaciones*, a shift from one national dominance to another, or to a multi-national population, is keenly noted and may have a significant effect on the local services and networks of support, e.g. a denominational congregation may disperse, as is happening in Malta, or a family doctor of the previously dominant nationality may move away.

Another issue is how the competition between international retirement and other social or economic functions will evolve in different areas. It has been noted that the intensification of tourism often leads to the displacement of migrants to suburbs and rural hinterlands. However, more and more tourists also seek greater peace and quiet while remaining accessible to tourism facilities, as shown by the increasing numbers seeking self-catering holidays in villas, or purchasing second homes. As a result, many of our interviewees – particularly in the Costa del Sol – complained that the character of suburban *urbanizaciones* had changed, with villas being rented out to tourists whose behaviour clashed with that of the permanent or seasonal residents. Of particular interest is the future use of the large stock of foreign-owned housing. What proportion will be inherited by children or other legatees living in northern Europe? How many will be retained as holiday homes; and if these greatly multiply, what will be the effect on the areas in which they concentrate? For those that are sold, an important issue will be whether the purchasers are retired foreigners, retired nationals or local working people. It is already clear that many units in the *urbanizaciones* of the Costa del Sol are being purchased by Spanish families, some as first and some as second homes. A continuing convergence of incomes between southern and northern Europe will contribute to such 're-nationalisation' of the favoured destination areas, as also will increasing retirement migration within southern Europe. The latter is likely to arise from the ageing of the indigenous populations, enhanced pensions, and the spread of education and careerist lives, although the outcome is conditional on the extent to which the hitherto close-knit (and geographically proximate) inter-generational ties break down through a combination of secular, meritocratic and individualist tendencies.

Future changes in the social composition and residential structures of the major destinations also depend on the evolution of residential preferences, the availability of development land, and the local range of residential environments. Several recent shifts in residential preferences have been noted: in Malta, to Gozo and the western peninsulas; to the interior of the Algarve; beyond the coastal mountain range of the Costa del Sol; and to Umbria and Marche in Italy. The pattern replicates the experience of retirement areas in Britain and France. Over time, incoming retirees have shifted from the early resort towns such as Bournemouth and Exmouth to surrounding rural areas. There is little scope for further dispersal on Malta and Gozo, but there are few barriers in Tuscany and central Italy, although the balance of push and pull factors (including comparative house prices) may not quickly lure large numbers away from its highly valued landscapes and culture. The Algarve has already seen a substantial inland displacement, although the mountain ranges will constrain further inland expansion; few British retirees can be found in the Alentejo to the north, if only because of its more extreme climate. On the Costa del Sol, the key issue is the extent to which the amenities and social opportunities of progressively more adapted and supported foreign communities, and enduring language barriers, will counteract the repellant effects of rising population densities, congestion and functional diversification.

Over the Horizon: The Future of IRM from Northern to Southern Europe

Phillipson (1998: 55) states that 'historians and sociologists have argued that the "triumph of retirement" only took place in the period following the Second World War'. A derivative question is whether we have yet witnessed the zenith of international retirement migration, particularly from northern to southern Europe. The nearest parallel is the development of retirement migration to Florida. Its present scale suggests that IRM in Europe is still in the early stages. Despite some broadening of the social character of UK retirement migration to southern Europe since the 1950s, it remains socially selective in terms of income, social class and wealth. A large majority of the British population still do not participate in IRM. The polarisation of incomes amongst Europe's elderly populations suggests, however, that although a widening band will be able to engage in foreign tourism and retirement, a limit to the penetration of these practices is not too far away.

On the one hand, increasing numbers of successive retirement cohorts will have relatively long international tourism careers, while the continuing integration of the European economies is also likely to increase international skilled labour migration, adding to the pool of those with experiences of living abroad, a factor that we have identified to be of increasing importance in determining IRM streams. Furthermore, teleworking is becoming more important, so that increasing numbers of workers could be residentially footloose in future. Both cost and amenity considerations are likely to make southern Europe attractive to many such workers; this would increase the potential pool of northern Europeans who later will retire *in situ* in the south. On the other hand, the higher levels of unemployment over the last twenty-five years will depress the proportion with high-value occupational pensions and substantial housing assets. Nonetheless, the weight of the evidence is that the zenith of IRM is yet to come. Concrete evidence of a substantial latent demand has been collected by a German building society survey which found that currently almost 600,000 Germans own homes abroad, but that a further 1.1 million had plans to make such purchases in the next three years.[4]

The relative attraction of southern Europe in the near future will be a function of economic development, environmental degradation and the pace of globalisation. First, will the increasing development of the Mediterranean region make it less attractive as a destination for IRM? Most relevant in the areas favoured for retirement will be the continuing pressures for tourism expansion and the compatability of the resulting developments with the lifestyle and functional advantages that retirees seek (Montanari 1995). Secondly, will Mediterranean climates and landscapes continue to be highly valued, or could fashions and attitudes turn right round? Intense sun is increasingly seen as a health hazard, the Mediterranean Sea many regard as too polluted, and the summer atmosphere of the 'tourist traps' is seen by many as a nightmare to be avoided. Finally, will the recent globalisation of tourism lead to the globalisation of the retirement market? If, for example, the next generation of aeroplanes significantly reduces travel times to the western USA or even to Australia, will this lead to increased amenity-led retirement migration to these English-speaking destinations? Such possibilities should be set against predictions of further growth in tourism numbers to the Mediterranean region (Jenner and Smith 1993: 16).

The other major consideration in the destiny of southern Europe as an IRM destination lies in the future of welfare provision. To date, the socially selective nature of IRM (in terms of financial resources and personal skills) has meant that most migrants have made a success of their moves, and coped with any difficulties encountered. It may be that the most severe challenges for most of these migrants have yet to be faced as they age and many experience sickness and incapacity. Few have yet required sustained support from local health and welfare services. Such support is even more likely to be required if retirement to southern Europe attracts those with lower incomes. There could be greater need, at different stages of the life course, for state income benefits, for home-care services, and for publicly-funded residential care. These are all areas which currently fall outside the competence of the EU. To some extent then, further extension of IRM may depend on the outcome of the contested division of social policy powers between national states and the EU. An intriguing possibility is that expatriate retirees will themselves be the agents of the extension of EU citizenship's meaning to the domains of retirement entitlements and the promotion by governments of the quality of later life.

Finally, we reiterate points made in the preface and introduction. International retirement migration is not new but its manifestation as a large-scale, amenity-led movement from northern to southern Europe is novel. Remarkably little was known about this phenomenon at the time when this research began, but we hope that this book has made a contribution to an understanding of the determinants and forms of the process, and of the motivations and characteristics of the participants. International retirement migration will pose increasingly substantial challenges for social policy, welfare practice, environmental management and international cooperation. This volume might therefore best be seen as an infant in a programme of research that requires nurture, a long and productive life and a fulfilled maturity.

Notes

1. Strictly comparable data are elusive. The 1994 figure is a collation of Haskey's (1994) estimate that before reaching their sixtieth birthday, '6 per cent of all children [had] become step-children of a married couple and 7 per cent of a cohabiting couple.' For sources and more details see Falkingham (1997).
2. Charles Darwin was describing his reactions to the climate of central Chile after six months in Tierra del Fuego. The respondents' quotations are drawn from in-depth interviews in Malta.
3. The replies to this set of questions were weighted 1 for 'definitely', 0.5 for 'more likely', and positive for 'stay', negative for 'leave'. The possible range of the aggregate scores was -9 to +9.
4. Paper presented by Claudia Kaiser at the first workshop of the European Science Foundation Workshop on International Retirement Migration, held at Palma, Majorca, 6-10 May 1999.

Bibliography

Acton, H. (1986), 'Introduction', in H. Acton and E. Chaney (eds), *Florence: a Traveller's Companion*, London: Constable, pp. 30-55.

Almeda, E. and Sarasa, S. (1996), 'Spain: growth to diversity', in V. George and P. Taylor-Gooby (eds), *European Welfare Policy: Squaring the Welfare Circle*, London: Macmillan, pp. 155-76.

Andrews, F. M. and Withey, S. B. (1976), *Social Indicators of Well-Being: Americans' Perceptions of Life Quality*, New York: Plenum.

Anthias, F. (1992), *Ethnicity, Class, Gender and Migration*, Aldershot: Avebury.

Arber, S. (1996), 'Gender roles', in J. E. Birren (ed.), *Encyclopaedia of Gerontology*, Vol. 1, San Diego: Academic Press, pp. 555-66.

Ardagh, J. (1988), *Germany and the Germans*, London: Penguin.

Ballard, J. G. (1996), *Cocaine Nights*, London: Flamingo.

Balm, R. (1996), 'Big holes in a small place: the stone quarrying dilemma in the Maltese islands', *Geography*, 81(1): 82-6.

Barke, M. and France, L. (1996), 'The Costa del Sol', in M. Barke, J. Towner and M. T. Newton (eds), *Tourism in Spain: Critical Issues*, Wallingford: CAB International, pp. 265-308.

— and Towner, J. (1996), 'Exploring the history of leisure and tourism in Spain', in M. Barke, J. Towner and M. T. Newton (eds), *Tourism in Spain: Critical Issues*, Wallingford: CAB International, pp. 3-34.

Barnard, C. (1993), 'Malta', in Europa Directories, *Western Europe*, London: Europa, pp. 393-9.

Beeley, B. W. and Charlton, W. A. (1994), 'Maltese patterns of dependence: an historical perspective', *Scottish Geographical Magazine*, 110(2): 112-20.

Benefits Agency (1998), *Your Social Security Insurance, Benefits and Health-Care Rights in the European Community, and in Iceland, Leichtenstein and Norway*, Newcastle-upon-Tyne: Benefits Agency, Leaflet SA29.

Betty, C. (1997), 'Language problems of older British migrants on the Costa del Sol', *Generations Review*, 7(2): 10-11.

— and Cahill, M. (1999), 'British expatriates' experience of health and social services on the Costa del Sol', in F. Anthias and G. Lazaridis (eds), *Into the Margins: Migration and Social Exclusion in Southern Europe*, Aldershot: Avebury, pp. 83-113.

Bhabha, H. K. (1994), *The Location of Culture*, London: Routledge.

Black, A. (1996), 'Negotiating the tourist gaze: the example of Malta', in J. Boissevain (ed.), *Coping with Tourists: European Reactions to Mass Tourism*, Oxford: Berghahn Books, pp. 112-42.

Blanchard, F. S. (1952), *Where to Retire and How: A Comprehensive Guide*, New York: Dodd, Mead and Co.

Blouet, B. (1993), *The Story of Malta*, Valletta: Progress.

Boissevain, J. (1977a), ' "When the saints go marching out": reflections on the decline of patronage in Malta', in E. Gellner and J. Waterbury (eds), *Patrons and Clients*, London: Duckworth, pp. 81-96.

— (1977b), 'Tourism and development in Malta', *Development and Change*, 8(4): 523-38.

Boldrin, A., Jimenez-Martin, S. and Peracchi, F. (1999), 'Social security and retirement in Spain', in J. Gruber and D. A. Wise (eds), *Social Security and Retirement Around the World*, Chicago: University of Chicago Press, pp. 305-55.

Bond, E. J. (1996), *Ethics and Human Well-Being: An Introduction to Moral Philosophy*, Oxford: Blackwell.

Brendon, P. (1991), *Thomas Cook: 150 Years of Popular Tourism*, London: Martin Secker and Warburg Ltd.

Brugiavini, A. (1999), 'Social security and retirement in Italy', in J. Gruber and D. A. Wise (eds), *Social Security and Retirement Around the World*, Chicago: University of Chicago Press, pp. 181-238.

BTA (1969), *Patterns in British Holidaymaking 1951-68*, London: British Tourist Authority.

BTA/ETB (1996), *Digest of Tourist Statistics*, London: British Tourist Authority/English Tourist Board.

Buller, H. and Hoggart, K. (1994), *International Counterurbanization: British Migrants in Rural France*, Aldershot: Avebury.

Burgess, E. W., Hoyt, G. C. and Manley, C. R. (1955), 'The construction of scales for the measurement of migration after retirement', *Sociometry*, 18(4): 616-23.

Burns, J. (1994), *Spain: a Literary Companion*, London: John Murray.

Butler, R. W. (1980), 'The concept of a tourist area cycle of evolution: implications for management of resources', *Canadian Geographer*, 14(1): 5-12.

Byron, M. and Condon, S. (1996), 'A comparative study of Caribbean return migration from Britain and France: towards a context-dependent explanation', *Transactions of the Institute of British Geographers*, 21(1): 91-104.

Bytheway, W. R. (1995), *Ageism*, Buckingham: Open University Press.

Carbonin, P., Bernabei, R., Zuccalà, G. and Gambassi, G. (1997), 'Health-care for older persons, a country profile: Italy', *Journal of the American Geriatrics Society*, 45(12): 1519-22.

Carmichael, M. (1901), *In Tuscany*, London: John Murray.

Cashmore, E. E. (1994), *The Dictionary of Race and Ethnic Relations*, London: Routledge.

Casolani, H. (1924), *Make Malta Prosperous – A Series of Articles from the 'Malta Daily Chronicle'*, Valletta: Vanity.

Castellón, R. H. (1991), *The Aging Population of Cuba*, Valletta: International Institute on Aging.

Castles, S. and Miller, M. J. (1998), *The Age of Migration*, London: Macmillan.

Cavaco, C. (1980), *Turismo e Demografia no Algarve*, Lisbon: Editorial Progresso Social e Democracia.

— (1993), 'A place in the sun: return migration and rural change in Portugal', in R. King (ed.), *Mass Migration in Europe: the Legacy and the Future*, London: Belhaven, pp. 174-91.

Central Statistical Office (1991), *Social Trends 1991*, London: HMSO.

Cerase, F. P. (1974), 'Migration and social change: expectations and reality. A study of return migration from the United States to Italy', *International Migration Review*, 8(2): 245-62.

Choi, N. G. (1996), 'Older persons who move: reasons and health consequences', *Journal of Applied Gerontology*, 15(3): 325-44.

Clarke, L. (1995), 'Family care and changing family structure: bad news for the elderly?' in I. Allen and E. Perkins (eds), *The Future of Family Care*, London: HMSO, pp. 19-49.

Clews, S. J. A. (ed.) (1998), *The Malta Year Book 1998*, Sliema: De la Salle Brothers.

Cohen, E. (1972), 'Towards a sociology of international tourism', *Social Research*, 39(1): 164-82.

Cribier, F. (1970), 'La migration de retraite des fonctionnaires parisiens', *Bulletin de l'Association Géographique Française*, 381: 119-22.

— (1982), 'Aspects of retirement migration from Paris', in A. M. Warnes (ed.) *Geographical Perspectives on the Elderly*, Chichester: Wiley, pp. 111-37.

— and Kych, A. (1993), 'A comparison of retirement migration from Paris and London', *Environment and Planning* A, 25(12): 1399-1420.

Cuba, L. (1991), 'Models of migration decision-making re-examined: the destination search of older migrants to Cape Cod', *The Gerontologist*, 31(2): 204-9.

Daciuk, J. F. and Marshall, V. W. (1990), 'Health concerns as a deterrent to seasonal migration of elderly Canadians', *Social Indicators Research*, 22(2): 181-97.

Damer, S. (1997), *British Expatriates: the Parameters of a Community*, Report to the ESRC on Project No. R000221644.

Darwin, C. (1997), *The Voyage of the Beagle*, Ware, Hertfordshire: Wordsworth (reprint of the 1845 edition).

Dench, G. (1975a), *The Maltese in London,* London: Routledge & Kegan Paul.

— (1975b), 'The Maltese in Britain', *New Society,* 32(654): 135-7.

Department of Education and Science (1983), *Education Statistics for the United Kingdom 1983,* London: HMSO.

Department of Health (1997), *Health Advice for Travellers,* Wetherby: Department of Health.

Doccioli, P. (1992), 'L'agriturismo in Toscana', in G. B. Meneghel (ed.), *Agriturismo in Italia,* Bologna: Pàtron Editore, pp. 163-88.

Dooghe, G. (1991), *The Ageing of the Population in Europe: Socio-Economic Characteristics of the Elderly Population,* Brussels: Ministerie Vlaamse Gemeenschap, Centrum voor Bevolkigns en Gezinsstudien.

Dunford, M. (1997), 'Mediterranean economies: the dynamics of uneven development', in R. King, L. Proudfoot and B. Smith (eds), *The Mediterranean: Environment and Society,* London: Arnold, pp. 126-54.

Eaton, M. (1995), 'British expatriate service provision in Spain's Costa del Sol', *Service Industries Journal,* 15(2): 251-66.

Economist Intelligence Unit (1993), 'Europe's senior travel market', *Travel and Tourism Analyst,* 4: 37-56.

Elliott, R. (1995), *Enjoying Good Health-Care on the Costa del Sol,* Málaga: BUPA International.

Erikson, E. H., Erikson, J. M. and Kivnick, H. Q. (1989), *Vital Involvement in Old Age,* New York: W. W. Norton.

Esping-Anderson, G. (1990), *The Three Worlds of Welfare Capitalism,* Oxford: Polity.

— (ed.) (1996), *Welfare States in Transition: National Adaptations in Global Economies,* London: Sage.

Europa Directories (1998), *Europa World Year Book,* London: Europa Directories.

Eurostat (1996), *Statistics in Focus: Population and Social Conditions 1996,* Luxembourg: Eurostat.

Evandrou, M. (ed.) (1997), *Baby Boomers: Ageing in the 21st Century,* London: Age Concern.

Falkingham, J. (1997), 'Who are the baby boomers?' in M. Evandrou (ed.), *Baby Boomers: Ageing in the 21st Century,* London: Age Concern, pp. 15-40.

Farnocchia-Petri, F. (1995), *Risorse e Popolazione: Settant'Anni di Emigrazione dalla Garfagnana e Media Valle del Serchio 1921-1991,* Lucca: Accademia Lucchese di Scienze, Lettere e Arti.

Favell, A. M. (1998), *Philosophies of Integration,* London: Macmillan.

Ferrera, M. (1996), *The Four Social Europes: Between Universalism and Selectivity,* Florence: European University Institute, RSC No. 96/36.

Fillenbaum, G. (1985), *The Wellbeing of the Elderly: Approaches to Multidimensional Assessment,* Geneva: World Health Organization, OP 84.

Findlay, A. M. (1995), 'The future of skill exchanges within the European

Union', in R. Hall and P. White (eds), *Europe's Population: Towards the Next Century*, London: UCL Press, pp. 130-41.

Fischer, P. A., Martin, R. and Straubhaar, T. (1997), 'Should I stay or go?' in T. Hammar, G. Brochmann, K. Tamas and T. Faist (eds), *International Migration, Immobility and Development*, Oxford: Berg, pp. 49-90.

Flower, R. (1988), *Chianti: the Land, the People and the Wine*, London: Christopher Helm.

Fontaine, P. (1994), *A Citizen's Europe*, Luxembourg: Office for Official Publications of the European Communities.

Foster, D. M. and Murphy, P. (1991), 'Resort cycle revisited: the retirement connection', *Annals of Tourism Research*, 18(3): 533-67.

Fournier, G. M., Rasmussen, D. W. and Serow, W. J. (1998), 'Elderly migration: for sun and money', *Population Research and Policy Review*, 7(2): 189-99.

France, G. (1997), 'Cross-border flows of Italian patients within the European Union: an international trade approach', *European Journal of Public Health*, 7(3): 18-25.

Fussell, P. (1980), *Abroad: British Literary Travelling between the Wars*, Oxford: Oxford University Press.

Garrett, M. D. and Scerri, M. (1994), 'Community services for the elderly in Malta', in J. Kosberg (ed.), *International Handbook of Community Services for the Elderly*, New York: Greenwood.

Gaspar, J. (1993), *The Regions of Portugal*, Lisbon: Ministry of Planning and Administration of the Terrritory.

Geoideia (1998), *Os movimentos migratórios externos e a sua incidência no mercado de trabalho em Portugal*, Lisbon: Geoideia.

George, L. K. (1992), 'Economic status and subjective well-being', in N. E. Cutler, D. W. Gregg and M. P. Lawton, (eds), *Aging, Money and Life Satisfaction: Aspects of Financial Gerontology*, New York: Springer, pp. 69-99.

Gibbons, J. (1936), *Playtime in Portugal: An Unconventional Guide to the Algarve*, London: Methuen.

Giddens, A. (1992), *The Transformation of Intimacy, Sexuality, Love and Eroticism in Modern Societies*, Cambridge: Polity.

Glaser, K. and Grundy, E. (1998), 'Migration and household change in the population aged 65 and over, 1971-1991', *International Journal of Population Geography*, 4(4): 323-40.

Gordon, C. (1986), *Patterns of Support for the Elderly: the Case of London's Working Class in the 1930s*, London School of Economics: unpublished MSc. thesis.

Griffin, J. (1986), *Well-Being: Its Meaning, Measurement and Moral Importance*, Oxford: Clarendon.

Grundy, E. (1995), 'Demographic influences on the future of family care', in I. Allen and E. Perks (eds), *The Future of Family Care*, London: HMSO, pp. 1-18.

Haas, W. H. and Serow, W. J. (1993), 'Amenity retirement migration process: a model and preliminary evidence', *The Gerontologist*, 33(2): 212-20.

Halsey, A. H., Sheehan, J. and Vaizey, J. (1972), 'Schools', in A. H. Halsey (ed.), *Trends in British Society Since 1900*, London: Macmillan, pp. 148-91.

Hamilton, O. (1982), *The Divine Country: The British in Tuscany 1372-1980*, London: André Deutsch.

Hammar, T. and Tamas, K. (1997), 'Why do people go or stay?' in T. Hammar, G. Brochmann, K. Tamas and T. Faist (eds), *International Migration, Immobility and Development*, Oxford: Berg, pp. 1-20.

Hantrais, L. (1995), *Social Policy in the European Union*, London: Macmillan.

Harlan, W. H. (1954), 'Community adaption of the presence of aged persons: St Petersburg, Florida', *American Journal of Sociology*, 59(3): 332-9.

Harrop, A. and Grundy, E. (1991), 'Geographic variations in moves into institutions among the elderly in England and Wales', *Urban Studies*, 28(1): 65-86.

Hoggart, K. and Buller, H. (1993), 'Estate agents, British buyers and rural regeneration in France', in E. C. A. Bolsium, G. Clark and J. G. Groenendijk (eds), *The Retreat: Rural Land Use and European Agriculture*, Amsterdam: Netherlands Geographic Studies 172, pp. 96-107.

— and Buller, H. (1995), 'Retired British home owners in rural France', *Ageing and Society*, 15(3): 325-53.

Hooper, J. (1994), 'Paradise bought up', *Guardian*, 5 August.

Hunt, J. and Martin, M. (1997), 'Hospice in Spain', in C. Saunders and R. Kastenbaum (eds), *Hospice Care on the International Scene*, New York: Springer, pp. 179-89.

Hutton, S. (1993), 'Incomes and assets of older people', *Ageing and Society*, 13(3): 427-36.

— (1996), 'Current and future incomes for older people', *Ageing and Society*, 16(6): 775-87.

— (1998), 'Incomes in retirement in the UK: changes in the debate since 1996 and prospects for the future', *Ageing and Society*, 18(5): 611-26.

Instituto Nacional de Estadística (1994), *Censo de Población 1991*, Madrid: INE.

Instituto Nacional de Estatística (1992), *Recenseamento Geral da População 1991*, Lisbon: INE.

Jenner, P. and Smith, C. (1993), *Tourism and the Mediterranean*, London: Economist Intelligence Unit.

Johnson, P. (1993), Income. Chapter 5 of Carnegie Inquiry into the Third Age, *Life Work and Livelihood in the Third Age*, Dunfermline: Carnegie UK Trust, pp. 35-51.

— Disney, R. and Stears, G. (1995), *Pensions: 2000 and Beyond, Volume 2, Analysis of Trends and Options*, London: The Retirement Income Inquiry.

— Conrad, C. and Thomson, D. (eds) (1989), *Workers versus Pensioners: Intergenerational Justice in an Ageing World*, Manchester: University of Manchester Press.

Jurdao, F. and Sánchez, M. (1990), *España, Asilo de Europa*, Barcelona: Editorial Planeta.

Karn, V. A. (1977), *Retiring to the Seaside*, London: Routledge and Kegan Paul.

King, R. (1979), 'The Maltese migration cycle: an archival survey', *Area*, 11(4): 245-9.

— (1993a), 'Recent immigration to Italy: character, causes and consequences', *GeoJournal*, 30(3): 283-92.

— (1993b), 'Why do people migrate? The geography of departure', in R. King (ed.), *The New Geography of European Migrations*, London: Belhaven, pp. 17-46.

— (1997), 'Introduction: an essay on Mediterraneanism', in R. King, L. Proudfoot and B. Smith (eds), *The Mediterranean: Environment and Society*, London: Arnold, pp. 1-11.

— and Black, R. (eds) (1997), *Southern Europe and the New Immigrations*, Brighton: Sussex Academic Press.

— and Montanari, A. (1998), 'Italy: diversified tourism', in A. M. Williams and G. Shaw (eds), *Tourism and Economic Development: European Experiences*, Chichester: Wiley, pp. 75-100.

— and Patterson, G. (1998), 'Diverse paths: the elderly British in Tuscany', *International Journal of Population Geography*, 4(2): 157-82.

— and Rybaczuk, K. (1993), 'Southern Europe and the international division of labour: from mass emigration to mass immigration', in R. King (ed.), *The New Geography of European Migrations*, London: Belhaven, pp. 175-206.

— and Took, L. (1983), 'Land tenure and rural social change: the Italian case', *Erdkunde*, 37(3): 186-98.

— Warnes, A. M. and Williams, A. M. (1998), 'International retirement migration in Europe', *International Journal of Population Geography*, 4(2): 91-111.

Kirby, P. F. (1952), *The Grand Tour in Italy 1700-1800*, New York: S. F. Vanni.

Kliot, N. (1997), 'Politics and society in the Mediterranean Basin', in R. King, L. Proudfoot and B. Smith (eds), *The Mediterranean: Environment and Society*, London: Arnold, pp. 108-25.

Larizgoitia, I. and Starfield, B. (1997), 'Reform of primary health-care: the case of Spain', *Health Policy*, 41(2): 121-37.

Laslett, P. (1989), *A Fresh Map of Life: The Emergence of the Third Age*, London: Weidenfeld and Nicolson.

Law C. M. and Warnes A. M. (1973), 'The movement of retired persons to seaside resorts', *Town Planning Review*, 44(3): 373-90.

— and Warnes, A. M. (1977), *The Migration Decisions of Individuals at Retirement*, London: Department of Geography, King's College London, Final Report to the SSRC.

— and Warnes, A. M. (1982), 'The destination decision in retirement migration', in A. M. Warnes (ed.), *Geographical Perspectives on the Elderly*, Chichester: Wiley, pp. 53-81.

Lazaridis, G., Poyago-Theotoky, J. and King, R. (1999), 'Islands as havens for retirement migration: finding a place in sunny Corfu', in R. King and J. Connell (eds), *Small Worlds, Global Lives: Islands and Migration*, London: Pinter, pp. 297-320.

Lewis, J. R. and Williams, A. M. (1988), 'No longer Europe's best kept secret: the Algarve's tourist boom', *Geography*, 74(2): 170-2.

— and Williams, A. M. (1998), 'Portugal: market segmentation and economic development', in A. M. Williams and J. R. Lewis (eds), *Tourism and Economic Development: European Experiences*, Chichester: Wiley, pp. 125-50.

Libreri, J. (1972), 'The economic implications of foreign settlers in Malta', *Cobweb: Journal of AIESEC (Malta)*, 3: 15-23.

Litwak, E. and Longino, C. F. (1987), 'Migration patterns among the elderly: a developmental perspective', *The Gerontologist*, 27(3): 266-72.

Lockhart, D. G. and Mason, K. T. (1988), 'Malta: the 1985 census', *Geography*, 73(3): 261-5.

Loda, M. (1994), 'Il turismo rurale extra-alberghiero nella compagna toscana', *Rivista Geografica Italiana*, 101(2): 251-76.

Longino, C. F. (1992), 'The forest and the trees: micro-level considerations in the study of geographic mobility in old age', in A. Rogers (ed.), *Elderly Migration and Population Redistribution*, London: Belhaven, pp. 23-34.

— (1994), 'Where retirees prefer to live: the geographical distribution and retirement patterns of retirees', in A. Monk (ed.), *The Columbia Retirement Handbook*, New York: Columbia University Press, pp. 405-16.

— (1996), 'Migration', in J. E. Birren (ed.), *Encyclopedia of Gerontology*, vol. 2, San Diego, CA: Academic, pp. 145-50.

— and Marshall, V. W. (1990), 'North American research in seasonal elderly migration', *Ageing and Society*, 10(2): 229-36.

López Carno, D. (1995), *Málaga: Atlas Sociodemográfico Provincial*, Málaga: Librerías Prometeo y Proteo.

Madden, L. (1999), *Making Money in the Sun: the Development of British- and Irish-owned Businesses in the Costa del Sol*, Brighton: University of Sussex, Research Papers in Geography 36.

Maddox, G. L. 1992, 'Aging and well-being', in N. E. Cutler, D. W. Gregg and M. P. Lawton (eds), *Aging, Money and Life Satisfaction: Aspects of Financial Gerontology*, New York: Springer, pp. 53-67.

Malmberg, G. (1997), 'Time and space in international migration', in T. Hammar, G. Brochmann, K. Tamas and T. Faist (eds), *International Migration, Immobility and Development*, Oxford: Berg, pp. 21-48.

Marchena Gomez, M. J. and Vera Rebollo, F. (1995), 'Coastal areas: processes, typologies and prospects', in A. Montanari and A. M. Williams (eds), *European Tourism: Regions, Spaces and Restructuring*,

Chichester: Wiley, pp. 111-26.

Markwick, M. (1997), 'The population of the Maltese islands: census 1995', *Geography*, 82(2): 179-82.

McDonald, M. (1987), 'Tourism: chasing culture and tradition in Brittany', in M. Bouquet and M. Winter (eds), *Who From Their Labours Rest: Conflict and Practice in Rural Tourism*, Aldershot: Avebury Press, pp. 120-34.

McDowell, T. Y. and Newell, C. (1987), *Measuring Health: A Guide to Rating Scales and Questionnaires*, Oxford: Oxford University Press.

McElroy, J. L. and de Albuquerque, K. (1988), 'Migration transition in small northern and eastern Caribbean states', *International Migration Review*, 22(3): 30-58.

— (1992), 'The economic impact of retirement tourism in Montserrat: some provisional evidence', *Social and Economic Studies*, 41(2): 127-52.

Mellado, P. R. (1996), 'El turismo residencial en la Costa del Sol', in *El Sector Turístico en la Provincia de Málaga Vol 1*, Málaga: Colegio Oficial de Economistas de Málaga, pp. 183-91.

Meyer, J. W. and Speare, A. (1985), 'Distinctive elderly mobility: types and determinants', *Economic Geography*, 61(1): 79-88.

Michener, J. A. (1971), *The Drifters*, London: Secker and Warburg.

Mintel (1998), *Seasonal Holidays Abroad: Winter*, London: Mintel Marketing Intelligence.

Misiti, M., Muscarà, C., Pumares, P., Rodríguez, V. and White, P. (1995), 'Future migration into southern Europe', in R. Hall and P. White (eds), *Europe's Population: Towards the Next Century*, London: UCL Press, pp. 161-87.

Montanari, A. (1995), 'The Mediterranean region: Europe's summer leisure space', in A. Montanari and A. M. Williams (eds), *European Tourism: Regions, Spaces and Restructuring*, Chichester: Wiley, pp. 41-66.

Mortimer, J. (1988), *Summer's Lease*, London: Penguin Books.

Mullan, C. (1992), *The Problems of the Elderly British Expatriate Community in Spain*, London: Help the Aged.

Myklebost, H. (1989), 'Migration of elderly Norwegians', *Norsk Geografisk Tijdschrift*, 43(3): 191-213.

Niero, M. (1996), 'Italy: right turn for the welfare state?' in V. George and P. Taylor-Gooby (eds), *European Welfare Policy: Squaring the Welfare Circle*, London: Macmillan, pp. 117-35.

O'Reilly, K. (1995a), 'A new trend in European migration: contemporary British migration to Fuengirola, Costa del Sol', *Geographical Viewpoint*, 23: 25-36.

— (1995b), 'Constructing and managing identities: "residential tourists", or a British expatriate community in Fuengirola, southern Spain', *Essex Graduate Journal of Sociology*, 1: 25-38.

— (2000), 'Trading intimacy for liberty: British women on the Costa del Sol', in F. Anthias and G. Lazaridis (eds), *Gender and Migration in Southern Europe*, Oxford: Berg, pp.227-48.

OECD (1976), *Measuring Social Well-Being: A Progress Report on the Development of Social Indicators*, Paris: OECD.

Office of National Statistics (1997), *The Health of Adult Britain 1841-1994*, 2 volumes, London: HMSO.

— (1998), *International Migration 1996*, London: HMSO, Report MN23.

— (1999), *Social Trends 1999*, London: Survey Office.

OPCS (1976), *Mortality Statistics 1974*, London: HMSO.

— (1983), *Mortality Statistics 1981*, London: HMSO.

— (1991), *Mortality Statistics 1989*, London: HMSO.

— (1992), *General Household Survey 1990*, London: HMSO.

Okun, M. A. (1987), 'Life satisfaction', in G. L. Maddox (ed.), *Encyclopedia of Aging*, New York: Springer, pp. 399-401.

Owen, D. and Green, A. (1992), 'Migration patterns and trends', in T. Champion and T. Fielding (eds), *Migration Processes and Patterns*, London: Belhaven, pp. 17-38.

Palagiano, C. (1994), 'Southern Europe: health in areas that have undergone recent development, demographic and epidemiological issues', in D. R. Phillips and Y. Verhasselt (eds), *Health and Development*, London: Routledge, pp. 289-99.

Paniagua Mazzorra, A. P. (1991), 'Migración de noreuropeos retirados a España: el caso británico', *Revista Española Geriatría y Gerontología*, 26(4): 255-66.

Parfitt, J. (1997), 'Questionnaire design and sampling', in R. Flowerdew and D. Martin (eds), *Methods in Human Geography*, Harlow: Addison Wesley Longman, pp. 76-109.

Phillipson, C. R. (1998), *Reconstructing Old Age: New Agendas in Social Theory and Practice*, London: Sage.

Pina, P. (1988), *Portugal: O Turismo no Século XX*, Lisbon: Lucidus.

Pollard, J. and Domínguez Rodríguez, R. (1995), 'Unconstrained growth: the development of a Spanish resort', *Geography*, 80(1): 33-44.

Porter, R. (1990), *English Society in the Eighteenth Century*, London: Penguin.

Premble, J. (1987), *The Mediterranean Passion: Victorians and Edwardians in the South*, Oxford: Oxford University Press.

Quirino, P. and Leone, M. (1993), *Gli stranieri in Italia: fonti statistiche*, Rome: ISTAT Note e Relazioni, 4.

Raison, L. (1983), *Tuscany: an Anthology*, London: Cadogan Books.

Ravenstein, E. G. (1885), 'The laws of migration', *Journal of the Royal Statistical Society*, 48: 167-235.

Rees, J. (1996), 'Beyond the pot of Basil', *Independent on Sunday*, 28 April, pp. 26-7.

Reynolds-Ball, E. (1899), *Mediterranean Winter Resorts*, London: Kegan Paul, Trench, Trüber and Co.

Rhodes, M. (1996), *Globalisation and the Western European Welfare Model*, Florence: European University Institute, RSC No. 96/43.

Rodríguez, V., Fernández-Mayoralas, G. and Rojo, F. (1998), 'European retirees on the Costa del Sol: a cross-national comparison',

International Journal of Population Geography, 4(2): 183-200.

Rogers, A. and Castro, L. J. (1981), 'Age patterns of migration: cause-specific profiles', in A. Rogers (ed.), *Advances in Multiregional Demography,* Laxenburg, Austria: International Institute for Applied Systems Analysis, Research Report RR-81-6, pp. 125-59.

— Frey, W. H., Rees, P. H., Speare, A. and Warnes, A. M. (eds) (1992), *Elderly Migration and Population Redistribution: A Comparative Study,* London: Belhaven Press.

Ross, C. J. (1997), *Contemporary Spain: A Handbook,* London: Arnold.

Rowles, G. D. (1978), *Prisoners of Space: Exploring the Geographical Experience of Older People,* Boulder, CO: Westview.

Ryff, C. D. (1996), 'Psychological well-being', in J. E. Birren (ed.), *Encyclopedia of Gerontology,* vol. 2. San Diego, CA: Academic, pp. 365-9.

Serrano Martínez, J. M. (1992), *Jubilados Extranjeros Residentes en la Costa Calida,* Murcia: Departamento de Geografía, Universidad de Murcia.

Silva, J. A. and da Silva, J. (1991), 'Algarve – crescimento turístico e estruturação geografica do concelho de Faro', *Sociedade Território* 13: 22-32.

Smith, V. L. (ed.) (1977), *Hosts and Guests: an Anthropology of Tourism,* Philadelphia: University of Pennsylvania Press.

SOPEMI (1995), *Trends in International Migration,* Paris: OECD.

— (1997), *Trends in International Migration,* Paris: OECD.

Stillwell, J., Rees, P. and Duke-Williams, O. (1996), 'Migration between NUTS Level 2 regions in the United Kingdom', in P. Rees, J. Stillwell, A. Convey and M. Kupiszeski (eds), *Population Migration in the European Union,* Chichester: Wiley, pp. 275-307.

Terribile, F. (1996), 'Portugal: reforming the social security system', *OECD Observer,* 201: 36-8.

Theroux, P. (1995), *The Pillars of Hercules: A Grand Tour of the Mediterranean,* London: Hamish Hamilton.

Thrift (1987), 'Manufacturing rural geography?' *Journal of Rural Studies,* 3(1): 77-81.

Tucker, R. D., Marshall, V. W., Longino, C. F. and Mullins, L. C. (1988), 'Older anglophone Canadians in Florida: a descriptive profile', *Canadian Journal on Aging,* 7(2): 218-32.

— Mullins, L. C., Béland, F., Longino, C. F. and Marshall, V. W. (1992), 'Older Canadians in Florida: a comparison of anglophone and francophone seasonal migrants', *Canadian Journal on Aging,* 11(2): 281-97.

Urry, J. (1990), *The Tourist Gaze,* London: Sage.

Valenzuela, M. (1998), 'Spain: from the phenomenon of mass tourism to the search for a more diversified model', in A. M. Williams and G. Shaw (eds), *Tourism and Economic Development: European Experiences,* Chichester: Wiley, pp. 43-74.

Valero Escandell, J. R. (1992), *La Inmigracion Extranjera en Alicante,* Alicante: Instituto de Cultura Juan Gil-Alberte.

Van Kersbergen, K. (1997), *Double Allegiance in European Integration: Public, Nation States, and Social Policy,* Florence: European University Institute,

Working Paper 97/15.

Vesperi, M. D. (1985), *City of Green Benches: Growing Old in a New Downtown*, Ithaca, NY: Cornell University Press.

Victor, C. R. (1991), *Health and Health-Care in Later Life*, Buckingham: Open University Press.

Walker, A. and Maltby, T. (1997), *Ageing Europe*, Buckingham: Open University Press.

Wall, R. (1995), 'Elderly persons and members of their households in England and Wales from preindustrial times to the present', in D. I. Kertzer and P. Laslett (eds), *Aging in the Past: Demography, Society and Old Age*, Berkeley, CA: University of California Press, pp. 81-106.

Warnes, A. M. (1983), 'Migration in late working-age and early retirement', *Socio-Economic Planning Sciences*, 17(5-6): 291-302.

— (1991), 'Migration to and seasonal residence in Spain of Northern European elderly people', *European Journal of Gerontology*, 1(1): 53-60.

— (1993), 'The development of retirement migration in Great Britain', *Espace Populations, Sociétés*, 1993-3: 451-64.

— (1994), 'Permanent and seasonal international retirement migration: the prospects for Europe', *Netherlands Geographical Studies*, 173: 69-81.

— (1996), 'Migration among older people', *Reviews in Clinical Gerontology* 6(1): 101-14.

— (1998), 'Population ageing over the next few decades', in R. Tallis (ed.), *Increasing Longevity: Medical, Social and Political Implications*, London: Royal College of Physicians, pp. 1-15.

— (1999), 'UK and west European late-age mortality rates: trends in cause-specific rates, 1960-1990', *Health and Place*, 4(1): 111-18.

— and Ford, R. (1995), 'Migration and family care', in I. Allen and E. Perkins (eds), *The Future of Family Care*, London: HMSO, pp. 65-92.

— and Patterson, G. (1998), 'British retirees in Malta: components of the cross-national relationship', *International Journal of Population Geography*, 4(2): 113-33.

Wensing, M., Mainz, J., Ferreira, P., Hearnshaw, H., Hjortdahl, P., Olesen, F., Reis, S., Ribacke, M., Szecsenyi, J. and Grot, R. (1998), 'General practice care and patients' priorities in Europe: an international comparison', *Health Policy*, 45(3): 175-86.

Wilkin, D., Hallam, L. and Doggett, M-A. (1992), *Meaures of Need and Outcome for Primary Health-Care*, Oxford: Oxford University Press.

Williams, A. M. (ed.) (1984), *Southern Europe Transformed*, London: Harper and Row.

— (1993), 'Portugal: the economy', in Europa Directories, *Western Europe*, London: Europa, pp. 463-8.

— (1995), 'Capital and the transnationalisation of tourism', in A. Montanari and A. M. Williams (eds), *European Tourism: Regions, Spaces and Restructuring*, Chichester: Wiley, pp. 163-76.

— (1997), 'Tourism and uneven development', in R. King, L. Proudfoot and B. Smith (eds), *The Mediterranean: Environment and Society*,

London: Edward Arnold, pp. 208-26.

— King, R. and Warnes, A. M. (1997), 'A place in the sun: international retirement migration from Northern to Southern Europe', *European Urban and Regional Studies*, 4(2): 115-34.

— and Patterson, G. (1998), 'An empire lost but a province gained: a cohort analysis of British international retirement migration in the Algarve', *International Journal of Population Geography*, 4(2): 135-55.

— and Shaw, G. (1998), *Tourism and Economic Development: European Experiences*, 3rd edition, Chichester: Wiley.

Wiseman, R. F. (1980), 'Why older people move: theoretical issues', *Research on Aging*, 2(2): 141-54.

— and Roseman, C. C. (1979), 'A typology of elderly migration based on the decision-making process', *Economic Geography*, 55(2): 324-37.

World Bank (1997), *World Development Report*, New York: World Bank.

Wuerpel, C. (1974), *The Algarve: Province of Portugal*, Newton Abbot: David and Charles.

Index

Wall, R., 12
welfare state
      European models 168–9
      future of 215–16
      support for elderly 13–14, 15
well-being, variations 192–7

Lightning Source UK Ltd.
Milton Keynes UK
UKOW052214211212

204018UK00002B/24/P